How We Survive Here

Families Across Time

A Memoir

CLAIRE GEBBEN

Letter translations by Angela Weber

coffeetownpress

Kenmore, WA

coffeetownpress

For more information go to: www.coffeetownpress.com
www.clairegebben.com

This is a work of nonfiction. Real names have been used with permission;
others have been changed.

Cover design by Sabrina Sun

Cover photo:
pictured in foreground: Angela Weber and Claire Gebben
pictured in background: Circa 1889, Mary Crolly Schuster and Lucy Harm
(the author's great-grandmother) at the Schuster residence, 186 Tod Street,
Cleveland Ohio

Map courtesy of Maria Brown, Kroll Map Company

How We Survive Here

ISBN: 978-1-60381-701-1 (Trade Paper)
ISBN: 978-1-60381-702-8 (eBook)

Library of Congress Control Number: 2018950034

Printed in the United States of America

Contents

Family Tree

HANDRICH-HARM FAMILY TREE
(Not all family members are represented)

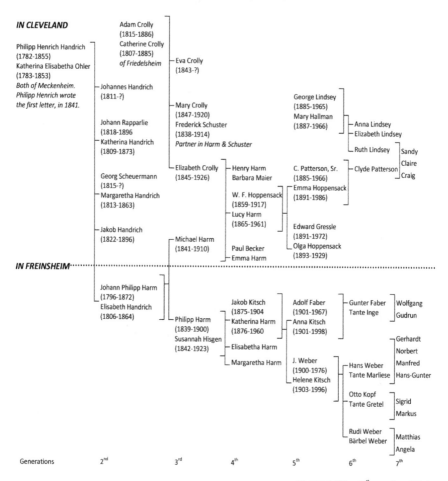

IN CLEVELAND

Adam Crolly (1815-1886)
Catherine Crolly (1807-1885) *of Friedelsheim*

Philipp Henrich Handrich (1782-1855)
Katherina Elisabetha Ohler (1783-1853)
Both of Meckenheim.
Philipp Henrich wrote the first letter, in 1841.

Eva Crolly (1843-?)

Johannes Handrich (1811-?)

Mary Crolly (1847-1920)
Frederick Schuster (1838-1914)
Partner in Harm & Schuster

George Lindsey (1885-1965)
Mary Hallman (1887-1966)

Anna Lindsey
Elizabeth Lindsey

Johann Rapparlie (1818-1896
Katherina Handrich (1809-1873)

Ruth Lindsey

Sandy
Claire
Craig

Elizabeth Crolly (1845-1926)

Henry Harm
Barbara Maier

C. Patterson, Sr. (1885-1966)
Emma Hoppensack (1891-1986)

Clyde Patterson

Georg Scheuermann (1815-?)
Margaretha Handrich (1813-1863)

W. F. Hoppensack (1859-1917)
Lucy Harm (1865-1961)

Jakob Handrich (1822-1896)

Michael Harm (1841-1910)

Edward Gressle (1891-1972)
Olga Hoppensack (1893-1929)

Paul Becker
Emma Harm

IN FREINSHEIM

Johann Philipp Harm (1796-1872)
Elisabeth Handrich (1806-1864)

Philipp Harm (1839-1900)
Susannah Hisgen (1842-1923)

Jakob Kitsch (1875-1904
Katherina Harm (1876-1960

Adolf Faber (1901-1967)
Anna Kitsch (1901-1998)

Gunter Faber
Tante Inge

Wolfgang
Gudrun

Elisabetha Harm

Margaretha Harm

J. Weber (1900-1976)
Helene Kitsch (1903-1996)

Hans Weber
Tante Marliese

Gerhardt
Norbert
Manfred
Hans-Gunter

Otto Kopf
Tante Gretel

Sigrid
Markus

Rudi Weber
Bärbel Weber

Matthias
Angela

Generations	2nd	3rd	4th	5th	6th	7th

Spouses and children of 7th generation not listed.

BELGIUM

BAVARIAN PALATINATE
circa 1848

Mosel R.

RHENISH PRUSSIA

London

ENGLISH CHANNEL

Havre

Paris

Hamburg

Frankfurt

Munich

FRANCE

Frankfurt

Freinsheim

Kaiserslautern

Bad Dürkheim

Mannheim

Ladenburg

Meckenheim

Neustadt

Neckar R.

Speyer

Heidelberg

Haardt Mountains

Forbach

BADEN

Rhine R.

Part One

The discovery of ancestral letters propels the author on a challenging journey to write about her family history. Narrative includes over a dozen 19th-century letters written by German immigrant blacksmiths and wagon-makers to Cleveland, Ohio

For a complete list, see Index starting on page 317.

———— ◆ ————

Chapter 1

The packet of letters tucked away in my father's belongings, unearthed amid stacks of decades-old travel brochures and mildew-dusted books, were bound with a tight cross of string, the way a gift is wrapped with ribbon. Folded and compressed, the pages were airmail thin, dense with tidy cursive in a language not my own. Letters in German, saved from a correspondence of my grandmother with two of her German cousins.

I sat there in Dad's apartment, his accumulation of a lifetime piling around us, and my first instinct was to dismiss them. These letters, the stuff of history, made me impatient. On the cusp of 50 years old, I was setting my sights on the future. Maybe one day, I told myself, I'd have time to dig backward into the past, but that time was not now.

With the kids nearly launched into their young adult lives, I'd recently quit my day job as a psychotherapist's assistant to write novels, a dream I'd harbored since childhood. I'd been at it for a couple of years, but it hadn't been going well. I'd written a first book—a great book, I thought—but no agent or publisher seemed to agree. When the letters in German materialized, I was looking ahead, still struggling to find my voice. Delving back into family history was Dad's thing, not mine.

Three years later found me standing at the foot of the graves of the two women in Germany who'd written those old letters. Their gravestones were polished and glinting, almost winking at me, the cemetery as a whole well-tended, suffused with silence and a pervading sense of the past. My grandmother in Cleveland, Ohio had corresponded with these two cousins in Freinsheim, Germany, her entire adult life. Yet she'd gone to her eternal rest never having met either of them.

Still, their correspondence spurred a unique and abiding exchange among subsequent generations, especially between me and my German cousin Angela. I'd come here to Germany at Angela's invitation, although for this particular outing, she had not accompanied me. This afternoon in Freinsheim,

I'd gone out for a stroll and entered the cemetery as an afterthought, stumbling my way along as usual, unsuspecting and unprepared.

And there I found them, dug into stillness amid granite and sandstone monuments, beneath a garden of clipped hedges, benches and a proliferation of ivy. The graves of the two letter writers were not side by side, but in proximity, scattered among the headstones bearing the names of other German relatives I recognized. For well over a year, so many of these former lives had preoccupied my thoughts.

If the dead were all knowing, I mused, the spirits of these previous generations could see me plainly for who I was—a pretender. I'd traveled all the way to this rural town in Germany, ingratiating myself into the lives of their children and grandchildren and great grandchildren. I'd been welcomed, encouraged and supported with warm hospitality, all on the promise I was writing a historical novel based on our common ancestors. I had a terrible secret. What I'd written was all wrong.

God knows, I was trying. So far, I'd researched and sweated through 150 pages of the book. But what I'd learned here on my research trip in Germany had clued me in to a worst case scenario—I'd completely missed the mark. All that work, all the help I'd been receiving, so many now counting on me, the relatives here, as well as friends and family back home. What if I couldn't do this? What if I failed?

Regardless, I had little choice but to keep pretending. I owed it to everyone, including these two women long gone to the grave. Standing before their headstones, I thanked them for continuing the connection all these years. For the strange, challenging, weirdly satisfying journey their letters had sparked so far.

Turning, I pushed open the black iron cemetery gate and stepped out onto the path. The meditative gloom of the graveyard had brought me some peace, but not entirely. Heading back toward Freinsheim, I gazed out over the green vineyards tinged with yellow autumn, the orange-red rooftops of Freinsheim clutched in the center.

A knot of anxiety bunched in my throat. *If only I don't let them all down.*

Chapter 2

Time was short. The year was 2007, and I'd flown from Seattle to Cincinnati with only one week to help my Dad move from independent to assisted living at the Scarlet Oaks Retirement Community. He and I were on a mission to make headway. The piles of belongings in his one-bedroom apartment rose around us as we sorted out what to keep, what to store, and what to give away. My brother Craig and sister-in-law Cheri were on vacation at the time. I had agreed to come to Cincinnati from Seattle to housesit, and to help out Dad while they were gone.

In our immediate family, only my brother and I were around to look after the elder generation—my father and my mother's younger sister Grace Elizabeth Lindsey. My mother had died in 1999. By that summer of 2007, my father was 84 years old and suffered from Parkinson's disease. Craig had brought Dad to Cincinnati from Cleveland to have him close by. Essentially, Craig had taken on the role of being Dad's primary caregiver. I understood this was a huge job, so however I could, I tried to help out. My goal during that week was to make decent progress on Dad's move to assisted living before Craig and Cheri returned from vacation.

We sat across from each other in Dad's dimly daylit apartment just outside his jam-packed closet, a humid breeze rustling the papers and piles growing around us as a thunderstorm grumbled in the distance, clearly tumbling our way. Of course, he had air-conditioning, and of course, he chose not to use it. But I didn't point this out. I was trying hard to keep us focused.

It was slow going. The advanced nature of Dad's Parkinson's made opening boxes and thumbing through papers a chore. He'd always been trim, but with the constant shaking, his body now gave the impression of being wiry and intense. His neck and jaw moved stiffly as he looked up again and again to tell me stories. Like an expert on Antiques Roadshow, he held forth on each object, year purchased, by whom and why.

When we unearthed a packet of letters, I foresaw yet another delay.

Dad recognized them as belonging to his mother, my grandmother Emma Patterson. A cursory glance revealed the letters were written in German, mostly by Helene Weber and Anna Faber, two women of my grandmother's generation. I didn't know German, and Dad knew very little. *Thank goodness,* I thought. *At least we won't lose precious time on this.*

"We should mail these to the relatives in Freinsheim," Dad said, blinking his gray eyes at me through wire-rimmed frames. Freinsheim[1] is a small village in Germany southwest of Frankfurt, which I'd visited once in 1988. Dad had visited almost every decade since the 1950s. "I'm sure they'd like to have them," he added, his tone wistful.

We both knew Dad wouldn't ever be able to visit Freinsheim again. His trip from independent to assisted living was another inevitable step away from freedom and mobility, his world growing ever smaller and more confined.

My brother Craig tried to keep Dad from feeling too isolated, by taking him out to restaurants, movies and such whenever he could. Craig was a compassionate caregiver for our father. He took on the responsibility without complaint, in part because he and I had struck a deal. We both knew our Aunt Elizabeth would need help one day, too. Aunt Elizabeth was then 86 years old. She'd never married, and lived independently in East Lansing, Michigan. Craig had taken on Dad. In return, if and when Aunt Elizabeth needed help, that duty would fall to me.

This deal suited us both, since our aunt tended to be snappish, especially with men. She adored Craig, and with good reason. Craig had traits of Mom's Lindsey side of the family, good-humored and practical, his hair dark and curly, his eyes brown. He was tall like the Lindsey's, too. His strapping physique could be a bit intimidating, but Craig was no bully. With Aunt Elizabeth he was tolerant and kind, and cracked jokes that made her chuckle. But she could be hostile, too. She felt free to criticize, about Craig hanging art too high on his walls, for instance, or taking too many photos of his daughters.

"They're too used to it," she declared to me once, within earshot of Craig. "See?" She nodded her head towards Craig's daughters Erica and Lisa as they paused in their game to smile for another photo.

Craig and I both let this pass. We were used to her cutting mannerisms.

Regardless, I deeply admired Aunt Elizabeth. And she seemed to adore me. As a young girl, I saw her at Christmas and sometimes Thanksgiving, a time when she infused our family with gifts of the very best of books, classics like *The Lonely Doll* and *One Morning in Maine.* "The pictures are by Robert McCloskey," she called across the living room as I leafed through gorgeous illustrations in the latter. When I grew older, she presented me with *Island*

---

1 Pronounced *Frynz-hime.*

of the Blue Dolphins and *My Side of the Mountain*, books I remember and treasure to this day.

With her dyed-red hair and abrupt, authoritative way of speaking, Aunt Elizabeth blazed her own path through life as a single woman. She showed an undying curiosity for learning and a deep appreciation for cultures vastly different from our own. Whenever she saved up a little money on her modest librarian salary, she'd head off to Yugoslavia, or Machu Picchu, or Ethiopia. When she visited us at the holidays, she'd show off her latest mementos—carved olivewood, jade figurines, a Coptic cross, a pair of maracas—and regale us with stories and humorous anecdotes. After her trip to Scotland, she was especially proud to show off her wool blanket of the Lindsey tartan. Mom's side of the family, the Lindsey sisters, had the Scots-Irish blood. Dad's side had the strong German roots.

That afternoon in Cincinnati, Dad and I paused in our work as the lightning and thunderstorm bowled in. It rained often in the Pacific Northwest, where I was living and raising a family, but rarely arrived with such pummeling. As the downpour subsided and I gathered my things to drive back to Craig's, Dad handed me the German letters and told me to mail them to Manfred Weber, one of the Freinsheim relatives. I knew Manfred, he was of my generation, but both he and Dad shared a professional interest in architecture, which gave them a special connection. They corresponded frequently.

By the end of our week together in Cincinnati, Dad and I managed to get quite a bit accomplished. Once Craig and Cheri returned, I flew back to Seattle, bringing with me the packet of letters, which I dutifully mailed off to Manfred in Freinsheim.

LATER THAT SAME YEAR, EMAILS began arriving from Angela Weber, my German relative and friend who lived in Marburg. Angela had grown up in Freinsheim, Germany and moved away to Marburg for university studies. I'd first met Angela in the 1990s, when she was in her early twenties and I was in my mid-thirties, a time when she'd spent a year in the Northwest. Despite our age difference of almost twelve years, we'd formed a lasting friendship. Although we emailed instead of writing letters, we kept up a long distance correspondence much as our grandmothers had.

November 14, 2007

Dear Claire,

It has been a while since we talked. I didn't tell you then, I had traveled to Canada in October with a group of Ph.D. students in Canadian studies. When I came home a pile of work and life waited for me ... I started reading and transcribing the old letters. Haven't translated them yet though .... These letters between the cousins in the 1920s are quite intense in many ways. Maybe I should translate them one after another and send them to you.

Yours Angela

Enough time had passed since helping Dad that at first, I wasn't sure what letters Angela was talking about. It took me a moment to remember how I'd mailed the German letters off to Manfred. But now Angela had them? It sounded as if some kind of hand-off had occurred, maybe when Angela had gone to Freinsheim to visit her mother Bärbel[2] Weber and brother Matthias who still lived there, as did Manfred. Somehow, I supposed, Angela had convinced her cousin Manfred to let her have the letters.

I replied that same day:

Dear Angela,

Sounds like a fascinating trip to Canada .... I am going at Christmas to see my dad and brother, so if you have translated any of the letters by then, it would be nice to be able to share one or two with them ... but it is a big task, and I understand if there is not time.

Much love,

Claire

Every time I emailed Angela, I felt grateful I could write to her in English. My paternal grandmother, Emma Patterson, was raised in a bilingual home. Her parents spoke English, but her grandparents, who also lived in the home, spoke to her in German. Even later in life, Grandmother still understood the language well enough to write German letters to the relatives in Freinsheim, who didn't know English. Now the tables had turned: I spoke next to no German, but Angela spoke fluent English.

THAT CHRISTMAS IN 2007, MY husband Dave and I and our teenage children George and Vivian all flew together to Cincinnati for the holidays. Dad would turn 85 that January. His Parkinson's had advanced considerably since my visit the previous summer. He now had difficulty going up and down the

2   Pronounced *bear-bel*.

stairs in Craig's home.

At age 86, Aunt Elizabeth probably shouldn't have driven the 300-mile trip from East Lansing, Michigan to Cincinnati, Ohio by herself, but she'd done it anyhow. Her mannerisms hadn't softened any with age. She kept such a surly demeanor at Craig's that I noticed the dogs growled whenever she rose from her chair.

Our immediate family that holiday numbered only ten—my family of four and Craig's family of four, plus Dad and Aunt Elizabeth. At some point that week, I checked my email and found one from Angela with three letter translations attached. Dad was having trouble with his eyesight, so I printed them out and read them aloud to him and others gathered in the living room. The first one had been written from Freinsheim by Katherina Kitsch, Angela's great-grandmother.

> 20th of March 1922
>
> Dear relatives!
>
> Peculiar will it seem to you, after such a long time, to read something from your dear uncle's place of birth .... For all that it has been such a long time, since our dear uncle had stayed with us (1893)! ... At that time, we still had blessed times in Germany. Then this horrible war broke out, which nobody among the people wanted; then after four years of wrestling and fighting, this peace and now this terrible dearth from which even the small children suffer, who are surely not guilty for the war. I have often said, I am only glad that our dear uncle didn't have to witness this humiliation of his old fatherland, as he has always stayed a good German, also in his new homeland ....

As I read the letter aloud in the somewhat stilted English, it felt as if the voices of these persons long gone were practically in the room, a kind of resurrection.

"Who is the uncle she's talking about?" I asked Dad.

"That's Michael Harm, your great-great grandfather."

I felt confused by the reference. Uncle? 1893? Throughout my childhood, I'd heard about great-great grandfather Harm, how he'd crossed the Atlantic in 1857 at age 15 to come to Cleveland, Ohio and apprenticed as a blacksmith. I'd never heard he'd gone back to Germany, though.

I did have a romanticized image of Michael Harm, based on reminiscences of him by my grandmother. She used to say he was her favorite grandfather, that during the Cleveland winters, he would harness the horses to the sleigh, tuck a lap robe around her legs against the cold, snap the reins and whisk the family off through the snow, sleigh bells ringing. Her childhood in Cleveland captivated me. It sounded so alien compared to my 20th-century "rust belt" upbringing, getting around in winter not on sleighs, but in station wagons on salt-encrusted, potholed roads.

For Dad's benefit, I read all three letters aloud. They described the sons in the German family who'd been injured or taken prisoner of war. They told how the Freinsheim families did not starve, only because they worked hard in the fields to grow their own food. How they did not have money for things like clothing and shoes. How the daughters had boyfriends, but were waiting to marry until better times. The third letter included thanks for a "present."

Dad brightened at this last, and repeated the story I'd heard many times, how his mother and grandmother had assembled care packages with clothes and food and money to send to the German relatives during those hard post-war years. They'd mail one shoe of a pair in each of two separate packages to ensure they would not be stolen before arriving at the intended destination. While the Freinsheim correspondent's reference to a present did not specifically mention shoes, I wanted to believe the letter corroborated the oft-told oral history.

Overall, Dad wasn't as excited about the letters as I'd hoped. It was hard for me to watch him age like this, to see his former passions wane. I think the Parkinson's had taken over. Dad's focus had shifted to making it through each day.

Aunt Elizabeth didn't seem interested either, or maybe she didn't have her hearing aids on. While I was reading the letters, she rose from her chair and left the room. She'd been more frail in general that Christmas, I'd noticed. It was time to precipitate her move closer to me. As we spent the holiday together, I convinced her to come look at options in the Seattle area that coming spring.

I emailed my thanks to Angela and she replied about how the letters had affected her:

> ...This Christmas was very different to me in a certain sense. When I was sitting in the old church of Freinsheim, time seemed to shrink and I wondered how many generations of family have been sitting there and what their hopes and wishes were for Christmas and for their lives. And if they carried along their children and if their children "behaved" and how and if they doubted at one

point that God was male, as I definitely doubt, and what
did they do without electric lights after all.

Angela went on to say she'd spoken with a historian who said personal
letters from rural women in the 1920s in Germany were rare, making them
even more valuable. She intended to ask around about the other half of the
correspondence, letters my grandmother would have written from Cleveland
to Freinsheim. Searching for them, she said, would be her next project.

I did not realize when I read Angela's email that her project would
initiate a project of my own, the writing and publication of my first novel,
The Last of the Blacksmiths. Before I began, I expected writing a book to be
pretty straightforward—research, write, then publish. Instead, it unfolded as
I now understand most such undertakings occur, with piecemeal discoveries,
serendipitous encounters, and creative imaginings, a journey full of
inevitability, opportunity and love.

Chapter 3

As we returned from Cincinnati to Seattle and welcomed in the New Year, it looked as if 2008 would have many milestones. Son George had turned 18 and would be graduating from high school in June. Daughter Vivian was deep into volleyball season and would start her junior year next fall. My husband and his long-time law partner were parting ways after twenty years, so Dave would be moving his office from Bellevue to Seattle.

As for me, it was time to jumpstart my writing career. Ever since I'd graduated from college, I'd been working at various jobs, as a desktop publisher, communications director, and most recently as a psychotherapist's assistant. Finally, three years earlier in 2005, I'd quit that job to pursue my childhood dream of writing novels. I remember discussing it with Aunt Elizabeth at the time, during a call to Michigan to see how she was doing.

"Why are you doing that?" she asked, as usual, getting right to the point.

"I've always wanted to, but we needed my income to help pay bills. This last job really wasn't doing it for me. I was screaming inside. I'm 47 years old. If I don't start following my dream now, I figure I never will."

"Get started right away," she said. "Otherwise, you'll never get around to it."

I was surprised by how my aunt zeroed in on just the thing I needed to hear. I'd quit my job months ago, but I'd let the summer take over my schedule and not yet gotten around to writing. What's more, once I confessed my plan to Aunt Elizabeth, I felt the pressure of her expectations. She'd been cultivating my reading interests all my life, continuing every Christmas to gift us with the latest books, for instance Frankel's *The Times of My Life and My Life with The Times*, Chernow's *Alexander Hamilton*. I was aware of her high standards and hoped I wouldn't disappoint her. To get started, I signed up that fall for a fiction certificate at the evening extension program through the University of Washington.

Three years later in 2008, I'd completed a manuscript of a first novel, but it felt like I wasn't getting anywhere. I couldn't interest any literary agents, and while I could see the problems in the book, I didn't know how to fix them. The more I learned about writing, the more I realized I had a lot to learn. That January, as a New Year's resolution, I applied for a graduate-level Creative Writing program. Based on nearby Whidbey Island, the program had been recommended to me and sounded like a good way to earn a Master of Fine Arts degree. In the process, I could either fix my current manuscript or write a new novel. If accepted into the program, both my son and I would be paying college tuition come September, but Dave and I talked it over and decided I should go ahead and apply. I felt more than ready to focus on my future.

Around the time I was filling out my application, I received an email from Angela, a follow-up about the letters, and also news of an impending visit.

February 8, 2008

Dear Claire,

I have read almost all the letters of the 1920s now and have asked Tante [Aunt] Inge, Onkel [Uncle] Gunter's wife for the corresponding letters from Cleveland to Freinsheim. But, as it turned out, her package of letters was much older than that, it contained a package of letters from 1841 onward until 1900. And this really surprised me as I never knew: Michael Harm wasn't the first one to go of his family. His grandparents of his mother's side had gone as early as the 1840s with all their children except his mother. They are originally from another village, Meckenheim, some 15 km south of Freinsheim …. Well, and this totally changed my image of Michael Harm's dream as a young man of 16 to go to America, he was no runaway but was welcomed there and learned his profession with his uncle.

I will transcribe and translate more, somehow the project grows and grows. At the same time I started seriously with a thesis work on North American indigenous interpretations of art history. I even got a travel scholarship from the Association for Canadian Studies for this coming summer to do research at Vancouver and Victoria.

So we are busily thinking now: could we maybe visit you in summer when Christoph would also come with the children. What do you think?

So much for today, I hope you're all fine and well,

Yours, Angela

Angela's information about the letter discovery was hugely exciting, but somehow, the revelatory nature of it zipped right past me. In my life-long understanding of the story, Michael Harm traveled alone from Freinsheim to America in 1857. What Angela said about earlier relatives and people in Meckenheim made no sense. Angela must be confused, I remember thinking. Perhaps she translated the letters too fast. Perhaps these new letters came from some other branch of her family.

When my eyes scanned down to the final paragraph about how Angela might come for a visit that summer, the other contents of the email were back-burnered. I emailed back that I thought it would be great to see them, and our subsequent emails became enmeshed in her travel arrangements, a complicated schedule of planes, trains, and automobiles. She'd be coming in the end of June, when I'd get to meet Christoph and their two daughters Carlotta and Luzi for the first time.

MEANWHILE MARCH ARRIVED, THE TIME when my 86-year-old Aunt Elizabeth would visit us for almost a week, mainly to tour retirement homes in preparation for her possible move. Frankly, I was unsure about how this would go. It felt like a job interview in a way, a visit to assess if I'd pass muster as her caregiver and power of attorney. Aunt Elizabeth had known me my entire life, from the time I was a clueless kid. Since I'd become an adult and a parent we'd seen each other rarely. Would she truly be able to trust me enough, I wondered, to make such a huge move to the Northwest?

Part of my doubts stemmed from knowing I wasn't her first choice. Once Craig had ensconced Dad at Scarlet Oaks Retirement Community in Cincinnati, Aunt Elizabeth suggested she also move to the Cincinnati area, even to the same place. Like she trusted my brother more. Craig and I both thought it was a terrible idea to move them into the same facility. Dad and Aunt Elizabeth were like oil and water, often sniping at each other at family gatherings. Gently, Craig had deflected her proposal, urging her to come to Seattle instead.

Aunt Elizabeth seemed to be cooperating, but I feared she was doing it grudgingly. In working out the details of her visit to Seattle beforehand, our conversations over the phone had been limited due to her ever-worsening hearing. She'd chosen not to enter the Internet age, still handwriting snail mail, sending me dashed off, cryptic notes. "Hi ho—flying in March 18, Flt. 331." So I really couldn't be sure of her intentions. Was my aunt truly planning to move? Or, was she coming to the Northwest to drop some bombshell or other about how she'd decided to make other plans?

When I picked her up at the airport that Tuesday in mid-March, though, my worries dissipated. Just being in Aunt Elizabeth's presence always raised my spirits. For one thing, she possessed the telltale traits of the Lindsey sisters, the super soft skin and wide hips. My mom had had a large nose, and Aunt Elizabeth did too, but hers was even larger, and more hawkish. There were plenty of differences between the sisters. Mom had been gawky in build and often unkempt in appearance. No matter how classy her dress, there was always something wrong, a spot on the front, or a fraying hem. My mom's younger sister Elizabeth was short and compact, her clothing unfailingly tasteful and sophisticated. Aunt Elizabeth's eyes were blue, whereas Mom's had been dark brown.

Yet, to be in my Aunt Elizabeth's presence made me feel as if a part of my mom had come back to me. Maybe it was the same, slightly crooked Lindsey smile, which Aunt Elizabeth would turn into a comical grimace, looking askance when something didn't seem right. Like Mom, Aunt Elizabeth had a tendency to erupt in a low belly laugh, especially in recognition of some foible of human nature, including her own.

"I'm so glad to see you," I said, as Aunt Elizabeth plodded slowly through the exit gate. She didn't smile, but gave me a pleased nod, then tilted her cheek toward me for a kiss.

As we waited at baggage claim, I observed my aunt had just been to the hairdresser, her signature color touched up to an unsubtle red, commanding us all to take notice. Abruptly, Aunt Elizabeth pointed to her suitcase, spurring me to action. I lifted it off the conveyor.

"That's pretty," I said, remarking on how the handle had been jauntily decorated with ribbons.

"They say it helps distinguish it from the others," she said, reaching for it.

"No, I'll get it," I said.

"Thank you," she said, and took my arm as we headed at a slow, measured pace for the garage.

As I helped her climb into the rather high passenger seat of our red Odyssey van, Aunt Elizabeth said "Thank you" again. I couldn't recall her ever being so polite. Then it occurred to me. My aunt was as nervous as I was about this visit. I was trying to be well behaved for her, and she was trying to be well behaved for me.

That week I drove Aunt Elizabeth to three different retirement homes, the ones around town she might possibly be able to afford on her limited savings. She accepted the paperwork from each, but was generally noncommittal.

Mostly, our family visit with Aunt Elizabeth was relaxed and cordial.

My mom Ruth Lindsey (Patterson) and little sister Elizabeth Lindsey in 1925 in Berea, Ohio.

Some evenings, we played Scrabble, a favorite game of hers. I learned early on not to play seven-letter words.

"Eileen's always doing that," she snapped, referring to her best friend Eileen, with whom she'd traveled often over the years.

From then on, to keep the game fun, I tried not to over-achieve.

My aunt was a huge fan of all things Michigan State University, it being the centerpiece of East Lansing, her beloved home town. The NCAA basketball tournament was gearing up at the time of her visit, with MSU the No. 2 seed. Dave let her know when the MSU game was on. Aunt Elizabeth sat down to watch it with him, but kept a crossword puzzle going at the same time.

"Look Elizabeth, MSU's about to take the lead," Dave said to her at one point, nonplussed that she wasn't really watching.

"Ooo, I can't look," she said, putting her hand up to block her eyes. She cared about her team so much that the tension was too much for her.

Dave was charmed.

Aunt Elizabeth left without saying anything conclusive regarding where, or when she'd come to Seattle. I didn't push her. She was still mentally fit, and could walk on her own, and drive herself where she needed to go. The decision was up to her.

NOT LONG AFTER MY AUNT's departure, I received the news that my application to pursue an MFA in Creative Writing had been accepted, and the busy pace of family events continued without pause. That June, in honor of son George's high school graduation, his grandparents on the Gebben side came out from Michigan to celebrate with us. While they were visiting, we enjoyed showing off the University of Washington campus where he'd be attending school that fall, and took a drive across the Cascade Mountains to deliver daughter Vivian to her camp counselor job.

Around the time of Grandpa and Grandma Gebben's departure, Angela and her family arrived, and the summer months kicked off in earnest.

"I've brought the letters," Angela announced that first afternoon of our time together. I remember we were standing in my office by the book shelf and desk. In one corner, the computer screen gleamed, beckoning with untouched emails and files. I'd been too busy of late to get much of my own work done. Just then George hopped down the stairs next to the office in a muffled series of thuds. Dimly, I could hear Christoph and Dave talking in the kitchen.

The Lindsey sisters—Ruth, Elizabeth, and Anna, in 1941. My mom, Ruth, was the only sister to marry, at age 36 in 1954.

"Letters?" I had an odd sensation I should know what she was talking about.

"The ones from Tante Inge's attic. I thought we could translate some together while I'm here."

A faint memory of our email exchange surfaced. "Right, the letters." I paused, mentally conjuring specifics. "But I thought you said they were written by people who lived in a different village. Are you sure they're from our family?"

"Yes, this is the best part, they're relatives from Meckenheim. That means the Freinsheim and Cleveland Harms are all descendents of another previously emigrated family."

I must have looked baffled. Patiently, Angela set her cloth-woven satchel on the desk and pulled out a bunch of folded papers. "The earliest one is signed by someone named Heinrich Handrich," she added, sifting through them.

"Who?"

She held up the letter. "Heinrich Handrich. See?"

I didn't see. The handwriting was loopy and illegible. To me, it looked like "ff Gaurif Famruf." The whole letter was written in the same crazy cursive.

"How can you even read that?" I knew I'd never be able to.

"That's another thing, these are written in Old German Script. Sütterlin, they called it later. Tante Gretel and Onkel Otto can read it—they were reading some of the letters out loud to me." Angela's mention of her elderly aunt and uncle conjured a memory of an aging but articulate couple I'd once met, long ago in 1988 in Freinsheim. "The contents are really very interesting, about the arrival of the family, their first years in Cleveland. The whole family went, the father and mother and all the sons and daughters except Elisabetha. Probably

Box of 19th century letters found in Tante Inge's attic in Freinsheim, Germany.

because she was already married. I have been studying the old script from an alphabet I have, to learn how to read it myself. I'm beginning to get it, but I'm really slow."

I was impressed, and intimidated, that Angela had worked with her relatives on the letters, and by now could decipher some of the weird old script. Plus, her English was so good. I'd only studied German for one semester in college. I felt bad that I'd really be no help at all.

"So, what does this say?" I squinted at the faded black ink of the last page, still puzzling over the signature.

"Heinrich Handrich. Plus a Ph in the beginning, which I think stands for Philipp. In Old German Script, the 'h' looks like an 'f.' But he has only written the first letter. Most are written by a man named Rapparlie."

"From Meckenheim? Dad never mentioned that village."

"There seems to be some sort of relationship between the villages. Maybe from a previous marriage. Many people emigrated based on letters they received from families who had emigrated before. Chain migration, they call it."

Despite her young-looking appearance in her baggy beige wool tunic and loose-fitting brown corduroy pants, Angela's intelligence and authority rang through loud and clear in her voice, and in the thoughtful reflection in her gray-blue eyes. Over the years of our friendship I'd learned not to argue unless I had darned good reasons. Mentally, I cast about for why I thought these letters weren't part of my ancestry.

"Handrich isn't a family name," I said at last.

A frown creased Angela's forehead. "You haven't seen your father's family tree? He gave me a copy. I saw the names written there."

Family tree? Now that she mentioned it, I did remember a family tree, something Dad had mailed to me some years ago. I rummaged through my densely packed file cabinet and located it—a sheaf of 8-1/2 x 14 pages, a clutter of felt-tipped pen calligraphy. My dad, the architect, lived his profession in every facet of his life, particularly with this distinctive thick black lettering.

Angela skimmed the earliest generations of the tree with her finger, her light-brown hair draping over her cheek like a curtain. Her finger alit near

the start, at the third column.
I leaned in to see for myself.
Among the names listed were
those of the letter writers,
Handrich and Rapparlie. Well,
Rappli, as Dad had spelled it.
Phonetically, though, Rapparlie

*Henrich Handrich's signature,
1841.*

and Rappli sounded similar. In the mid-19th century generation, Michael's
name (1841-1910) was written beneath Philipp's (1839-1900). Michael's older
brother. Their parents were listed as Johann Philipp Harm and K. Elisabeth
Handrich. At last, I understood. Handrich was the maiden name of Michael's
mother.

That day, my family ties with Angela fit together as they never had before.
All along, I'd known she and I were related somehow, but I'd always taken
the relatives in Freinsheim for granted. I hadn't truly understood. Angela's
great-great grandfather was Philipp Harm of Freinsheim. My great-great
grandfather was Michael Harm of Cleveland. Two brothers of the same
family. One brother, Philipp, had stayed in Germany, and the other brother,
Michael, had come to America. Since this 1841 letter writer was Philipp's and
Michael's maternal grandfather, that meant he was Angela's and my 4x great
grandfather. The people named Handrich and Rapparlie, the people who'd
written the letters Angela held in her hands, *were* relatives of mine.

Oddly, I'd never before made the Harm connection. None of the relatives
I knew in Freinsheim had that last name. My grandmother used to tell me
about her favorite grandfather Michael Harm. Vaguely, I understood he'd
emigrated from Freinsheim, but had never thought through the relationships,
how her grandfather had left an older brother Philipp behind. These relatives
in Freinsheim with whom my grandmother had been corresponding, relatives
whom I had visited, and many of whom had visited me, were all descendants
of Philipp Harm.

Angela, for her part, pointed out that she'd always understood about the
two brothers Philipp and Michael. However, she'd always believed it was her
great-great uncle Michael Harm who was the first, and probably the only
ancestor on that side of the family to leave for America. An uncle, rather
than a direct descendant. That her 2x-great grandfather Philipp's maternal
grandparents, and his uncles and aunts as well, had emigrated earlier than
Michael Harm was a revelation. It was the first time Angela realized that she,
too, had direct ancestors buried in American soil.

I'd always imagined such a dramatic "aha!" moment occurring in isolation,
perhaps in the library after long and focused study. Instead, it came crashing
in amid the hubbub of everyday life. As Angela and I stood working this out

Clyde Patterson's family tree in calligraphy.

in my office, her four-year-old daughter Luzi and nine-year-old daughter Carlotta were waiting for her in the next room, poking their heads in regularly to make incomprehensible requests in German. My husband Dave was milling around in the kitchen, waiting for me to tell him the plan for dinner so he could get started on it.

"I thought we could spend time while I'm here translating some of these," Angela said again, indicating the packet of letters on my desk. She looked at me expectantly, perhaps sensing my faltering resolve.

It did seem like a lot to tackle. Not to mention I had little genuine interest in history and no idea what I'd get out of it. Even so, I told her I was willing to try.

Chapter 4

When Angela and her family first arrived at our house that summer of 2008, she and Christoph were concerned about their nine-year-old daughter Carlotta who'd become ill with digestive problems earlier on their trip in Canada. Until Carlotta felt better, Angela and Christoph didn't think it was a good idea to travel. Besides, they had no pressing plans except a visit to a friend in Regina, Saskatchewan later in July, so Angela consulted with me, wondering if they could stay on for the next month, or at least until Carlotta was feeling better,

By that time, over a decade into my friendship with Angela, we knew each other well enough that I was happy to oblige. In the early 1990s when I first was getting to know this German cousin from Freinsheim, I was in my mid-thirties and pregnant with my second child. Her visit to us and other acquaintances in the Pacific Northwest had been brief, but we'd enjoyed each other's company. A year later in 1993 Angela returned to stay for a year at Neah Bay on the Pacific Coast, in order to volunteer at the Makah Cultural and Research Center, one of the first indigenous museums in the United States.

Dave and I saw Angela numerous times in 1993-1994. She'd come for a holiday or long weekend break from her work at Neah Bay, full of energy and stories. She was a welcome guest. I was older than Angela by twelve years, but the age difference seemed to matter very little. She and I would work together in the kitchen preparing meals or cleaning up, getting into lengthy, rambling conversations on all manner of subjects: her studies in cultural anthropology and fine arts, my interests in writing and psychology. She asked me questions about my upbringing in Cleveland with my parents and brothers, people Angela knew since they'd visited her family in Freinsheim over the years. She'd been to my parents' home in Ohio that year on her way out to Neah Bay.

When her year in the Northwest ended and Angela returned to Germany, she and I had continued to correspond, exchanging letters at least once a year much like our grandmothers had. So when Angela talked to me about staying on at our home for an extended time that summer of 2008, it sounded fine to me. I had no job to go to per se, not since I'd committed to being a writer and started working from home. Dave went off to work weekdays, son George was mostly independent by then, orbiting in and out of the house on his own schedule, and Vivian was away working as a camp counselor.

In fact, Angela's need to linger seemed serendipitous, a time for me of relatively few distractions. Every so often in the ensuing days, while Angela's husband Christoph watched over Carlotta and Luzi, she and I would hole up in the office to work. The office area of our home was walled on three sides by mid-century modern built-in bookshelves and stained-wood paneling, on the fourth side by a large picture window. It was an ideal getaway, far enough removed from other activity, but still within reach if needed.

By clearing Dave's and my other projects off the desk, Angela and I could work side by side. Many times, though, Angela preferred to sit by the natural light of the window to better examine the faded handwriting and thin pages, which the ink often bled through. Usually, I sat at the computer ready to receive her dictation.

Angela approached the translations like a true scholar. In advance of her visit, she'd made an inventory: thirteen complete letters, two partial letters, and one postcard, which together spanned the years 1841 to 1900. Beside each date and year, she'd entered who'd written the letter, to whom, page count, letter condition and relevant notes. Most of the earliest letters were written by John (Johann) Rapparlie. Our 4x great grandfather Handrich had written only the first, also one of the most faded and difficult to read. It was directed to Johann Philipp Harm in Freinsheim.

"Cleveland, 21st September, 1841," Angela translated aloud, her index finger skimming the first lines. "Dear daughter—literally, it says 'daughterman.' " She looked up at me. "I've never heard that expression before. It must be an old one. I think he means 'dear daughter's husband,' don't you think? Because he's writing to Johann Philipp Harm, the husband of his daughter?"

Honestly, I didn't know what to think. I still didn't have all the relationships straight in my head. I knew Johann Philipp Harm was the father of Michael and Philipp Harm, hence, Angela and my 3x-great grandfather. But the word daughterman made no sense to me at all.

"Should I type daughter's husband, then?" I asked, fingers poised over the keyboard, a blank document on the screen.

"Let's do both, until we know for sure how it should be written," Angela said.

And so I typed:

Cleveland,[1] 21st September, 1841

Dear daughter's husband ("daughterman")!

[Author's note: At the time of this first translation, and each translation following, Angela and I knew next to nothing of the information footnoted in this book. These were details we discovered during ensuing years of research. The letter writers were spare with punctuation; in some cases, periods and commas have been added for flow.]

> Your letter I did indeed receive in 26 days, and I intended to let you know through this letter that we are all well, and we are healthy. When you write to us, then I would like to learn what my brother-in-law and his wife are doing, and next their girls[2], if they are all healthy, and the girls are still in unmarried state. My sons are working here as coopers[3] and earn 5 Thaler[4] a week and my daughter Margaretha[5] is here in service at innkeeper Risser's.[6] We have in mind to stay here still for some time as we don't have perspective on better properties to buy. We are waiting to look around for at least one more year.
>
> My sons have learned their profession with Filius[7] and still work for him and we have good reason to be thankful to him. Regarding the death of Jacob Ohler[8] I indeed feel sorry. One quarter of a year before, I have already suspected that something would happen to one or the

1   The population of Cleveland in 1840 was 6,000 persons.
2   Reference unknown—The letter writer Philipp Henrich Handrich's sister presumably lived in a village in the region of Freinsheim, most likely in Meckenheim, but the sister's married name is not provided.
3   Barrel-makers
4   Apparently, the Germans used the values of the Thaler and dollar almost interchangeably (1 Thaler = 1 dollar).
5   K. Margaretha Handrich, younger sister of Rapparlie's wife, born 12/12/1813 in Meckenheim, Bavarian Palatinate (Bayern-Pfalz)
6   Possibly Jacob Risser, bakers & confectioners, 12 Superior Lane, listed in the First Directory of the Cities of Cleveland and Ohio City, 1837. A Daniel Risser is also mentioned in Jacob Mueller's *Memories of a Forty-Eighter*, (Western Reserve Historical Society, 1996).
7   Presumably, a German American barrel-maker in Cleveland.
8   Ohler is the maiden name of letter writer Ph. Henrich Handrich's wife, Catherina. Jacob Ohler is possibly her father or brother.

other of the couple. If Daniel Ohler wants to send his son into this land here later, he should let him first learn a profession with which he can advance well here. Tailor, shoemaker or coopers are the best professions here, the former two still better than the latter.

I also let you know that my daughter Katharina[9] is married to Rabalier[10]. He is working in his profession and has 22 Thaler a month.

So you will know about where I live I want to tell you that when my wife and I want to make a change, once in a while we drive 6 miles from here, that is, a 2 hour journey to the Umbstädters, the Bletschers or the Leises[11]. That you have informed me about Stützel's son I have to tell you that I haven't heard anything yet. I have gotten letters from Hans Philipp Herr and Wilhelm Stenzel and Hans Martinger.[12]

They are still in this land, namely in Cincinatti [sic] [and] are well off. The letter which I had taken along from Wernz[13] into this land, I have sent away but not yet received an answer. Through a tailor's apprentice from Böhl[14] I have heard that he has left half a year ago from Cincinatti. Yet Jacob Höge was still there.

I ask you please to inform me which people are here in this land from Meckenheim. Since I don't know anything

---

9   Katherina Margaretha Handrich the elder (two daughters had the exact same name) born 8/16/1809 in Meckenheim, married to Johann Rapparlie on 12/12/1840 in Cleveland, Ohio.

10   Johann Rapparlie, born 10/5/1818 in Rheingönnheim.

11   Jacob Mueller writes in *Memories of a Forty-Eighter* about 1830's German immigrants who "wanted nothing to do with the sandy soil of Cleveland, so they bought their farms in the nearby townships of Newburgh and Parma." John Umstader is recorded in the 1840 census in Parma, Ohio, located approximately 6 miles south of downtown Cleveland. Mueller notes the Laises and the Pletschers as two of the first farm families to arrive in the area.

12   An example of how people frequently hand-carried letters and news from place to place.

13   A Meckenheim Philipp Jacob Handrich married Anna Maria Wernz (Walter Mattel, Meckenheim genealogist), so perhaps this Wernz is somehow related to that family.

14   A neighboring village to Meckenheim.

else to write of importance, I wish you further all the best
and greet you, and all good friends and acquaintances,
many times cordially, as well as greetings from my wife
and the children

Ph.[Philipp] Heinrich Handrich[15]

It's so nice to have the letter translated here on the page, all in a seamless flow. Back in 2008 as Angela and I worked our way through this 1841 letter sentence by sentence, we often stopped to ponder and speculate on the contents.

"How far is Meckenheim from Freinsheim?" I asked Angela as I wrestled to picture these people and former times.

"About twenty minutes by car, maybe 15 kilometers," she said. "To me, the family name Ohler is most interesting. If these Ohlers are family back then in Meckenheim, something really funny could result: I could be a relative of my school dance prom partner, whose last name was Ohler! He was a classmate from a neighboring village, not Meckenheim, but that doesn't mean anything, since people married and moved between the villages. And Ohler is a rare name."

"How could it be a family name?" I was mystified. Angela seemed to have a much a better grasp of all this than I did.

"I think perhaps Ohler was the maiden name of Handrich's wife."

I accepted her hunch, wondering vaguely how she and Dad obtained this kind of family tree information. I knew absolutely nothing about genealogy.

Handrich mentioned many names in his letter. For having just arrived in Cleveland, he seemed acquainted with a surprising number of people. Also puzzling were his references to the employers of his sons and daughter, as if the Freinsheimers to whom he wrote would know who he was talking about. Not at all how I'd pictured the immigrant experience. Previously, I'd imagined people tearing up roots and leaving everything behind to arrive in a completely alien world—faced with a different language and different customs amid total strangers, having to learn everything on their own. Based on this letter, though, the new arrivals knew all kinds of people, some well

15 Ph. is an abbreviation for Philipp. Angela and I would later learn that Henrich, not Heinrich, is the most common spelling of our 4x-great grandfather's name. Ph. Henrich Handrich was born 3/7/1783 in Meckenheim. His wife Katherina Elisabetha Ohler was born 11/18/1782 in Meckenheim. They were married in 1801. They emigrated in 1840 with four adult children, leaving behind the eldest daughter Elisabetha, then married to Johann Philipp Harm of Freinsheim.

enough to go out visiting them on Sunday afternoons.

"'We have in mind to stay here still for some time as we don't have perspective on better properties to buy,'" Angela read out. "'We are waiting to look around for at least one more year.'" She looked up and out the window, her expression thoughtful. "It sounds like they originally planned to be farmers." Angela's grandparents in Freinsheim had been farmers, carrying on the long family tradition. Angela still owned a remnant of that land, a small plum field she'd inherited, a hold-out of trees engulfed by vineyards. She told me how she had decided at one point to leave the old trees as long as they survived, to only replant the ones that died naturally. "When Onkel Otto and Tante Gretel were reading through the letters with me, we found out the Handrichs ended up staying in the city. I wonder why they never got a farm," she added.

It seemed to me a mystery we'd never solve. I pictured the vast geographical distances between Handrich and his eldest daughter Elisabetha in Freinsheim, married to a farmer named Johann Philipp Harm. What had it been like for her, the one left behind? Her parents had voyaged across the ocean to North America to an unimaginable place called Cleveland, Ohio. For the rest of Elisabetha's life, she'd miss the important milestones and everyday life events of her parents and siblings, and they'd miss hers.

The letters in Angela's inventory showed that, at times, many years passed between letters. Mail in those days took months to cross the Atlantic. If letters or news didn't arrive, letters bearing news of marriages, births and deaths, the information might even be years after the event occurred. Even if Elisabetha had expected the news of the death of her parents, when it finally arrived, the abrupt finality of it would have been wrenching. She must have felt terribly far away.

EVEN IN OUR MODERN, HIGH-TECH lives, we sometimes aren't able to bridge great distances. When my mother died in Cleveland, Ohio on October 29, 1999, I was living in the Seattle area, where I'd settled with Dave over a decade earlier.

The last time I saw Mom had been that summer of 1999, on the occasion of her eightieth birthday, a time when, coincidentally, our German relative Manfred Weber had been visiting Cleveland, too. In my photo album I have a picture of the event. Her birthday was in July. On that hot humid Ohio afternoon, Dad brought Mom home from the Somerset skilled nursing facility. Mom's hair was beautifully styled, a perm that highlighted the elegant gray at her temples.

In the photo she's sitting in a red, soft-patterned dress, party balloons strung on the wheelchair handle behind her. Mom was once a bright woman. She'd been Valedictorian of her high school class. When I was growing up, she was a teacher at a local high school, a woman who kept a sharp eye on current events and was an avid reader, especially of murder mysteries. I used to love the haphazard attention she gave her glasses, perpetually crooked and slipping down her nose, visible proof that her priorities lay elsewhere, less in how she looked, more in reading and learning and doing things she cared about. It cut me to the quick to see her without them.

Mom's Alzheimer's had advanced to the point that she didn't know where she was. Once a gracious and smiling hostess, at her birthday party she sat in the center of dear friends and family amid the laughter and talking, her expression wistful, sad and lost. I hovered protectively around her, all the while missing her desperately, stricken by a massive sense of guilt I'd not been there for her long before now, back when she'd still had her mind.

"It's your responsibility to look after your family," Mom always told me. I should have listened. Ever since I'd turned eighteen, I'd been living in different cities miles away, only visiting once or twice a year, not really looking after her at all.

Maybe it's a sign of our current era, how I blithely put such distances between myself and my parents without thinking ahead to the inevitable outcome, imagining I could hop on a plane whenever I chose. It's a huge regret of mine that when Mom died later that fall, just two months shy of the new millennium, I was not by her side.

Mom's admonition to take care of family was a compelling reason I'd started prodding Aunt Elizabeth to move to a retirement community in Seattle. I admired my aunt's alertness, her mental and social competence, and didn't want to take her away from her life in East Lansing. I knew she wasn't eager to leave, especially not her close friends. They'd always looked after one another, but now all of them were octogenarians, failing in health and physical ability.

As Angela and I translated the 1841 letter, I thought about how, perhaps, my attitude about moving great distances had been handed down to me from these ancestors. The senior Handrichs had migrated with their entire family from Meckenheim to Cleveland. Michael Harm had made the choice to emigrate across the Atlantic, too, in 1857, just as I'd made the choice to leave my family in Ohio when I'd turned 18 in 1976, eventually settling thousands of miles away in the Pacific Northwest.

I knew Angela saw it as very important to keep ties with her home and family. Although she lived in Marburg two hours north, she went back often to see her mother and brother in Freinsheim and had not let go of her plum field there. Perhaps Angela also saw my tendency to live far from home as a family trait handed down from the Handrichs and Michael Harm. If so, she kept the observation to herself.

TRANSLATING THAT FIRST LETTER TOOK several days, in part due to Angela's disciplined word analysis. She concentrated hard to figure out the words that best reflected the original intentions of the letter writers. If I'd been doing it alone, I'm sure I would have tried to cut corners and been less precise about the German to English word meanings.

Angela's ability with languages was advanced, not just in English, but in Spanish, too. She had no problem discussing in-depth, complex subjects in English. I realized that no matter how hard I tried, my language skills could never match hers, so I was grateful for her patience in unraveling the dense script.

She and I differed not only in personality and language ability, but in clothing styles as well. Around Angela, I noticed my culturally American habits, my tendency toward brighter colors while Angela dressed in earth-tones, my form-fitting clothes compared to her looser, baggier ones. My blow-dried, shoulder-length brown hair looked carefully composed and coiffed next to her longer, lankier light brown tresses. Overall, I'm pretty average looking, brown hair, brown eyes and well-fed build, my melting pot genetics stirred into a German and Scottish stew.

As a trained cultural anthropologist, Angela enjoyed studying cultural differences between societies and peoples, especially their customs and ways of thinking and behaving. She and I often discussed these topics—I held a Bachelor of Arts in Psychology, so our areas of knowledge intersected. We didn't focus as much on the dates and facts we were gleaning from the letters as we did on the historical and cultural context surrounding the lives of those previous generations. But because I am an American and she a German, our observations could be radically different.

I began noticing the disconnect in cultural perspectives back in our earliest encounters. During one of Angela's 1994 visits, when I brought my son home from preschool, he carried into the house with him a flimsy paper plate adorned with an assortment of glittered pasta shells. Angela leaned over to admire his art project and her pleasant expression faded to dismay. She looked up, taking the plate from him.

"You teach your children to waste food?" She asked, holding it up for me to see.

I bridled, but I also saw her point. I'd not thought of it that way. I'd made pasta collages when I was a child. Pasta is inexpensive, comes in fun nature shapes, and poses little danger to toddlers if swallowed. Then again, in other parts of the world, and in my own country, too, many people go hungry. How horrifying it would be, I realized, even cruel, for them to see their potential meal, food that might have filled their hungry stomachs, coated in glitter and glued on a plate. We were sending our children a mixed message.

Such experiences were both jarring and enlightening. The 1922 letters Angela had first translated, letters that told of the terrible "dearth" in those years in Germany, were a case in point. For generations, Angela's family had lived in a rural farming community and maintained a strong connection to the land. She and I discussed how her parents and grandparents stressed the importance of not wasting anything. They'd been forced to survive in a land torn by war, and subject to the continual capriciousness of bad weather and poor harvests. The hardships her family had endured in the past still influenced her present-day perspectives.

My American family history, on the other hand, had not included farming for generations. I'd tried to garden, but I never felt as if I knew what I was doing, and the results were evidence of my inadequacy. My mother had gardened, too, with similar, lackluster results. As Angela and I worked on these letters I began to wonder. Did my remoteness from food sources trace back to the earliest arrival of my immigrant ancestors? Did our ineptitude stem back generations? Already in the first, 1841 letter from Cleveland to Freinsheim, it seemed as if family attitudes and values toward the land were shifting. From 4x-great grandfather's statement about looking around for land to buy, it appeared he'd intended to continue farming. But he hadn't done so, and, according to Angela, never would. Clearly, I didn't experience as keenly as Angela the potential for scarcity and hunger, something her grandparents endured. It seemed a good thing, to be more aware of this cultural difference. If I should ever experience dearth in my lifetime, I would be ill-equipped to handle it.

Chapter 5

Gradually, Angela and I were falling into a rhythm. Before diving into the tedium of line by line translation, we speculated first about the letter writer and his purpose in writing. The next letter chronologically, written in 1847, was written by Johann Rapparlie a full six years after the first one by Handrich. After some discussion, Angela and I determined Johann Rapparlie was Handrich's son-in-law, the Rabalier mentioned in Handrich's 1841 letter: *"I also let you know that my daughter Katharina is married to Rabalier. He is working in his profession and has 22 Thaler a month."* That made three spellings of the same name: Rappli, Rabalier, and Rapparlie.

In this 1847 letter Rapparlie (the spelling the man himself uses) wrote three dense pages of news. Why was Rapparlie writing the letters now, we wondered, and not the elder Handrich? Had the father come to some sort of incapacity, or even died since 1841? The letter hadn't been sent in an envelope; instead, the lengthy address had been scrawled on the blank backside of the third and last page, to Philipp Harm[1], Freinsheim Rheinkreis[2], Kanton Dürkheim an der Hard[3], Europa [Europe].

> 10 November, 1847
>
> Much loved brother-in-law and sister-in-law[4],
>
> With great joy I pick up the feather [quill][5] to let you know

---

1   Johann Philipp Harm, father of Philipp (8 years old) and Michael (6 years old) Harm.
2   Rheinkreis—the Palatinate/Pfalz region to the west of the Rhine River, then a province of Bavaria.
3   Canton Dürkheim at the foot of the Haardt Mountains was the district for the village of Freinsheim.
4   Johann Philipp Harm and K. Elisabetha Harm, maiden name Handrich.
5   By 1850 use of the feather quill for writing had faded, replaced by pens with steel nibs. However, the term "feather" continues to be used by the Germans

about our happy affairs, how all of us are amongst each other here in Cleveland. We have already waited for two to three years for a letter from you since my brother[6] has left from home as we have already written two letters to you and never received an answer. Therefore, we thought you didn't want to write us but when my sister came from Germany she was upset because you hadn't received

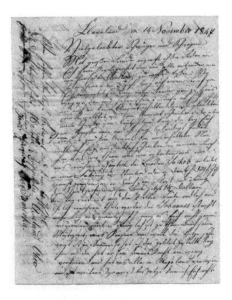

First page of 1847 letter

any answer from us. Now I especially want to write to you in my letter what we are doing, what we are working, how we survive here. Namely, brother Jakob[7] works in a factory where steamboats are being fabricated[8] where, because of his diligence and skill in the blacksmithing profession, he earns now an income of $1.50/day and sincerely and honestly indulges the two old people.[9]

Further, Johannes[10] is no longer with us, I don't exactly like to express it because it is impossible to do so. Due to the indifference of his body and because the heat is very

---

in this and subsequent letters.

6 Possibly Adam Rapparlie, listed in Cleveland directories in the mid 1800s.

7 There are apparently two Jacob Handrichs in the family. "Brother" Jakob Handrich is possibly the youngest brother of Rapparlie's wife Katherina Handrich, born 2/24/1822 in Meckenheim, Bavarian Palatinate (Bayern-Pfalz). The identity of the other Jacob Handrich is not elucidated in this and subsequent letters.

8 Possibly, the Cuyahoga Steam Furnace Co. founded in 1827.

9 Philipp Henrich Handrich and Katherina Elisabetha Handrich (maiden name Ohler), who emigrated with four of their adult children. (This letter is addressed to their eldest daughter and her husband.)

10 Johannes Handrich was the eldest brother of Rapparlie's wife, Katherina Handrich, born 8/2/1811 in Meckenheim, Bavarian Palatinate (Bayern-Pfalz)

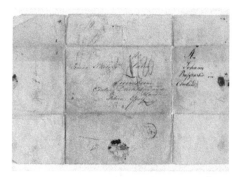

Address on 1841 letter.

big in the summer so his blood has rebelled and this has allegedly made him lose the power of his senses a little bit and he has abandoned us all in Cleveland and where he has gone I cannot describe to you. We have already heard different times where he should have been and he should be again pretty much in order.

Further, Margaretha[11] is married with Georg Sheuermann[12] from Weisenheim am Sand[13] and she has one child that is a boy. He is also rightly and honestly supporting himself, also earns his $7-$8/week. They are healthy and fine.

Further, I myself have had now my own blacksmith and wagon builder business already three years. I now have two men for making the wood work in the wagon building work place and have two fires burning in the Schmidschob or blacksmith's workshop. I'm now manufacturing wagons and chaises, everything ready so that one can put on the horses, as it is the fashion here to have everything done by one man. I now have my own property in the middle of town. [14] It cost $600, one house on it and two workshops. And thanks be to God and we are all quite happy that we don't see the German mean-spirited cheaters of Europe anymore and don't wish to see them, either.

Further, the old mother[15] has lain in bed sick this summer

---

11 K. Margaretha Handrich, younger sister of Rapparlie's wife Katherina Handrich, born 12/12/1813 in Meckenheim, Bavarian Palatinate (Bayern-Pfalz).

12 Georg Scheuermann was born in Weisenheim am Sand in approximately 1815. His marriage with Margaretha occurred in Cleveland on 2/14/1844.

13 Weisenheim am Sand is a village just 3.5 kilometers from Freinsheim.

14 RAPPARLIE, J. Seneca St., corner of Michigan and Seneca, carriage mfr., listed in Cleveland's Knight & Parson's City Directory 1848-1849.

15 Katherina Elisabetha Handrich, maiden name Ohler, born 11/18/1782 in Meckenheim, Rheinland-Pfalz

very long, that is, she didn't leave the bed for 13 weeks but has been treated right by doctors and is quite well again now. The old man[16] has not been sick yet since he's here. Thanks be to God we are all quite healthy and have only one child that was two years old on the 19th of March this year and is called Elizabetha but whereas earlier, before her, two have died to us. The first was but only eleven days old. The second nine months. The third has never been sick yet.

Next, two lads from Meckenheim arrived on the 4th of November, namely Nicholaus Räder and Philipp Häuser who both work as laborers close to Cleveland and who also brought us your dried cherries and they have spent several days with us and we have learned of much news from Meckenheim. Further, dear unknown brother-in-law, whom I have never seen, now if I may, while not knowing you, ask you, if you should have the goodness to tell this letter or the other few lines to my brothers-in-law in Rheingönheim. When my sister arrived, I have written them a letter but they might not have received it so you might let them know my matters.

Dear brothers-in-law, the paper is getting small now. My sister Elizabeth[17] has arrived here in Cleveland healthily and happily and has told the entire circumstances of how everything is for you. In case you should travel to America, start your way early in spring and don't do a ship contract at home in between and wait until you get to Havre.[18] Then you can get a way fast and cheaper. When you arrive in New York, don't make contracts farther than from station to station, namely from Havre till Neuyork [New York], from there till Allbargie [Albany], from there till Bufalo [Buffalo][19], from there till Kleveland [Cleveland]. Later go asking for John Rapparlie. I hope you will have gotten the letter sent earlier.

---

16 Ph. Henrich Handrich
17 Presumably, this Elizabeth Rapparlie is from Rheingönnheim, the same birthplace of her brother Johann Rapparlie.
18 Le Havre, France
19 Presumably, Rapparlie is referring to the Erie Canal route

Dear brother-in-law Harm, if you get to Rheingönheim[20] just ask for Martin Scherer[21]. I don't know any further news but that it is always good to send fruits. I want to close my writing and hope it will meet you in as good health as it has left us.

Johannes Rapparlie

NOTE: We hope for an answer soon and no delays and the address is:

John Rapparlie, Cleveland, Ohio, North America.

NOTE: I greet you many thousand times. Jacob Handrich.

As Angela deciphered each sentence, I was being drawn in, like a time traveler getting a firsthand glimpse into a former time. From his detailed explanation of their Cleveland life, it seemed to me Johann Rapparlie enjoyed writing letters. He brimmed over with news, as if to convince his readers in the Old Country just how great life was in the New World.

Several sections were especially challenging to translate.

"The closest meaning to this phrase," Angela said, "I'm just not sure." Laboriously, she read out the words. "...*sind alle recht froh daß wir daß deutsche lumpische spitzbübische Europa nicht mehr sehen und auch nicht mehr verlangen zu sehen.*" (Angela was referring to a passage near the middle of the letter, when Rapparlie writes, "we are all quite happy that we don't see the German mean-spirited cheaters of Europe anymore and don't wish to see it, either.")

Rapparlie's word *lumpische*, she went on to explain, was most likely a variant spelling of *lumpig*, which translates as "mean." *Spitzbub*, we discovered in my German-English dictionary, meant "scoundrel."

"Oh, sure," I agreed, "that makes sense. Mean scoundrels of Europe."

"Really?" Angela shifted her gray-blue gaze to stare out the window. I could almost see her brain mentally rummaging through vocabularies and word meanings. "*Lumpig* in German, it means something more, I think. Not just mean like a bully, but mean in the heart, in one's whole being."

After further discussion, we settled on "mean-spirited" as the closest translation. Then we moved on to *spitzbübische*. Angela asked me for my best English definition of scoundrel. I explained what I thought it meant, something akin to rascal.

20 Rheingönnheim is near Mannheim, approximately 30 kilometers from Freinsheim, and the town of Johann Rapparlie's family.
21 Presumably the name of one of Rapparlie's relatives.

"No, that's not quite right, either," she said. "I think Rapparlie is not just saying they're trouble-makers, I think he means they're cheating people out of what belongs to them."

"Well, how about mean-spirited cheaters, then?"

Angela nodded agreement, so I typed it in. We wondered aloud about European history in the 1830s and 1840s, what could have prompted Rapparlie to write such a thing. Neither of us knew much of anything about 19th-century European history, so our conversation petered out quickly. When it came to U.S. history, we weren't much better off. Although I'd grown up in Cleveland, it had never crossed my radar that the city once had a steamboat factory. And how come so many letters hadn't reached Ohio from Germany? Were shipwrecks that common? It didn't seem likely.

Angela grew especially excited about Rapparlie's detailed description of his shop. "I'll bet this letter is of scholarly interest to historians of material culture and of trades," she said. "Rapparlie talks about the number of workers, the dimensions of the building. I'm surprised there were women. What work did they do?"

We both appreciated the news supplied in the letter that the elder Handrich and his wife, ("the old mother" and "the old man") were still living. One particular sentence in the 1847 letter remained with me long after Angela and I had finished the translation. "Now I especially want to write to you in my letter what we are doing, what we are working, how we survive here." In German, that last verb: *sich ernähren* is more closely translated as: to keep oneself, or to sustain oneself with food. As Angela and I discussed the translation at the time, though, "how we keep ourselves" sounded awkward in English. Plus, I couldn't think of an equivalent expression in English for "how we sustain ourselves with food." Initially, we settled on the phrase "how we survive here," which to me had an especially thought-provoking ring to it.

In 1847, about six years after the arrival in America, the family seemed to be surviving well, in business and employment endeavors, anyway. Yet they'd also suffered hardships, the old mother sick all summer, and the eldest son Johannes abandoning them, and two infant deaths. In that light, Rapparlie's insistence that their third child was in good health, announced practically in the same breath as the tragedies of losing two babies, stood out like a prayerful mantra against future calamity.

While I'd begun this translation project reluctantly, now I was hooked. What would happen to these ancestors? How would they survive? I longed to find out whatever story the letters had to tell.

Chapter 6

The disappearance of Johannes Handrich was one strong hook drawing me into the lives of these long-ago relatives. The letters we'd translated so far mentioned two Handrich brothers—Johannes and Jakob. According to Rapparlie's account, the younger brother, Jakob, was working "with diligence and skill" as a blacksmith and also "indulging the old people," which Angela and I took to mean he was the primary caregiver of the Handrich parents. Johannes, the eldest, on the other hand, was struggling. In the 1847 letter, Johannes was reported to be a source of heavy concern: "…Due to the indifference of his body and because the heat is very big in the summer so his blood has rebelled and this has allegedly made [Johannes] lose the power of his senses a little bit and he has abandoned us all in Cleveland and where he has gone I cannot describe to you."

Lordy, I understood about the very big heat in the Ohio summers, which I'd experienced again the previous year when housesitting at Craig's and helping Dad. That heavy, sweltering humidity built and built, then exploded in a torrent of wind, thunder and lightning. In the days of no air-conditioning, it must have been terrible. Especially in a blacksmith shop, working over a forge fire.

But the summer heat in Ohio was not the main impression this account made on me. It was how the eldest son, Johannes, had disappeared, a long-ago event that struck me with a sense of immediacy. The same thing had happened in my own family. In the mid-1980s, my older brother, Sandy, also "lost the power of his senses" and "abandoned" us.

Sandy was born in 1955, the eldest of the three Patterson children of Clyde Patterson and Ruth Ellen Lindsey Patterson. I am the middle child, born in 1957, and Craig the youngest, born in 1959. Sandy was the first son, first to learn to ski, first to go hiking and camping, first to head off to college. At Michigan Technological University in Houghton, Michigan he studied geological engineering. Early on at his time there, he joined Campus Crusade for Christ. As Sandy became more and more indoctrinated, his behavior grew increasingly odd. He studied the Bible and prayed constantly, and often went on fasts. Sometimes when he was home on a school break, I'd come across him sitting up late at night, his Bible open in his lap, refusing to go to sleep because "the devil invaded his dreams."

Naively, I attributed his behavior to religious zealotry. Mom used to argue endlessly with Sandy about his theology, but our parents basically accepted it. Perhaps they, too, believed it was a phase? Or hoped it was.

My grandmother was the one who recognized what was happening to Sandy before any of the rest of us. She

Sandy Patterson, Clyde Patterson, and Emma Patterson, circa 1986.

lived next door to our family, and I made it a habit sometimes, when delivering her mail, to stop and talk with her. My brothers did, too. She seemed to worry constantly, and since she lived alone, whenever we dropped in she'd start in about her latest concerns. After we went away to college, we continued the habit whenever we came home for breaks.

"Sandy was here to see me," she said almost the moment I stepped in the door one time. Grandmother was a small woman. Now in her eighties, she'd shrunk to almost half my size. She gazed at me with a forehead creased in concern, her pale blue eyes blinking through black-and silver-framed bifocals. "He told me his life had been changed by Christ. He said he never could sing before, but he'd prayed about it and God had given him a singing voice. Then he started singing hymns. He sang for a long time, in a high-pitched, bleating voice. It was like he wasn't right in the head."

"He just started singing?" I had trouble imagining this. He and I had just missed each other on visits home that summer, so I hadn't seen him in a while. Sandy had done some strange things, but nothing that weird. I wasn't so much worried, though, as mad at Sandy for upsetting Grandmother. She was old and frail. She didn't need him stirring her up like this.

Grandmother reached out her joint-swollen hand, trembling slightly, to the white Formica countertop for support. "We've never had anything like that in our family. It must come from your mother's side."

I suppressed a smirk. All my life, Grandmother had denied any wrongdoing, related to a misdeed, or a personal shortcoming, or a genetic flaw. Anything that couldn't be swept under the carpet had to be hung on someone else, usually Mom and her Lindsey side of the family. Even so, I loved Grandmother and listened to her worries. I did my best to calm her down, assuring her I thought Sandy would probably even out his more fanatic beliefs over time.

After Sandy earned a degree in Geological Engineering, he continued to devote his life to Christ. First, he spent a year printing Bible tracts in Switzerland, then he returned to work with Child Evangelism Fellowship at a summer camp in Michigan. When the summer ended, he went to Chicago to continue his ministry.

Although over-the-top in his Christian beliefs, Sandy was a loving, compassionate brother, and a storyteller with a great sense of humor. In Chicago, as he went from place to place holding Bible studies with inner city kids, he drove a heinous beige Ford Fairmont. It looked so rusted and awful one of his friends slapped a bumper sticker on it that said, "This Is Not An Abandoned Car." Sandy loved telling this story with a huge grin.

By that point, when he was in Chicago, I was living in Seattle. As the years passed, every time I saw Sandy he looked worse, more pale and skeletal. I rationalized that the cause of his thinness had to do with Bible dictates about fasting and prayer, and how little money he was making.

Eventually, Sandy wasn't making ends meet in Chicago. When Mom and Dad went to pick him up, they visited his apartment and realized he wasn't even able to take care of himself anymore. They brought him home and checked him into a mental health facility. At last, Sandy's mental illness received an official diagnosis—schizophrenia complicated by severe anorexia. My brother's mental illness had been right before our eyes, yet the diagnosis came as a shock.

Thank goodness his psychosis was being addressed at last, I thought. According to my parents' reports, my brother was a stellar patient. Then, as soon as he was released from the mental health facility, he disappeared. He left no note. Days passed, and he didn't return. My parents were crazy with worry. They had not the slightest inkling where he had gone.

Angela had met Sandy several times as a young girl when he'd lived in Switzerland and visited Freinsheim. I'd been honest with her about his mental health issues. So as we translated the part of the letter where Rapparlie reported on Johannes, I spoke my thoughts aloud.

"Sounds like manic-depression, or schizophrenia, just like Sandy."

"Maybe." Angela gazed up from the letter and into the distance. I expected her to say something about Sandy, but she went down a different track. "Rapparlie is the one writing this story about Johannes. To me, it sounds like Rapparlie has a set way of looking at the world. Maybe Rapparlie and Johannes didn't agree."

"What do you mean?"

"Perhaps Rapparlie was too pragmatic for Johannes. Maybe it was a difference of opinion, and Rapparlie drove Johannes away."

I tried to consider her point. Angela could be right—no doubt she could read into the German phrasings a tone of voice or other nuances that were lost on me. Maybe Rapparlie was a hard taskmaster. On the other hand, it also felt as if we'd run into a cultural difference of some kind, like my frankness about Sandy's diagnosis was breaking a cultural taboo. Later, when Angela reviewed this manuscript, she agreed. For many reasons, including the stigma against mental illness in the Nazi era, Angela told me she had a deep-seated discomfort with discussing the subject.

For my part, Rapparlie's account in his letter had hijacked my thoughts back to memories of my older brother. I had a clear recollection of how hard my parents had struggled to understand Sandy, and how distraught they were when he disappeared. I couldn't help imagining the Handrichs must have suffered a similar angst and despair.

Chapter 7

With eleven letters yet to go, Angela and I began to regret how soon her 2008 visit would be drawing to a close. Carlotta was feeling better, and the family needed to leave in a few days' time for their trip to Regina, Saskatchewan. It appeared we'd only be able to do one, or possibly two more letters.

"Next why don't we translate the one just after Michael Harm arrives in America?" Angela said. "He came in 1857, right?"

I cringed. Her inventory showed at least five letters we'd have to skip over. I longed to keep going with the story, to know if Johannes came back, and if the old people kept their health or had passed away in the ten years since 1847. Then too, I wanted to get to the part where my great-great grandfather Michael Harm arrived in Cleveland, the family history I'd heard so often.

Angela set aside letters dated 1849, 1850, 1852 and 1856, and picked up the one dated 1858. "I've looked at this already. I think at the end there is even writing in the hand of our great great great aunt."

So, leaping ahead eleven years, we started in on another letter written by the coach-maker John Rapparlie. The condition of this letter was worse than most, with creases and several holes, parts of it illegible.

> Cleveland 8 December 1858
>
> Much loved brother-in-law and sister-in-law,
>
> I can't keep myself from writing a few lines to you about how it goes with us. We are, thanks to God, all still quite healthy like we are here, but we don't know how our brother-in-law Jacob[1] is in California. I have received a

---

1 Jakob Handrich, the youngest son of the Handrich family. In 1858 he was 36 years old. By 1858, both parents had died. Elisabetha Katherina Handrich/Handrick died 2/20/1853 and Ph. Henrich Handrich/Hendrick

letter from him in August. He then had worked in San
Francisco and had a big income. That is, he wrote me
that he earned each day, when he worked, $62 and paid
only $7 for the week in room and board. He worked there
for a while, then he lost his job because times are really
very bad in California. On October 18, he wrote me again
that he was in Sacramento Sutte[2] but is still without work
and he wanted to go from there to the gold digging places
and try his luck there. He also wrote to me that because
he doesn't like it there and he doesn't have an opportunity
to work in his profession [blacksmith] he will want to see
us again soon, that is, approximately within two years.

Angela glanced up. "Soon? Two years is soon?!" We looked at each other,
marveling at the different perspectives about what constituted a short time
from their era to ours.

Dear brother-in-law and sister-in-law, Jacob is many
thousands of miles away from you and us. His journey
where he wants to go now is almost as far as the Black
Sea[3] but you can't get a grasp of such a journey. It may
be the case that he is very lucky as very many from here
have become rich people, but it could also be the case
that we will never see Jakob again. These are the words
he wrote to me: Dear brother-in-law, I am enormously far
away from you and don't know yet if I will be able to shake
hands with you again or not, and so on. Jakob didn't need
to undertake again such a journey since he has his own
house and property which they call house place[4], which
brings him each month $9.00 of rent. He has also cash
money besides. This journey costs him at least $400 and

died 4/20/1854. Both were laid to rest at Erie Street Cemetery in downtown
Cleveland.
2   Perhaps this refers to Sutter's Mill or Sutter's Fort near Sacramento, where the
Gold Rush began in 1848.
3   The distance from Germany across Eastern Europe to the Black Sea is
approximately 2000 kilometers.
4   Angela and I are unsure of the meaning of this expression. Rapparlie could
be trying to express to his German relatives that houses in Ohio came with
property surrounding them, unlike in the German villages where houses
abutted one another.

is a very unstable life. But it may be his luck after all. It is like a lottery. Now I will close about Jacob.[5]

"One of my ancestors went to California during the Gold Rush?" I swiveled in my chair, opened my Internet browser, and typed in California Gold Rush. "The Gold Rush had been going on for ten years. It'd just about ended by 1858," I said. Angela didn't respond. Head bent in concentration, she stared at the handwriting, lips sounding out the words. "Didn't Jakob catch gold fever kind of late?" I prodded.

Angela looked up from her work. "Maybe he had to stay and care for the parents."

Such a practical point, but it hadn't occurred to me. I felt a twinge of guilt about Aunt Elizabeth, how it was too easy for me to forget how our elders need us. I thought maybe I should be pressing my aunt to make a change, that she might be putting off the move for too long. But I had plenty on my plate as it was. I wasn't eager to upset either of our lives, and besides, she seemed happy where she was.

Angela continued reading.

My two boys now already attend schools in German and English. They learn both reading and writing in two languages at the same time. Then our third one is not in school yet. We have had a portrait taken of our small daughter because she is the only female person from the Handrich family and we also hope to be able to educate her if God allows it.

Dear brother-in-law, this man, namely George Wekerling, who carries this letter will be able to tell you much personally about how it goes for all of us here in America. I also want to write to you about how it's going with your son Michael. He is learning the business from me and will have to learn for three years. Then he'll get from me in three years $130[6] plus room and board.[7] In the beginning it came hard to him to swing the heavy blacksmith hammer but now I think he is pretty turned around and knows no other things than work. I think he has been doing little

5 Rapparlie switches between Jacob and Jakob in spelling, but is clearly referring to just the one Jakob.

6 In apprenticeship arrangements, this end-of-training payment was known as "freedom dues."

7 *Für Wasch und Kost*—for washing and expenses?

hard work earlier because he didn't know much about working but I think in three years when his apprenticeship is over he will become a good craftsman. Our brother-in-law Georg Scheuermann and Margaretha are also very well and their two boys are also quite healthy.

Dear brother-in-law, the man will probably want to buy some wine in the area. Please be good enough to be a little bit helpful to him so he won't be cheated. He is my next and best neighbor. If the wine is very cheap and good, then you can buy me again a barrel of about 80-100 liters and write my name twice on the barrel and should the man buy wine and he's pleased with the wine, then you can send it along with him. In case you should buy for me, don't buy inexpensive bad wine because it costs freight. I don't know any further news except that we have bad times in America and it has never been as bad as now.

I hope that these few lines will reach you in as a good a health as they leave us.

We stay your true ones

John Rapparlie, Katherina Rapparlie nee Handrich

[Note following signature[8]]

Dear parents and brother,

I can't keep myself from also writing a few lines to you, how I am and how I like it. I am still very fine and am healthy and am enjoying the business. My contract for the

---

8   Additional notes at the bottom:
A nice greeting to cousin Daniel Ohler, and we all greet many thousand times and also let him know how we and Jacob are.
[written in pencil on the letter, perhaps a copy of a response, by Johann Philipp Harm:]
Also cousin Daniel's [son] Bernhard has entered the second marriage, where I have as well been attending at the wedding and they also send you many greetings. Also cousin Johann Michel's [daughter] Anna Maria has started her marriage with Michael Selzer. I don't know any further news. Now I want to close my writing and we remain your faithful ones and your brother who loves you Philipp Harm

time of my apprenticeship you can read in uncle's writing.
I can't write further news, since you can read all about
Uncle Jakob in Uncle's writing I will close my writing and
remain your faithful son,

Michael Harm

There it was, at the very bottom of Rapparlie's long missive. A message to
Freinsheim from my great-great grandfather. In 1858, he would have been 17
years old.

"Why is Michael's part so brief?" I wondered aloud. "Just one paragraph
after being gone a whole year? If that's the first and only time his parents
heard from him, I feel very sorry for them." The terseness of the message even
seemed to hint at some kind of falling out, I thought. Perhaps Michael had
even run away. On the family tree, Dad had recorded the oral history, how
Michael Harm hated farm work, so left his hoe in the field and followed a
music band to Cleveland.

"I think it shows Michael was having a hard time," Angela said. "Remember
what Rapparlie wrote?" We scanned back through the letter and reread that
paragraph.

'In the beginning it came hard to [Michael] to swing the
heavy blacksmith hammer but now I think he is pretty
turned around and knows no other things than work.'

"Johann Rapparlie seems to be telling the parents their son is a *Luftikus*."
"*Luftikus*? What does that mean?"
Angela didn't know the English translation so we looked it up: Happy-go-
lucky.

"Hmm. Is that the closest American expression?" Angela didn't look
convinced. "Happy-go-lucky sounds like a compliment."
"You're right, happy-go-lucky, laissez-faire. That's not necessarily a bad
thing."
"In Freinsheim, when someone says a person is a *Luftikus*, it's not a
compliment. It means they aren't serious, they don't know how to work."
"So Rapparlie is being insulting about Michael to his parents?" I found
it hard to imagine, especially if Michael ran away. Wouldn't it have been
Rapparlie's own fault for taking him on?
"Remember what he wrote in the other letter? How Jakob worked in a
factory with 'diligence and skill' but the other brother, Johannes, had been
indifferent and lost his senses and abandoned them? Like Rapparlie didn't
think much of somebody who couldn't stick with their job."

"I thought Rapparlie sounded genuinely concerned about Johannes," I said. I couldn't bear the thought of anyone being unkind to a person who was losing his mind. Watching my brother Sandy lose his mind had been both frightening and distressing. I'd felt powerless to help in any way.

Regarding Rapparlie's reference to "bad times in America," we embarked on another Internet search. It didn't take long to hit on the "Panic of 1857," spurred by a bank failure that led to a severe economic depression. These letters, I was beginning to understand, were loaded with clues, bread crumbs leading into the dim forest of the past. As I cut and pasted info about the Panic of 1857 at the bottom of the letter translation, Angela flipped the letter on its side and studied a note scribbled in different ink along the margin.

> I also want to write you the name of my daughter. Her name is Katharina Rapparlie just like her mother. I also want to write you how my wooden leg works. It works very well and I can work and walk with it well. But it cost a lot of money besides my travel from Cleveland to Philadelphia.

"Below this part about the wooden leg, it's signed Katherina Rapparlie." Angela looked up from the letter. "Rapparlie's wife had a wooden leg?!"

We stared at each other, dumbfounded.

"I wonder what happened," I said. "Perhaps there's an explanation in an earlier letter—or in one that didn't arrive? But why would she have to journey all the way to Philadelphia for a wooden leg? Why couldn't she get one in Cleveland?"

"A better hospital, maybe?"

Angela's idea made sense. Back then, Cleveland would have been a pioneer town, whereas East Coast cities like Philadelphia no doubt offered more sophisticated universities and hospitals. On the Internet, I searched for money equivalencies to get a clearer idea of the cost. In general, one dollar in 1858 was equal to $29 dollars today. So the $150 wooden leg cost the Rapparlie's approximately $4,300. No wonder Rapparlie mentioned the expense. Continuing to calculate equivalencies, I learned that Jakob's journey to California cost him $400, which in today's dollars equaled $11,600. If he could earn $62 per day as the letter said, that sum would have been equal to a staggering $1,800.

As fascinated as we were becoming with these translations, Angela and I were nearly out of time. Her family would leave in just two more days.

Chapter 8

We debated which last letter to translate before Angela's departure, and settled on a short, one-pager from 1849, the only letter written by Jakob Handrich. On Dad's family tree, only Jakob's name was listed. No date of birth or death. On the outside, Jakob had addressed his letter to Philipp Harm[1] in Freinsheim, but it seemed as if he was mainly writing to Johann Philipp's wife, his older sister Elisabetha, who had remained behind when the family emigrated. Apparently, the letter had accompanied a package bearing gifts.

> November 10, 1849
>
> Beloved sister and brother-in-law,
>
> I wish that these few lines will meet you in as good health as they leave us. I have been working now for six years at a place in the factory where steaming kettles and machines for steamboats and railways are being built[2] and I earn one and one half dollars per day. Last winter I made a journey into the southern states, approximately 2000 miles. I met in Cincinäti [Cincinnati], in Mobiel [Mobile], in Neu Orlians [New Orleans], in Sängt Luis [St. Louis] all our good acquaintances.
>
> As far as we all are concerned, we are all quite healthy and we are all quite fine and Father and Mother[3] are still with me and we live in my house which I built myself last

1 It was the custom in this region to call persons by their middle names, so Jakob was writing to Johann Philipp Harm.
2 This may be the same factory mentioned in Rapparlie's 1847 letter. He may have been employed by the Cuyahoga Steam Furnace Co. founded in 1827. Less likely—the Detroit & Cleveland Steamboat Company, founded in 1846.
3 Presumably, Philipp Henrich Handrich and Katherina Handrich.

year. The property and house cost me $600 in cash and as I have the opportunity here with this man, also I will send you a small package that is vests for you and your two boys and one pair of shoes for your daughter.[4]

Beloved sister, it should not make you sad that I don't send anything to you. I will send something for you until next spring with [Herr] Selzer[5] who is also here in town and his sister.

The shoes, that is the work which the wild people or the brown Indians make. I close my writing. Greetings to you from all, Father, Mother, brothers and sisters, brother-in-law and especially a greeting from your brother and brother-in-law.

I am now still unmarried and will marry soon and then I am politely inviting all of you for that.

Greetings to you

Jakob Handrich

[Backside]

Soldier drawing and the date Freinsheim, June 24[6]

As Angela and I wrapped up this translation, it felt to me as if the mystery had deepened. Back in 1849, Jakob Handrich gave no mention about the discovery of gold in California, nothing about the flood of gold seekers heading west to try their luck that would rope him in eventually as well. In the 1858 letter, it's reported that Jakob had gone searching for gold, so it must have been on his mind. Then again, based on his journey to the southern states, this letter revealed how much he loved to travel, a foreshadowing of things to come.

---

4 Philipp Harm, born 10/9/1839, Michael Harm, born 5/26/1841, Barbara Harm, born 12/8/1844.

5 Apparently, Selzer is from Freinsheim, and is referenced also in Rapparlie's 1850 letter (following). It's possible Selzer had established a trading business as he seems to have traveled often between Cleveland and Freinsheim.

6 On the backside partial phrases are also scribbled: "with joy I reach to [the feather?] ... "I cannot describe these things ..." and a list of numbers, accounting for some kind of bill or costs? Also, a note which seems to have been added later: Michael Harm 1854 // Philipp Harm 1854

The kind of journey Jakob took sounded like a steamboat journey down the Mississippi River. With well over a thousand steamboats plying the Mississippi by 1830, steamboats were in their heyday. In the first letter of 1841, I'd been impressed by how many people the Handrichs knew in Cleveland. According to this account, the network extended all the way down to the Gulf of Mexico at a time of limited communication based mainly on word of mouth and hand-carried letters. By the mid-1800s, it seemed, immigrants weren't arriving as strangers in a strange land after all.

I got especially excited about the mention of the vests and shoes. "How cool is that? Jakob sent Indian vests back to his nephews." The mere thought of it made me fond of him.

As a child, I'd fantasized that I was an Indian girl. I wore Indian beads constantly like a talisman and spent hours playing in the woods on our property with my imaginary "real family," my father the chief of the tribe, my mother an Indian squaw, our home a teepee. I wrote stories about it, and made paintings. The Indian girl in these fantasies was named Dark Cloud. When Jakob Handrich talked about the "wild people or brown Indians" in his letter, I pictured fringed leather vests, delighted by the thought that my great-great grandfather Michael Harm would have received such a gift from his uncle in America.

"It doesn't say they were Indian vests," Angela said. "I think they were probably regular vests, good clothes to be worn for church."

"Couldn't they have been leather vests? Just like the shoes?" I was crestfallen, and must have given away my disappointment with my tone.

Angela put her fingers to her lips, a gesture she often made when lost in thought. "You know, I think that would be really amazing," she said, smiling at me, going along with my fantasy. "Philipp and Michael would have really liked that. *Der Lederstrumpf*, *The Leather-stocking Tales*, are still very popular in Germany."

"*Leather-stocking Tales?*"

"The James Fenimore Cooper book."

"Oh, you mean, like, *The Last of the Mohicans*?"

"Is that what it's called here? There are also the Indian stories by Karl May." A pleased smile crossed Angela's face. "German children are still reading his books, although not so much as when my father was a child. Do American children read Karl May?"

I confessed I'd never heard of him. A little research into Karl May turned up a surprise. The author was a contemporary of Michael Harm. My great-great grandfather lived from 1841-1910. Karl May lived from 1842-1912. Karl May was best known for his books about the American Old West, which he wrote before he'd ever been there. Due to numerous thefts and frauds, and

Jakob Handrich's drawing of a soldier.

later, vagrancy, Karl May spent about eight years in jail, during which time he became an avid reader in the prison library, and also listened to tales of the American West told to him by fellow prisoners. Like others born in his day, Karl May had read the wildly popular works of James Fenimore Cooper, which were speedily translated into German as soon as they came out in English.

Angela had been fascinated by Karl May's books as a child like countless other Germans. However, May wrote the books without having ever met with tribal people. Many readers have taken May's books at face value, believing the descriptions to be true, thus perpetuating a false, romanticized image of Native Americans that continues to this day. Perhaps my childhood fascination was also fueled by romantic ideals, born of fictionalized TV episodes like "Daniel Boone," but even so, I found it intriguing and remarkable that both Angela and I shared this childhood fascination with the American Indian. Now, we'd discovered, American Indian shoes purchased by Jakob Handrich had made their way all the way back to the Harms in Freinsheim. The very idea of it gave me goosebumps.

The picture of the soldier on the flip side of Jakob Handrich's letter made little sense to us. The letter had been dated November 1849, but the date above the picture read Freinsheim, the 24th of June. How to account for the discrepancy? Angela thought the picture looked like a Bavarian or Prussian soldier, but we had no idea why Jakob would draw it there. Had Uncle Jakob been trying to entertain the boys?

In that summer of 2008, I did not know my history. I've since learned that Prussian troops invaded and occupied the small rural village of Freinsheim that June of 1849, due to peasant rebellions for democracy then sweeping Europe. Given the June 24 date, perhaps Jakob Handrich's drawing was of a Prussian soldier, his way of showing his sister and brother-in-law that the Cleveland Germans knew about the occupation without writing something that might be intercepted and put his sister's family at risk of arrest. At the time, not knowing any of this history, I naively attributed the drawing to playfulness.

And why were the American Indian shoes sent to a daughter? Dad's family tree listed no daughter in the Freinsheim Harm family, only sons. Was Jakob confused? Or, was it possible that the Freinsheim family had written

Angela and family's 2008 visit to Seattle.
Back row: Christoph Otterbeck, Luzi Weber, Dave and George Gebben.
Front row: Angela and Carlotta Weber, Claire and Vivian Gebben.

to America announcing the birth of a daughter? If they did have a daughter, what happened? Why wasn't she listed?

Looking back, I'm aware that the discovery of these letters was a blessing, a genealogist's dream-come-true. At the time, though, it seemed more like a daunting challenge, mainly serving to impress on me how little I understood about history, and about my own family.

"Isn't it amazing," I said to Angela "how these letter writers had all these experiences, but without the letters, we would not know any of it?"

"I think it is typical," Angela said. "History taught in schools follows broad strokes and leaves out so many experiences, especially the stories of individual families. That's the main point, how I found the letters in the first place. It happened because I understood what can be learned from oral history while living with Helen Peterson at Neah Bay."

I nodded in recognition. Angela had introduced me to Helen Peterson, an elder of the Makah Native Americans, with whom Angela had stayed for several months back in 1994. As Angela continued, her voice grew warm with excitement. She'd had a keen interest in cultural studies now for years, and as she visited with us in 2008, she was simultaneously in the process of deciding on the topic for her Ph.D. thesis.

"For a while I had the idea for my thesis to compare my grandmother's life to Helen Peterson's life story and to another old artist woman I had known in Germany—all filtered through the memories we have of them. Helen of the Makah, and my grandmother in Freinsheim, were the same age, but were born and lived through the 20th century in very different circumstances. But for doing research with the Makah, I would have had to go through an entire process of review of my purpose and questions, and honestly, I didn't even know what would be a topic which would be agreeable and interesting to both sides. *So*, I thought, *what about my own family? What about interviewing my own elders?*

"That's how it happened that I found these letters. I was in Freinsheim talking to Tante Gretel, asking her questions about what Onkel Hans and Tante Gretel experienced. While I was talking to Tante Gretel, she told me about the letters you had sent to Manfred, so I asked him for them. And later while I was talking to Tante Inge, she went to see if she could find your grandmother's letters, the responses, in her attic and came back with the tin box of much older letters. I wouldn't have found out about them otherwise."

Listening to Angela, it occurred to me that in a strange way, we weren't finding these letters as much as they were finding us. But for the moment, we'd run out of time. As Angela and her family departed that summer, she and I agreed she should take the letters with her, and somehow, she assured me, she'd try to find time to work on them from her home in Marburg, Germany.

Chapter 9

About a month after Angela and her family departed, I entered my Master of Fine Arts program on Whidbey Island. The Creative Writing program operated in a low residency format, which meant the bulk of the classes occurred online. A good thing for me, since I needed the flexibility of learning from home in order to be around for my family, especially for our daughter Vivian, who had just begun her junior year in high school.

But not everything happened online. Each semester began with face-to-face classes—the low residency part. For the first nine days of each semester, students came together from all over the country to attend daily morning classes, afternoon Profession of Writing seminars, and evening readings by faculty, guest faculty and students. I was starting the program at age fifty not as much to earn a graduate-level degree, although that would be great to have. My main interest had to do with the requirement for graduation: a book-length, publishable thesis.

The MFA residency was held at Camp Casey, located just south of Coupeville on Whidbey Island in an old military barracks that had been converted into classrooms and lodging. I was nervous at first. I hadn't been to college since receiving my BA at Calvin College twenty-eight years earlier. On the other hand, it felt so good to finally be pursuing my lifelong dream, to be meeting published and aspiring writers and begin learning what I needed to know about writing and the writing business.

The MFA program also offered something special—a more supportive than competitive environment, a place to celebrate writers and writing. Before returning home to the online classroom, students had the opportunity to meet our classmates face to face and get to talk with our professors in person. By the end of residency, we knew one another pretty well. It was a wonderful discovery, that through this MFA program, I would not only be learning to write, but would be connecting with other writers in a broader literary community.

Just after I returned home and my online coursework kicked off, the United States underwent events of historic proportions. In the end of August, the Democratic Party nominated Barack Obama for the highest office in the land. His upbeat, "Yes We Can!" presidential campaign was gaining momentum, which made it seem like something entirely new was happening in politics, in my opinion for the better.

But at the same time things were looking up, in mid-September the unthinkable occurred. America's fourth largest bank—Lehman Brothers – failed, and many other banks teetered on the brink of collapse. Shock waves, and the fear of another Great Depression, reverberated globally.

Angela and I had not been in contact since her summer visit, so I was glad to open my email one day and find a message from her.

October 9, 2008

Dear Claire,

It has been such a long time since I wanted to write to you and ask for news about your start into the writing classes, the rest of your summer and the pre-election atmosphere in Seattle, and now suddenly there are new questions. How are you at the West Coast receiving the bank crisis? Is there much fear and discussions or do people stay calm?

It is strange here. We hear worse news every day, but it doesn't seem to have affected everyday life yet. The German government has issued a new law to protect individual savings up to 50,000 Euro, to calm everyone down and avoid hectic reactions of getting one's money out of the banks.

Isn't it strange how we read these letters from former times of crisis ... [and] know that financially good times and years of crisis can follow each other so fast. How will people react? We saw one funny demonstration in front of some important building in New York (or was it Washington?), some people dressed up and wearing signs like: We, the billionaires, will solve this crisis!

Please let us know how you are doing and take good care!
Yours Angela

October 13, 2008

Dear Angela,

Great to hear from you. My schoolwork is going fine. I am editing and writing short stories and writing a paper on Salman Rushdie, plus still writing articles for the newspaper and keeping up with the kids. George is settled at college, and Vivian almost has her driver's license.

Yes, the financial situation is really frightening people— it's saturating the news and everyone's conversations and psyches. A friend of mine who works for a car company said they are taking work shifts away from people because no one is buying cars. It is just one example of the domino effect that will be going on for months, even years to come ....

Say hello to Christoph and Carlotta and Luzi from us. Love, Claire

October 31, 2008

Dear Claire,

Today I finally printed out the translations we did. We are going to Freinsheim for the weekend. Tante Gretel and Onkel Otto are the ones who are really interested, and they are looking forward to a book we are supposed to make out of our findings!!! Isn't this nice?

I visited the German Museum for Emigration in Bremerhaven last month and showed the letters to one of the scholars there. She said, these old ones are rare, because paper quality was often not so good ....

December 24, 2008

Dear Angela,

Thank you so much for the translations .... Yes, we have a project. Did Manfred tell you about the family tree web site he set up? I posted a lot of pictures there that I scanned when you visited.

My father is failing more and more, but he keeps in good spirits and Craig does a great job looking after him. I will bring my mother's sister Elizabeth to live in Seattle this summer. Merry Christmas to you and family,

Claire

P.S. YES WE CAN!

That fall, too, Aunt Elizabeth and I talked on the phone, and she let me know she'd sent paperwork to Bayview Retirement Community, one of the three we'd toured. She said she would move to the Northwest that coming summer of 2009. I was surprised that she wasn't hesitating, that she'd made the difficult choice to uproot her life. I was also pleased. Her decision to me felt like a vote of confidence. She trusted me enough to put her future in my hands.

That winter of 2008, my son George had settled in for his freshman year at the University of Washington and my daughter Vivian, now a junior in high school, was busy with volleyball and orchestra in addition to school assignments. For the moment, my time was more or less my own. I had a delightful first semester in my MFA program, taking classes on Craft of Fiction, and also Fiction Workshop, where we critiqued one another's work.

In that same time period, Angela was seeking an adviser to mentor her as she pursued her doctoral degree in Cultural Anthropology. As she and I both followed our educational pursuits while raising our children, it seemed in a way like Angela and I were leading parallel lives on either side of the Atlantic.

In January of 2009, at the start of the second semester of my MFA program, the hot air balloon of my new writing career seemed to be hovering off the ground, ready for lift off. That coming semester, in addition to craft and workshop classes, I'd enrolled in a course on the contemporary novel. The course description indicated we'd be reading one contemporary prize-winning novel a week and writing a five page paper on each. While the workload sounded daunting, I also could hardly wait.

Returning home from the January MFA residency on Whidbey Island, I dug into the online semester, and also began making calls to facilitate Aunt Elizabeth's summer move to Seattle. I met with the intake Counselor at Bayview and took photos of a studio apartment to help my aunt plan what furniture she'd bring along. I called around for estimates on estate sales and made inquiries into various moving companies. It seemed as if everything was on schedule.

But, on a freezing winter day in Michigan, Aunt Elizabeth slipped on ice by her car and severely tore a tendon in her knee. Her longtime friend Louise Sause called to deliver the news. My aunt needed surgery, then faced months of rehab. Even after she fully recovered, she would no longer be able to live in her second floor walk-up apartment. Louise gave me Elizabeth's phone number at the skilled nursing facility where they'd placed her. I dialed it right away.

"Where've you been?" Aunt Elizabeth said in customary, abrupt Elizabeth-speak. "I've been waiting to hear from you."

"I just got word. Louise tells me you're in good hands."

"There's a problem. You need to come."

"What kind of problem? Give me the specifics, and I'll make some calls."

"I need you here!" Aunt Elizabeth said, and hung up on me.

This behavior reminded me of the old Aunt Elizabeth, the less well-behaved aunt. Throughout my life, my aunt had often talked to me, to my whole family, like a queen commanding her court. When I was a young girl and she'd visit for the holidays, I'd sit by her chair and she'd start poking my arm with her nylon-stockinged toe. "Give me a foot massage," she'd demand from her easy-chair throne. She kept poking until I either moved elsewhere, or relented. "Gin and bitter lemon," she'd call to Mom, who was preparing dinner in the kitchen. Mom was not amused. While I viewed Aunt Elizabeth as teasing and playful, Mom and Dad saw her as a spoiled and selfish child.

On the phone call, though, beneath Aunt Elizabeth's bossy command I sensed a full-blown desperation. What could possibly have gone so wrong? I didn't see the urgency of rushing to Michigan, but reluctantly followed orders. Leaving husband Dave in charge at home, I flew to Michigan for a week to try to figure out my aunt's problem and what I could do to help.

Such, I soon discovered, was the beauty of being enrolled in an online program—I didn't have to miss classes at all. I could log in from anywhere. I stayed alone in Elizabeth's apartment in Michigan while she recuperated in skilled nursing at Burcham Hills. Each morning, I headed out for breakfast at Panera Bread and logged in to do class work. Afternoons and evenings I spent at Burcham Hills trying to untangle my aunt's difficulties.

As it turned out Elizabeth did indeed need me there. She showed me her

Elizabeth Lindsey, Gladys McKnight, and Louise Sause, July 2009.

health insurance paperwork. She had two different insurance policies, but to my dismay none of her medical bills were being paid. Elizabeth had made calls on her own to try to sort it out, but her hearing loss was so severe she couldn't hear what they were telling her on the phone. Medicare would not talk to me unless we put Elizabeth on the phone first and she gave her approval.

Together, we made the calls. I'd hand the phone to Elizabeth so she could agree to let me talk to them about her insurance. Since she really couldn't hear them, as soon as she got the receiver she would mutter: "Yes, this is Elizabeth Lindsey. Yes, my niece Claire Gebben can speak with you." Then she'd hand the phone back to me and I'd go from there. Due to a computer glitch, I finally figured out, Medicare had cancelled her coverage. The whole mess was shockingly complicated to fix, but eventually, I got it mostly sorted before I had to fly back home.

Aunt Elizabeth's troubles in Michigan cemented her move to Seattle, now scheduled later in the summer until after she'd completed rehab. Once I returned to Seattle, in the midst of all the other things going on, I put in motion the necessary arrangements for her move.

By July of 2009, I'd wrapped up another semester of the MFA, cheered my daughter on at her crew race in Vancouver, Washington (she'd switched allegiance from volleyball to rowing crew), and Dave's parents had been out for an extended visit to help with house repairs. It was time to bring my 87-year-old aunt to Seattle. First, I flew back to Michigan to pack up her apartment —everything not in the estate sale –for the moving truck. I understood the move would not be easy for her. Aunt Elizabeth was leaving behind a lifetime of connections, her dear friends, her regular haunts and associations. She loved the local WKAR classical radio station, and Michigan State University's Art Museum and libraries. She'd lived in East Lansing for over forty years.

Most of all, Aunt Elizabeth loved her friends. A couple of days before her departure, her octogenarian friends Gladys and Louise came to say farewell at her assisted living room at Burcham Hills. The furnishings were spare, so I snuck a bench from the hallway and placed it in front of the TV. While I sat on the bed, Aunt Elizabeth lowered herself into the second easy chair and

Gladys planted herself on the bench and pulled out a full bottle of Glenlivet Scotch.

"Hurray!" they exclaimed.

Elizabeth explained to me where to pilfer some glasses and ice. When I returned, Gladys poured hefty swigs for us all. I'd just bought Aunt Elizabeth some Pringles, so popped open the can and passed it around. We enjoyed an hour or so of conversation and laughter. When it came time to go, the women all

Scotch farewell at Burcham Hills in Michigan.

hoisted themselves up with walkers and canes. I was barely able to get them to pause for a picture before they were bustling out into the hallway and saying farewells. Louise could no longer drive, so she was depending on Gladys to get her home. *Feed them Scotch, send them home?* I thought, my concern for Gladys and Louise swarming in as I watched them head off down the elevator.

Later that evening, I stopped in again to see Aunt Elizabeth on another errand.

"Louise called," she said by way of greeting. "It was really very funny. For a moment Gladys couldn't remember where Louise lived and they sped past her apartment. 'There it goes,' Louise said. Eventually, Gladys got turned around."

I was relieved they'd gotten home safely. What's more, I could tell by the way Aunt Elizabeth recounted the story how much she loved and would miss her friends.

Although she'd resigned herself to leaving, and had calmed down since I'd fixed the tangled insurance problem, every so often Aunt Elizabeth's anxiety bubbled to the surface. I'd negotiated with Atlas Vanlines for a partial truckload. When I admitted to my aunt the total cost, she glared at me from her wheelchair.

"Too expensive. I don't have the money!" she snapped.

"I'm sorry, I couldn't find anything cheaper."

She sat back, clearly disgruntled. "You hold all the power."

Aunt Elizabeth had a point. She was giving up everything—her apartment, her car, her friends, the life she'd made for herself in East Lansing. In this latest blow, I was deciding how she'd spend her dwindling savings. I felt bad, but I couldn't help it. She didn't stay angry, though. Mostly, she did everything she could to help despite her immobile state.

Once Aunt Elizabeth arrived at Bayview Retirement Community, she seemed to adjust without much trouble. Perhaps she had complaints, but if so, she chose not to voice them. Soon enough, Aunt Elizabeth and I settled into a routine. Weekly, we'd go out for lunch, a time when she'd reminisce about her years growing up with my mom and her eldest sister Anna, about her escapades and Elderhostel travels with her good friend Eileen, and about my grandparents and the lives of the Lindsey family in Berea, Ohio. I soaked up the stories.

Chapter 10

That August of 2009, just before I returned to Whidbey Island for the start-up to my second year of the MFA program, I visited my aunt in her new independent living apartment. Her hair was looking great. The new stylist at Bayview, I was pleased to see, was doing a good job. Aunt Elizabeth's room had also improved since the move, due to the addition of a small, round contemporary table, low filing cabinet and two chairs, items we'd purchased on a shopping outing to IKEA. The furniture was finished in white, the chair upholstery sunny yellow. My aunt said she'd invited several residents in to have a look. They'd given it a thumbs up.

"One lady thought it was too bright," she told me. "But the one who's a sharp dresser thought it looked great."

That was Aunt Elizabeth, always noticing what people wore. "They really dress well here," she'd stage-whispered to me in the hallway on one of her first days at Bayview.

I told Aunt Elizabeth how, during my absence at MFA residency, Dave would fill in if there was an emergency, and I'd only be away for a little over a week. I couldn't tell if this worried her at all. She simply nodded and wished me well, saying she'd see me soon.

As excited as I was to be off, I took the ferry from Mukilteo across Possession Sound to Whidbey Island with a sense of trepidation. I'd really been enjoying my classes, teachers, and fellow students, but it was a two-year MFA program, so it was already time for me to declare a thesis topic, the book manuscript I'd have to write in order to graduate. I'd already decided not to revise the first manuscript, but to write something entirely new. But I still wasn't sure what I wanted to write about.

Late one afternoon during residency, my thesis adviser and published author Kathleen Alcalá and I held a meeting outside, sitting across from each other in folding chairs on the straw-colored lawn of Camp Casey. What with classes being held inside throughout the pleasant August day, it was a relief to

Elizabeth Lindsey, 88 years old.

sit outside, amid the gorgeous setting, the expansive blue sky, within view of long stretches of driftwood beach leading up to a forested bluff.

Kathleen and I met just before the dinner hour. That afternoon was sunny and warm, the breeze off Admiralty Inlet keeping us slightly cool. My thesis adviser was fair-skinned, and a couple of days of beach walks had turned her cheeks pink. She and I were both about the same age, but we played our roles of professor and student appropriately—Kathleen wearing a long skirt and cardigan sweater, me wearing jeans, a t-shirt, and a windbreaker suited for bicycling to and from classes. I bicycled out of necessity, in order to leave the car at home so Vivian could get around during my absence.

When Kathleen asked about my thesis topic, I told her I'd dreamed up four ideas.

"I thought I might write about the 1970s at Kent State University," I started in. "My dad was a professor there at the time of the shootings that year." Kathleen raised her eyebrows, but offered no comment, so I plowed ahead. "Or, something set in Ecuador and Peru in the 1980s? My husband and I were traveling there when there was a border war. I could do research and set a story then. I also have an idea for a thriller about a serial killer." All of these ideas, I realized as I said them aloud, had been born of MFA writing exercises and class assignments. I really hadn't begun to pursue any of them in earnest. What with parenting, moving Aunt Elizabeth, and taking three full-credit classes, all I'd managed to accomplish was turning assignments in on time. "Then there are these letters I've been working on with my German cousin. They're old family letters from the mid-1800s, written in German. I thought I might draw from them to tell the story of my great-great grandfather's life. He immigrated to Cleveland when he was 15."

Kathleen nodded at this last suggestion. I could almost see the gears turning in her mind. "Interesting. Do you have these letters in your possession?"

"Well no, Angela has them," I said. "My German cousin. Actually, she's the one who can read them. She's done all the translating."

Kathleen crossed her legs and swished her long brown hair back over her shoulder, a gesture I recognized from workshop as the moment when she was about to deliver her critique. "When it comes to the thriller idea, I'm not sure how much help I'd be. You and I would both have a steep learning curve with the genre. But the family letters ... as you know I've written books along those same lines. I could be of some help with that."

I'd read my professor's novels voluntarily by then, several books set in 19th-century Mexico and the Southwest based on the true story of her Hispanic/Jewish ancestry. I'd read them because she was my professor, not because I loved historical fiction. I enjoyed her books, but history was not my favorite subject. Years ago, in my freshman year as an undergraduate, I'd earned a "D" on my first history paper. I'd never fully recovered.

Second year start to MFA residency held at Camp Casey on Whidbey Island, August, 2009.

"The problem is, at least half the letters aren't translated," I said. "And I don't think Angela has the time to do the rest of them right now. So much would depend on her." Could I even ask her? It seemed unreasonable. Angela had young children, and graduate-level studies of her own to pursue.

"Do you speak German?"

"Hardly any. I took one semester in college."

Kathleen looked thoughtful. "That's not the end of the world. My Spanish is limited, but I've gotten by. And you can probably find someone in the U.S. to translate the letters. The main question is, will your cousin be willing to send you the letters? Can you even get them?"

"I'm not sure." I was beginning to regret I'd brought it up. These questions needed answers, and I would have to supply them.

Plus, I felt reluctant to write on this topic because my father and his mother—my grandmother Emma Patterson—had touted the German family ancestry to a fault, retelling the Michael Harm story over and over again. My great-great grandfather had been a German immigrant who apprenticed as a blacksmith. Would a novel about that really be all that interesting?

But Kathleen seemed keen on the idea. "Not all relatives are forthcoming with information." she said with authority, as if she'd experienced difficulties herself in that regard. "But let's say Angela is willing to share them with you. What do you think you'd write about? What's the story?"

I sighed. "Honestly, I'm not sure." Mentally, I sifted through the possibilities. "I know the most about Michael Harm—he came over in 1857. But from the letters Angela uncovered, we have some cool information about his grandparents and aunts and uncles who came in the 1840s. One uncle went off to the Gold Rush. And a woman lost her leg. The letters don't say how, at least not in the parts we've translated so far. She had to go to Philadelphia to get a wooden one." I paused, a weird sensation passing through me, an odd mixture of excitement and frustration. "I'm not even sure it should be a novel. I mean, I came into this program to write fiction, but this might be nonfiction."

"Well, you can figure that out later," Kathleen said, almost briskly. "Why don't you start by finding out how many facts you have."

"What kind of facts?"

"For instance, the ships they came over on. Do you have that information?"

"No. And I have no idea how to find out."

Kathleen thought for a moment. "There's a National Archives and Records Administration on Sand Point Way in Seattle. They have that kind of information. I'd start there." She gazed at me in a searching way then. My doubts must have been written plainly on my face. "I don't want to push you into it, though. Are you sure this is what you want to write?"

I hesitated, sifting through the emotions wrestling inside. Did I want to write about Michael Harm? The letters were enticing, and unique material to draw from. But this kind of book would be a huge step into the unknown. I'd never thought about writing historical fiction. And I couldn't do it without Angela's help. Then again, Angela and I had shared a fascination with the stories the previous summer, so maybe she'd be willing. And along the way, I'd have a thesis adviser as a resource when I ran into difficulty.

"The timing feels right," I said. "In a lot of ways. My father's getting older, and so are some of the relatives in Germany—in some ways it feels like it's now or never."

"You realize, if you do this, it will take you an extra year to graduate?" Kathleen said.

"Oh." I wasn't willing to consider the enormity of this. Not then, with so many other uncertainties boiling in my head. I knew Kathleen had experience with this. No doubt she knew better than I did. But I clung to the idea she was wrong. Once I had all the letter translations in hand, wouldn't the story practically write itself?

"I'll shoot for next year August anyhow," I told her.

Kathleen didn't argue, just assigned me the task of turning in an outline once I got home. Having the outline would be a help to her, she said, as I turned in chapters. *Outline? Chapters? First, I need the letters*, I thought, feeling slightly off balance as Kathleen and I rose and headed inside for dinner.

In the residency environment, with so many writers gathered together, we were always inquiring about one another's writing and plans. After my meeting with Kathleen, I had many opportunities to share with classmates, and faculty too, regarding what topic I'd chosen for my thesis.

"I'm writing about my German great-great grandfather, the blacksmith, based on family letters," I repeated again and again.

"Do you speak German?" many asked.

"No," I said, each time with that sinking feeling. I had no doubt I was out of my depth. "Then again, I don't blacksmith either. The learning curve here is steep."

One afternoon during general announcements, one of the fiction professors, Bruce Holland Rogers, stood up.

"I'd like to congratulate Claire Gebben," he said, grinning mischievously. "She's the only student so far who's committed to learning a new language— German, no less—in order to write her thesis."

I laughed along with everyone, while inwardly writhing. Bruce hadn't intended to make me worry, of course. In fact, he was encouraging me. When I'd spoken with him about my thesis over one of our meals, he'd told me about online language learning courses available for free with many library memberships. Bruce encouraged me to try Mango Languages, or a program called BYKI (Before You Know It), to start by tackling a little at a time. I appreciated his kindness, but knew in my heart I wasn't going to gain a proficiency in German along with everything else. If I didn't have Angela's help with German, I was certain this project would be dead in the water.

The whole concept of blacksmithing also eluded me. What did I know about shoeing horses? What kinds of things did I need to learn about the properties of metal? The tools blacksmiths used? What happened in a work day? At one point during a meal at residency, I confided my lack of knowledge to David Wagoner, one of the MFA poetry faculty in the program. David was a distinguished writer not only for his poetry, but also for his historical novels and screenplays. He looked up from his plate and beyond me, his blue eyes gazing deep into former times.

"In steelwork, everything is heavy, dirty, dangerous, and hard to handle," he said. "My father was a steelworker, in Ohio as a matter of fact." He paused, then gave a wry chuckle. "The scrap yard where my father worked had all kinds of scrap metal, anything iron, old parts. He would bring home play things for us. Scrap alloy, small gears and such."

David explained how his father worked in steel after the Bessemer process came along. Before then, it was time-consuming to transform iron into steel because it required such intense heat. I asked David if he could explain about Bessemer steelmaking.

"The Bessemer process was invented by a man named Bessemer, of course," David said. "It forced oxygen through molten metal to make the metal burn hotter and remove oxygen faster. The steel would get so hot it would become a mixture of white and blue. The smelter foreman's job was to determine when it was just the right color, then feed in the manganese or whatever. Sometimes there'd be a splash, and the worker would have to run with his hand on the back of his neck to keep from being burned. Oxygen in the iron is where the splashes come from. If a worker gets splashed from molten metal, he has to stand still. The metal is about the size of a raindrop or bb. It'll burn right through the pants. He can't touch it with his hands, he has to shake his leg to get it off. Workers also wear dark purple glasses to keep from looking into molten steel and damaging their eyes. Before the Bessemer process, the pounding of the blacksmith sledge on iron was used to change the crystal structure, to make the iron denser and stronger."

Now we were getting somewhere, I thought. Michael Harm hadn't worked in a factory, he'd been an old-fashioned blacksmith, no doubt pounding horseshoes with a hammer just as David described.

David also told me about growing up near Canton in northeastern Ohio. Back in the late 1800s, he said, there were still Native Americans around, hiding out in the forest, starving because they didn't have land to grow food. David's grandmother would give them vegetables from her garden, and they would thank her by leaving a deer on her back porch.

David's memories sparked all kinds of images and scenes. Listening to him, I realized I'd need to check out books on metallurgy and the history of the Native tribes in Ohio. By the end of residency, I returned home with a growing excitement about getting started, and an abject dread I wouldn't be able to pull any of it off.

Chapter 11

"I've decided to write about those letters found in Germany, the ones written by Dad's ancestors," I told Aunt Elizabeth in the end of August 2009 during my next visit to her apartment. I'd come up to the seventh floor to check out her room, as she wanted to discuss what color duvet, based on her new white and yellow furniture, might work for the bed.

Aunt Elizabeth pressed her lips together with a sour expression and averted her gaze. "Why don't you write about the Lindseys for once?"

Her disappointment reminded me of my initial hesitation. Hadn't we already heard everything there was to tell about Michael Harm? Aunt Elizabeth was right, I mused. Perhaps I should be writing about the Lindseys.

"Well, anyhow, I can't do it without Angela's help. Hopefully, she's willing," I said. "Besides, it'll be a good excuse to get those letters translated."

My reasoning didn't mollify Aunt Elizabeth, nor me either, but we left it at that. A few days later, I gathered my nerve and emailed Angela to ask for her help.

Thursday, September 3, 2009

Re: big news and a favor

Hi Angela—so your apartment is fixed, and you've moved back to Marburg? I hope all is well for you, and Christoph, and Carlotta, and Luzi.

I had SUCH a busy summer—I moved my mother's sister from Michigan to Seattle, and I visited my dad. Then I started my semester at Whidbey Island and spent 9 days there. I'm so glad fall is here and I can just stay home and write.

I begin my thesis this year. I took four ideas to my thesis adviser, and she picked my idea about a novel that draws from our German letter translations. I want to center the book around the German immigrant community in Cleveland Ohio in the mid-1800s.

So I need to ask a big favor. Will you send me the letters you brought with you last summer? I will carefully make very good copies of them, and then mail them back to you. I will send you money for the shipping cost if you like. I am very excited to begin.

Love,

Claire

September 4, 2009

Re: big news and a favor

Dear Claire,

Yes, we just moved and still live in boxes, and I just installed the internet with the result that I lost the letter I wrote to you. So just short for now: How exciting! I will help you as much as I can. Please write me if you have a deadline. Yours Angela

September 4, 2009

Re: Deadline

My outline for the whole book was due yesterday, so it would be very helpful to have the letters as a skeletal framework for the characters—not translated, just in German in their original form, so I can make photocopies of them. My thesis adviser says this is my first step, to get copies of the originals. I will mail them back in pristine condition, I promise, if you will just mail them as soon as you can.

Thanks and love,

Claire

September 15, 2009

Hello Claire,

I asked my mother to please send me the letters from Freinsheim and the little package didn't arrive for some days now ... I will ask at the post office tomorrow, maybe because of our new address??? Christoph thinks it's too dangerous to send them. I don't really think so, but these days with the package not arriving are strange ... I hope I can tell you better news tomorrow.

If you want, it might be helpful for you to talk on the telephone one of these days. I have attended a conference in May about 300 years of emigration to America from the Palatinate and there's a lot to tell. I also bought a book by one scholar at the Institut für Pfälzer Geschichte und Kultur who collected letters from emigrants in America to the family back in Rheinland-Pfalz. When I talked to him, he said our letters are rare, and he's interested in them, too, once I have transcribed all of them.

Tante Marliese, Uncle Hans's widow also told me an interesting thing this summer. She remembered that the family talked about visits from relatives from Meckenheim—they came in a horse cart, which means they were thought to be well off, because many people only had oxen carts. If you have certain topics and questions, I could be your "interviewer in the field"...

Well, before I lose this letter again, I'd better send it,

Yours, Angela

As I read through Angela's emails, I felt as if I'd won the lottery, as if one day I'd randomly rubbed off numbers and hit the right sequence. What were the chances? Not only did Angela want to help, but since she shared my interest in the letters, she was already working on research for both of us. All I had to do was await the arrival of the letters, and I'd be off and running.

WHILE WAITING, I DIDN'T SIT idly by. I started researching for the thesis, oddly enough, by reading *Moby-Dick*. The novel had been on my radar for years. *Moby-Dick* is referenced in most writing classes, but I'd never gotten around to reading it. I made the book my starting point because I felt the most challenged by my lack of knowledge of 19th-century reality. How did people see the world back then? What science was known and how did that influence their perceptions? What about religious views? I didn't see how I could set scenes in that time period and get into the minds of the characters without knowing the way people thought.

Melville's *Moby-Dick* was published in 1851, so I hoped it would provide me with insights. Cracking open the thick paperback, I thought for a minute I'd opened an encyclopedia of some kind. The table of contents listed chapters about sea and whaling ship life, from the cabin-table, the quarter-deck, and the ship's carpenter, to the monkey-rope and the battering-ram. And a chapter each on the blacksmith and the forge. Digging into the first chapter, I made a mental note that travelers—complete strangers—shared beds at inns, an unthinkable arrangement today. Queequeg's antics made me laugh out loud. Further along, though, the white whale did not appear and the novel became a slog. More often than not, I found something else to read.

In my hunt to brush up on anything about the 19th century, I went to Barnes & Noble and browsed the U.S. history shelves. To my dismay, almost every book focused on war—mainly the Civil War, but also the War of 1812 and European conflicts. What about peace time? I wondered. What about average blacksmith German immigrants like Michael Harm? Among all the titles, one book stood out, not just because it was three fingers thick. *What Hath God Wrought: The Transformation of America, 1815-1848,* by Daniel Walker Howe. The book jacket described unprecedented technological changes in that era, the advent of railroads, the telegraph, and steam, and many more inventions dramatically impacting human civilization. Here I'd been picturing the 19th century as backward and simplistic, a preconceived notion now blown apart.

But how did blacksmithing fit into the picture? German immigration? Cleveland and Ohio history? That fall, my son George had begun his sophomore year at the University of Washington, so one afternoon, while dropping off something for him on campus, I decided to stop in at the campus library to see what I could find. As I stepped through the grand, arched portals of Suzzallo, my task felt even more enormous. The place practically bulged with books and knowledge, and I had no idea where to start. I doubted they'd have much on Cleveland. Feeling discouraged before I'd even begun, I stopped first at the catalog terminal and searched for books on German immigration and Atlantic voyages, finding nothing of interest.

Next, I wandered to the Information Desk. Others stood in line ahead of me, but I didn't mind. I needed time to figure out how to explain my errand. When it was my turn, the reference librarian gazed at me expectantly, and I took a deep breath.

"I'm looking for books about the German immigrant community in Cleveland, Ohio in the mid-1800s," I spilled out. *How wide open was that?!* To my relief, the woman nodded agreeably enough and got busy clicking away on her keyboard. "Steamboats might be a keyword," I put in. "Or Erie Canal." I could feel myself getting warm. Was "complete idiot" stamped on my forehead?

"There are eleven entries," the librarian said. Her matter-of-fact voice had a calming effect. She swiveled the screen to allow me to look with her as she scrolled past entries for the Western Reserve, whiskey merchants and the Midwest. "You know, my family is mostly of German ancestry," she added. "They arrived in Ohio during that same time period."

"You're kidding. In Cleveland?"

"No, Toledo."

I took a closer look at this librarian then, at her Caucasian, clear-skinned, brown-haired features, as if there might be some outward sign of our similar origins. One hundred and fifty years ago this librarian's ancestors and mine had both crossed the Atlantic, wound up in Ohio, and now the two of us stood across from each other at this reference desk in Seattle, Washington. The coincidence seemed significant, but just how remained a mystery.

The reference librarian turned up Orth's *A History of Cleveland, Ohio*, jotting the shelf location on a slip of paper and handing it to me with an "x" on a map of the building. Now feeling hopeful, I wound my way through the maze of shelves and located it easily enough. Published in 1910, the tome touched briefly on the influx of German immigrants: "[Cleveland's] principal ethnic parts were the English, the Irish and the German, the last two greatly preponderating. Unfortunately, there are no reliable data of the earliest arrivals in Cleveland of these emigrants." Sigh.

Back home I reread the letters searching for more clues, then turned to the Internet to browse Cleveland and German history. The *Encyclopedia of Cleveland History*, a reference site created by Case Western Reserve University, popped up right away. It included excellent write-ups about German immigrants to Cleveland. But nothing under "B" for Blacksmithing, and nothing under "C" for Carriage Works. In fact, the term "carriage works," which my father and grandmother had used to describe Michael Harm's carriage-making business, did not appear to exist. I didn't find the term in the dictionary, and not on Google, either.

It wasn't until I searched on Google Books that I found the word, prevalent in old trade magazines and other publications from the 19th century. By the 1900s, the term seemed to have passed out of parlance. Was this because carriage works themselves ceased to exist? My great-great grandfather's carriage works had closed around that time, in the early 1900s, because by then people were hot to purchase newly-invented automobiles.

Weeks passed while I fumbled here and there through a vast amount of background information about Ohio and German history. How I'd use most of it in the book remained to be seen. Passing the time, I worked up a chronology of the key dates in the letters we'd translated so far—births, deaths, marriages, children—and cobbled together the start of a basic outline.

Still, the letters didn't come. I didn't want to press Angela, but where were they? I knew she was busy with unpacking from a recent move, plus looking after her family and her own studies. Even if I had the letters, I wouldn't have the translations. How would I go about getting that done? Should I hire someone in the U.S. to do it? I hated to depend entirely on Angela, especially if she was just too busy to help. The whole project hinged on these letters, which now seemed non-existent.

As for weekly progress reports to my thesis adviser Kathleen, I posted the following in our private thesis advising site, and also uploaded the outline.

September 4, 2009 post to Kathleen Alcalá

This thesis project will explore German-speaking immigrants to Cleveland, Ohio from 1840 to early 1900.

Background Note—My ancestors who arrived in Cleveland in 1840 were not, technically, "German immigrants," but "German-speaking immigrants," since in the 1840s there were an array of regions in what is now known as Germany, small feudal states dating back to Roman times .... My ancestral village of Freinsheim (located in southwestern portion of present-day Germany, the Rhineland-Palatinate) ... is still in existence today, a region of vineyards and wine-production ....

In 1840 in Cleveland, pop. 6071 (city founded 1796). Early start—Indians, early white citizens unpretentious and fun-loving. Turns out to be easy to find work, with steamboat/ship building businesses in full swing. In 1858 (Cleveland pop. Approx. 40,000), Michael Harm, 16-years-old, crosses Atlantic alone to start new life with uncle and aunt.

In addition to these first, broad strokes, my outline included eras of the families, the Handrichs and Rapparlie arriving first, then the misfortunes of

Rapparlie's business burning and infant deaths, then another section with Michael arriving in 1857. In that first outline, chapter one opened with Johann and Katherina Rapparlie in 1847 Cleveland ten years before Michael Harm arrived. At first, I wanted to tell the story from Katherina Rapparlie's point of view. Since she'd lost her leg, I thought that incident might make for an exciting event early on, and she could be the narrator of the story of Michael Harm.

To organize the sections, I used roman numerals and subheadings and listed characters and events. By the time I was finished, my multi-generational family saga of a thesis resembled McCullough's epic *The Thorn Birds*. Way too ambitious and long, but I turned it in anyhow.

"That's not an outline," Kathleen responded, to my surprise.

Well then, what kind of outline did she mean? Kathleen sent me a sample, which broke the story arc into chapters, each chapter containing a one-paragraph summary of the opening conflict, what happened in the plot, then the resolution of the conflict as the story transitioned to the next chapter.

Way more than I could handle just then. I could only think about research, not what might actually happen in the book chapter by chapter. The letters were only partially translated, and I didn't even have them yet. Plus, I still wasn't sure if I'd write a fiction novel, or a nonfiction account. I expressed these concerns to Kathleen.

"If it is fiction, I would go towards the character for whom you feel the most affinity. If it is nonfiction, towards the era and people on whom you have the most information," Kathleen wrote back.

I followed up with a request for more time to revise the outline. Fortunately, Kathleen granted it. However, she still pressed for chapters or scenes, so I forced myself to begin writing drafts of what might eventually become scenes and posted them on our thesis advising site.

BY THIS TIME IN THE MFA program, I'd developed a writing practice that worked best for me. I preferred the early morning hours, writing before I did any reading or posting of comments or assignments in the class forums. Sometimes, I arose before breakfast, at five or six a.m., and sat on the couch writing in longhand in a blue-ruled notebook. The sky outside the living room window would be black when I began, and as the hours passed, day gradually dawned in deep blue and yellow and sometimes rose. My husband Dave would come downstairs around then and I'd join him for breakfast. Later in the afternoon, I'd type up the day's cursive on the computer, editing and adjusting the text as I added it into a document file.

Experimentally, I tried writing a scene about how Katherina Rapparlie lost her leg. Maybe, I imagined, she'd been hit by a carriage while crossing the street? Or maybe while ironing, she'd dropped a hot iron on her foot? I knew a thing or two about ironing in the old days. My family still owned a couple of irons, heavy blocks of cast iron, arrow-shaped and solid. My grandmother told me the women heated the irons by the fire, then pressed them on dampened cloth over the wrinkled clothes. Those irons were heavy enough to do serious damage if dropped. In my house growing up, we used them as door stops and bookends.

But my first attempts with Katharina as the main character felt unsatisfactory. Her story wasn't grabbing my imagination, probably, I decided, because the letters were all written by men. Kathleen suggested it might be best if I focused on my great-great grandfather. I saw her point. If my main character was Michael Harm, I had not only the letters, but also my grandmother's stories to go on.

Even with a main character in mind, though, I had no idea how to grasp the realities of the mid-nineteenth century. At this juncture, a hobby of mine—maintaining a collection of old books passed down in the family—proved invaluable. Our bookshelves were lined with collections inherited from my parents and their ancestors, for instance, the complete works of Charles Dickens, Anthony Trollope, and George Eliot. I began breaking up the tedium of *Moby-Dick* and class assignments by starting in on Charles Dickens's *David Copperfield*. Then too, based on Angela's insistence that James Fenimore Cooper was so popular in Germany, I started reading *The Last of the Mohicans*. (Yes, I was reading all of these at once, and books for course assignments, too—books were stacked beside every chair and sofa in the house.)

But what about German novelists in the 19th century? None came immediately to mind. They seemed much less prolific in that era. Then I remembered something I'd learned long ago in an English literature class, how the novel was a relatively modern invention. In former times, people turned for reading pleasure to poetry and plays and essays. When I looked for German poets and playwrights of Michael Harm's era, I found a wealth of resources—Johann Wolfgang von Goethe, Friedrich Schiller, and Heinrich Heine, for starters. Goethe had written some novellas, I discovered, so I picked up a collection of those, and started in on his most well-known: *The Sorrows of Young Werther*.

This novella by Goethe, more than any other work, introduced me to the ideals of Romanticism. The book was published in 1774, and while Goethe was technically a Classicist of the rational Enlightenment, the protagonist Werther in his novella epitomized a man of the romantic era. In the story, young Werther is a victim of unrequited love, which makes him heavily pensive and introspective, dwelling on his suffering, longing always for the unattainable. When the Romanticism Movement hit full stride in the 1790s, it arrived in part as a reaction to Classicism with its formality and rules. Romanticism encouraged the collection of folk songs, ballads and folklore, and a heightened interest in the wild, unrestrained natural wilderness. Reading *The Sorrows of Young Werther* started me thinking about whether my great-great grandfather had been a romantic at heart. Whether he was or not, I decided it was a good character trait to build on.

IN THE MIDST OF THESE hit-and-miss early attempts, I followed Bruce Holland Rogers's advice and signed up for a library language learning program. Whatever happened, and no matter how much help I had from Angela, it felt to me as if I needed a better grasp of German. My progress online was slow— lessons for ordering food at a restaurant, buying tickets at a train counter— but at least it was something.

More weeks passed, and still the letters did not arrive. Then Angela called to say she'd made a visit to the post office looking for the package of letters her mom had mailed, and they hadn't turned up anything. Not what I needed to hear just then, but what could I do about it? During the call, Angela asked me about my progress on my thesis, what I thought so far, how I'd decided to tell the story. At that point, I doubted there'd even be a thesis, but I did my best to rally.

"I think maybe Rapparlie talked the Handrichs into emigrating," I told her. "I think maybe Rapparlie lived in Meckenheim too, and wanted to marry their daughter Katherina, and talked the whole family into going to America."

"Do you think so?" Angela's tone was doubtful. "It doesn't seem right. In the first letter, it says Rapparlie and Katherina married once they arrived in Cleveland. I think maybe they met on the boat. I have to go to the archives in Speyer one day and look for Rapparlie and the Handrichs. Do you have archives, to look up records there?"

"There might be some in Cleveland. I'm not sure."

"What else have you found out? What do you think is the reason Michael left?"

Now both Kathleen and Angela were expecting reports from me. I shifted in my chair, unable to answer with any certainty.

"It was always said in my family that he hated the farm work," I said, falling back on family lore, "and wanted to be a blacksmith. He probably ran away."

"Oh no, he couldn't have run away."

"Why not?" I was surprised by her confidence. I remembered his terse paragraph in the 1858 letter, how short he'd been with his parents. Michael Harm had written: "My contract for the time of my apprenticeship you can read in uncle's writing."

"If he ran away, we would not still be in contact. His parents would not have spoken to him again," Angela said.

She may have been right, but I had a hard time accepting it. Hadn't he left his hoe in the field and followed a music band to Cleveland? Both hating farm work, and following a music band sounded like running away to me. It made a big difference to the story, whether he ran away or was sent, and Angela and I didn't agree.

If only we had the letters to help us solve the mysteries. And what would I do, I wondered, if they didn't appear?

Chapter 12

I would have liked to spend full-time on my thesis, but instead had to work in fits and starts. That fall of 2009, in addition to thesis and my regular MFA classes, my husband moved to another law office, my senior-in-high-school daughter was applying to colleges and I had ongoing duties with Aunt Elizabeth.

My aunt was settling in, more or less. When she first arrived, she'd been on her best behavior, but as time passed some of her more imperious traits began to emerge. First, there had been a kerfuffle with the 7th floor resident liaison Nita, who couldn't understand why Aunt Elizabeth kept so much to herself.

Nita stopped me in the hall soon after we'd arrived and let me have it. "That aunt of yours. She doesn't attend floor meetings. I tried to talk to her about it and she pushed right past me!"

"Look, Nita, I'm sorry," I said, surprised by how protective I was feeling. "Elizabeth has lived alone her entire adult life. She never married, she has no children. She's just not used to being around people all the time."

"Oh my goodness, that explains everything," Nita said, "I'll keep that in mind and try not to pester her."

I was grateful for Nita's quick understanding, but also unnerved by how quickly she'd initially gone on the attack. As we said a pleasant good-bye, I hoped I'd brokered a lasting peace. I did worry that Aunt Elizabeth's personality might rub some people the wrong way, as it had my parents. If things started going sour, what would happen then? Would she start complaining and hate it at Bayview? Would we have to find her another retirement community?

A while later, another incident cropped up.

"Yesterday at breakfast, something went wrong," Aunt Elizabeth said as we sat in the van about to head off for our weekly errands. *Uh oh*, I thought. Breakfast was a sticking point for my aunt. She always, and I mean always, ate dry toast and black coffee, nothing more, nothing less. And she absolutely hated to wait for it.

Clyde Patterson, Jr., at Christmas in Cincinnati, 2007.

"I always sit at breakfast with these three other men. One of them is your friend from church, Herb I think his name is? I told the wait staff: 'Dry toast and coffee.' Only they brought buttered toast, so I had to send it back. Then the coffee was cold. Finally, I got the toast, but still no coffee. So I left."

"You got up and left?" I hoped that was all. If Aunt Elizabeth had made a scene, it would have been embarrassing for her. For us all.

"I went up to the room and ate crackers. But this morning, I went down again for breakfast, and I was walking toward the table, and it was really very funny, whoosh, in zips a girl with a plate of dry toast. Then whoosh, in comes this young man with hot coffee." Aunt Elizabeth chuckled to herself, clearly enjoying her victory.

"Sounds like you put the fear of God in them," I said, starting up the van. From the corner of my eye, I saw her nod with satisfaction.

With all the attention I'd been giving Aunt Elizabeth, I still needed to take pains not to neglect my father back in Cincinnati. I wrote him letters once a week, to which he replied almost as often. For my part, I rarely mentioned Aunt Elizabeth. I didn't want to give Dad the impression I cared more about his sister-in-law than I did about him. Even before Mom died, Aunt Elizabeth and Dad never managed to get along. The mere mention of her name worked like a Taser, making him tense and irritable.

I'd also been waiting to bring up my thesis topic. I assumed Dad would be delighted, but it seemed like too much to explain in a letter. Due to his Parkinson's, talking to Dad on the phone was problematic as well. His tremors had advanced to the point where he could barely keep his grip on the handset. Even so, by mid-October I'd drawn up a list of questions to help me get started on my thesis that I hoped Dad could answer. One afternoon I picked up the phone and dialed his number in Cincinnati.

"So Dad, you know those letters we found and sent to the relatives in Freinsheim? And then the old letters Angela found in Gunter and Inge Faber's attic? Guess what. I'm going to write about those people of the letters for my MFA thesis. My thesis adviser says it has great possibilities."

"Uh huh," Dad said. "I've spent more time on my autobiography, but I'm afraid you won't be able to make any sense of it." Dad's voice dropped out at this point. Perhaps he was fumbling for a better grip or had even lost hold of the phone. Dad had been working on his autobiography for years, which my brother reported was, indeed, a mess.

There was some shuffling on the other end, then Dad's voice again. "Are you there?"

"Yeah, Dad, I'm here." I wondered how reliable his memory would be about Michael Harm at this point. "Is now a good time? If you don't mind, I have some questions for you. Like, remember that story about Michael Harm carrying a gun on his way to work?"

"No, that was your great-grandpa Hoppensack. My mother's father. Before the E. 55th Street bridge was built in Cleveland, he had to go through Kingsbury Run to get to work at the bank. It was like a jungle down there. He had to carry a gun because there were vagrants, and robberies sometimes."

I hadn't remembered correctly. I was so glad I'd asked him, and made a mental note to change the outline. Then again, did I need to change the novel's plot? The struggle of writing something based on a true story was getting confused in my mind. When should I stick to the historical record, and when should I deviate? I hoped that, eventually, I'd figure it out.

"So did you ever hear any stories about people named Rapparlie and Handrich?"

"I heard my mother and G-G talk about those people a few times." G-G was the nickname for Michael Harm's eldest daughter Lucy, my Great Grandmother. "I think we visited them once, in Toledo," he added.

Toledo? That didn't sound right. But Dad rambled ahead, saying something about the Bihns in Toledo, some family picnic they'd attended. As Dad talked, I scribbled notes on a yellow pad as fast as I could.

"Do you remember Michael Harm's wife?" I asked when he paused. "Grandmother used to show me pictures of you as a baby sitting on Elizabeth Harm's lap."

"Yes. Elizabeth Crolly was living until 1926. I was only three when she died. I don't remember much, except that every month Ed Gressle would come pick her up, and G-G, too, and take them over to the Putnam Street Church where the women would quilt."

"Putnam Street Church?"

"That's what they called it. For years that church held services in German. It used to stand on Putnam Street. But at some point they moved it, the whole church building, stone by stone, over to 99th and Olivet."

All at once, I wished I could return to Cleveland with Dad, to retrace the terrain and glean what knowledge I could from him. Back when I'd had the opportunity, during decades of visits to Cleveland to see my parents, it had never occurred to me to suggest such a thing. I'd taken the family stories for granted.

Through the few letters Angela and I had translated, I was beginning to see Cleveland in a whole new light. Growing up, with the broken glass and tar paper and crumbling old brick buildings downtown, sights I witnessed during the Rapid Transit rides to and from Public Square, I had no idea of its 19th-century history. The letters were making me curious, about what Cleveland was like back then, about what the first German immigrants encountered.

But still, Angela's package of letters didn't arrive. In a progress report to Kathleen in our thesis advising site, I shared my concerns about this, but much to my wonderment, my thesis adviser seemed to think I could move forward anyhow.

October 8, 2009

Claire, don't necessarily count on your cousin sending the letters. This is where things can get tricky, so keep looking at other sources. Another thing that will come up is the idea of fictionalizing family stories, if that is the route you choose to go. Not everyone understands this …. The obverse of that is telling stories that relatives may consider shameful or demeaning.

Keep looking at other sources? I appreciated Kathleen's belief in my project, but I'd come across very little information on carriage-making. Worse, I'd checked out books on metallurgy and blacksmithing, but it still didn't make a lot of sense to me. In my opinion, things weren't looking great. My updates during that time reflected my lack of direction and sense of unease. My thesis adviser was patient with me. She suggested not taking on too much at once and narrowing the focus to Michael Harm. So in my next update, I included a synopsis of the story I hoped to tell about Michael Harm, drawn mainly from his obituary and the oral history.

Synopsis of Michael Harm's life

My great-great grandfather grew up in Freinsheim in the Bavarian Rhinelands fascinated with Indians because of childhood gifts he received from his uncle in Cleveland. He begged to go to America and left at age 15. First, he landed in New York, then continued on to Cleveland and Rapparlie's shop. Blacksmithing turned out to be harder than he thought. Eventually, he fell in love and married, and became ambitious about founding a carriage works of his own. As Michael raised his family and devoted his life to Harm & Schuster carriage works, Cleveland became more polluted, and violent enough that he had to carry a gun on his walks to work. With the introduction of the automobile, his carriage-making business began to fail. Later, his adult children turned their backs on their heritage, preferring American society to their German roots. In 1893, Michael Harm returned to Freinsheim to see his brother, and found a land resembling the romantic idyll of his youth, a lush, green, peaceful life he originally left his homeland to find. In the end, Michael thinks about his prospects and disappointments in Cleveland, and wonders if it was what he wanted after all.

In her reply, Kathleen assured me this storyline would be a good start.

ONE MORNING IN THE SECOND week of October, I was up early and sitting on the couch, trying to find my way through a massive amount of information. One of the books on the stack next to me was a fat tome of poetry by Johann Wolfgang von Goethe, which I'd checked out from the library. As I leafed through it, pausing here and there, I landed on a poem written in 1817, "Primal Words, Orphic." The poem covered the five phases of a person's life, almost like the five acts of a play. The five stanzas were titled: Destiny, Chance, Love, Necessity, Hope.

The poem evolved in lofty language. Perhaps due to the translation, it sounded stilted to my ears, but the progression spoke to me. Now that I saw it on the page, it seemed almost too obvious. In "Primal Words, Orphic," the stanzas fit well with the synopsis I'd just sent off to Kathleen: Michael Harm was born into one life, his Destiny to be a farmer, but wanted to be a blacksmith. He took a Chance, a big risk, and shipped off to America to pursue his dream. Next came Love, when he fell for my great-great grandmother, Elizabeth Crolly and started a family. Of Necessity, his life became consumed with his business, the growth and importance of his Harm & Schuster Carriage Works.

It all fit, except for the last part—Hope. Of that, I could not be sure. In the end, when Cleveland had become polluted by oil refineries and more violent, when cars were supplanting horsedrawn carriages and Michael was forced to close down his business, when his own children refused to speak German, only English, then what? Was my great-great grandfather glad that he'd left his homeland behind? Did he have hope for the future? Or did he think he'd made the biggest mistake of his life?

I did not know, but was excited to try writing my way to some kind of conclusion.

Chapter 13

At last, I was having breakthroughs. For my update in mid-October, I shared with my thesis adviser about my discovery of the Goethe poem, and something more.

October 16, 2009

Emails with German cousin—After I submitted last week's progress report, I got some crucial correspondence from my cousin Angela. Apparently, her mother had mailed the family letters from Freinsheim to Marburg and they'd been lost in the mail. After three weeks of searching at various post offices, they found them! The package had been wrapped in paper, the paper ripped off, so the address was gone. Angela is now emailing me scanned .jpgs of the letters.

October 17, 2009—Kathleen's reply

I cannot believe the story of those letters! And that they found them. Did you do the translation of the Goethe poem?

October 19, 2009—Claire's reply

I know! Really incredible. Angela said it occurred to her the letters had been stolen because of the value of the stamps. What a lucky break.

Translation? Heck no, I'm not that good. But I can tell even with my rudimentary German that the English version lacks the depth and nuances of the German one. I'm so excited about it. I wish I could just concentrate on this full-time.

With the near loss of the letters, we'd all learned a lesson. Angela couldn't bring herself to put them in the mail again. Instead, she promised to scan them page by page and send me the .jpg files via email. They weren't translated, of course, but at last I was beginning to feel as if I was on my way.

Angela emailed me an updated inventory of our progress, noting what we'd translated so far. Six were grouped between 1841 and 1858. Only a few covered the later years—the era of necessity, as I'd come to think of it, the time in Michael Harm's life when he had to focus entirely on his business and support his growing family. A letter in 1869, one in 1883, a postcard in 1893, one in 1900, and a partial, undated letter. If I wrote my thesis to include the Civil War and beyond, I'd have to make up just about everything, a challenge I didn't feel up to. I thought about cutting the story off when Michael Harm fell in love and got married, but I'd really begun to see the story arc in terms of Goethe's poem. If I could manage it, I longed to write the story of my German immigrant great-great grandfather from beginning to middle to end.

Angela started translating the letters immediately, starting with one of two written in 1850. When I saw it in my inbox, I admit to feeling slavishly grateful. This 1850 letter, written by Johann Rapparlie to the Freinsheim family, included additional information about the disappearance of the eldest son Johannes Handrich, almost as if we'd written to Rapparlie ourselves to ask.

Addressed to: J. [Johann] Philipp Harm

In Freinsheim

Dürkheim an der Haahrt

Baijer. [Bayern] Rheinkreis [Bavarian Rhine province]

Europa

Cleveland[1], 21 April 1850

Much loved brother-in-law and sister-in-law

We all have rightly received your letter from February 23rd

---

1   Between 1840 and 1850, the population of Cleveland nearly tripled, from 6,000 to 17,000 persons.

and have learned from it that you and your little children[2] are quite healthy. And that your wife has been sick for 5 years now. That is indeed very hard. And we also know very well here what kind of bloodletting you have had from the military[3], which we read about week after week in our newspapers of which I believe it must be even harder for a father of a family when he has a sick wife.

Now dear brother-in-law you write if grandfather[4] still has receipts so he should send them. He has no receipts here. But I can write you further information where you should go or with whom you have to deal. You have to deal with trader Heinrich's family but the old man has passed away so you have to deal with the young R.H. They shall open the books for you, so you will find that it is already paid 19 years since I have sold the old house, which was purchased by Franz Wilhelm Gros.

Dear brother-in-law you would like to know where brother-in-law Johannes[5] is. I want to write you the whole description about it. In the first year after we have come to America Johannes apprenticed in the cooper's[6] trade and earned quite some money as in that same time it was the best trade. All of a sudden he lost his senses and what means in German he became melancholic, we had big trouble with him. More than 1-½ years ago suddenly he stopped and said he would still have to make a journey that was the last he then put on his best clothes and a new coat that was the last time we saw him. And further we have learned that a man who knew him had seen him 130 miles from Cleveland and that was the last and we have already spent all kinds of efforts wanting to find out if he is still alive or dead or where he is.

---

2   Philipp Harm, born 10/9/1839, Michael Harm, born 5/26/1841, Barbara Harm, born 12/8/1844.
3   In 1849, Prussian troops occupied Freinsheim, followed by Bavarian troops several months later.
4   Philipp Henrich Handrich, penner of the first letter in 1841.
5   Johannes Handrich, mentioned in the 1847 letter, was the eldest brother in the Handrich family.
6   Barrel-maker

We have already made a journey but nothing to be heard or found it has been 6 years now in the month of March. That is all the information I can give you. Now I want to close this.

Now dear brother-in-law I also want to write you my circumstances how bad luck has hit me. Namely, the first [child] was named Margarethe, born the October 31 died the 12 November 1841. She only lived 10 days. The second [child] was named Katharina Margarethe, born March 9, 1843, died the 18 February 1844. The third [child] was Elisabetha, born March 19, 1845, died October 16, 1848 and was only sick for 10 hours. She knew all English and could talk. All three are in one grave. God may grant them the eternal peace. That is a hard thing not to keep any child. But God be thanked now we have a boy whose name is Johannes, born August 30th 1849 and is up till now quite healthy.

Further I can't complain I have my business in a good state now I work with 6 to 7 journeymen.[7] It is called Smith and Wagonmaker[8]. I think I earn now within one week as much as in Germany within 2 months. My brother-in-law Jakob is still unmarried but he has already bought himself a house and property, approximately $800 to $900 dollars in value. He has had to earn everything with his hands [illegible—page torn] me too. I have also bought 2 house properties which cost me approximately 13 hundred dollars. Further the bad luck has also hit me when two of my workplaces burned. The loss wasn't so big since the buildings were old. But I have surely built everything out of brick. The smith and wagonbuilder work spaces again are in one building 60 foot long 24 wide 2 ½ stories high. Above is the workplace for painters and saddlers[9]. God be thanked if I keep healthy for a few years then I can help myself.

7   A journeyman was a skilled craftsman who had accomplished an apprenticeship. In a wagon shop, the journeymen would have been blacksmiths, woodworkers, painters, and upholsterers.

8   Rapparlee, John, carriages. 52 Michigan St. h. 194 Seneca. Williston & Co.'s Directory, 1859, Cleveland.

9   Saddler is another word for an upholsterer, also known as a trimmer.

Further our brother-in-law Georg Scheuerman who is from Weisenheim am Sand[10] is also healthy and also has 2 children. He works in his profession and also already [saves] money. Now I want to close. I don't know any further news. Our parents-in-law are both quite healthy and live quite happily, and so forth.

Dear brother-in-law if you write again always write a letter for yourself. And don't let it be put into other letters as the costs aren't as high.

We stay your true ones and greet you many thousand times. And hope for an answer soon again.

Johann (Rapparlie)

Jacob Handrich

[Note below the signatures]

(I can't leave it to tell you that you should motivate your children to write read and count so it won't happen to them as it happened to me[11])

Angela noted the postscript was in a different handwriting than that of Rapparlie. Possibly written by the brother-in-law, Jakob? I thought back to the neat, professional appearance of his 1849 letter. It occurred to me perhaps when Jakob had decided to send the presents of vests and shoes back to his sister and her family, he had paid someone else to write the letter for him. One can only wonder what Jakob meant about what had happened to him as a consequence of a lack of education. Or, perhaps, he included the message as an attempt to inspire his nephews to be diligent at school?

As for this lengthy account from Johann Rapparlie, for all the "success" he claimed regarding his new American life, he reported an undue amount of hardship. Two times his business burned and he had to rebuild. Worse yet, he and his wife suffered the heartbreaking loss of three infant daughters.

---

10 In the 1847 letter, Georg was mentioned via his marriage to the Handrich daughter Margaretha. George and Margaretha had two boys, George and John.

11 Postscript in a different handwriting, possibly by Jakob or Katherina Handrich. There is nothing to suggest why Jakob Handrich (presumably this Jakob is the youngest son of the Handrichs) would not have learned to read, write and count. The 1849 the letter from Jakob Handrich is in a neat, very legible script, indicating he may have paid someone to pen it for him.

Rapparlie had mentioned the third, Elisabetha, in his 1847 letter. Now she was dead as well. How awful. Even so, Rapparlie's pen drove forward with conviction. Close on the heels of the news of his bad luck he announced that he earned in one week what it would take two months to earn in Germany. In the same sentence about the hard reality of three infant deaths, he expressed joy at the birth of a new baby boy.

What captivated me most, though, were the additional details about the disappearance of Johannes. By the time of this letter in 1850, Rapparlie said it had been six years, so apparently Johannes left in 1844. Still, the family had no word about what had happened to him. Did they ever learn? How common was such an experience in those days, for a person to wander off and never be heard from again? With my older brother Sandy, when he disappeared without a trace, even in these times of better communication, there was a real possibility we might never find him.

IN 1988, AFTER SANDY DISAPPEARED, Mom and Dad called me in Seattle to let me know. They described how they'd put out a police report and called everyone they knew, but turned up nothing. When I received this news, I was living in Seattle and felt helpless to be of any use. I suggested maybe he'd gone to see our brother Craig, but my parents had talked to Craig already, and Sandy wasn't there.

A week or so later, Sandy's former landlords, the Davidhuizers in Chicago, called to tell my parents Sandy had resurfaced there. They'd encountered him on the street only by chance. They said my brother hadn't told them where he was living. From what they could tell, he didn't have a job or a place to stay.

"We have to go bring him back," Mom said, reporting to me by phone from Ohio. It all felt so terribly sad, for Mom and Dad, for Sandy, who was thirty-two years old at the time, for me and Craig. I understood that by escaping to Chicago, Sandy was sending us the message that he wanted to be treated as an adult, to make his own decisions regardless of the consequences. But my older brother needed medical help for his severe schizophrenia.

"We have to at least try," Mom said.

I agreed, but had no idea how they'd ever find him. Chicago was such an enormous city. Plus, I figured if Sandy did not want to be found, he'd probably manage it. But I kept my misgivings to myself and hoped and prayed they'd have success in the search.

Shortly after talking with me, Dad and Mom set out on their desperate journey, driving from Cleveland to Chicago to try to find their oldest son and bring him home. They spent several days there, visiting Sandy's former haunts, searching for any sign of him to no avail.

Then came an odd twist of fate.

"We had given up and were driving down the street toward the highway to come home, and there he was," Dad said, when they phoned later to tell me what happened. "Just walking down the sidewalk. Plodding along like a lost soul."

Sandy wasn't glad to see them, Mom confided to me later. "He was so upset with us. He did everything in his power to keep living in Chicago, to not go with us. But how could we leave him? He couldn't care for himself. He was so sick. I didn't see any other way."

Less than a year later, after an endless string of anti-psychotic medications that did little to manage his schizophrenia, in June of 1989, my brother took his own life. My parents had struggled so hard to save him, we all had. But nothing worked.

ALTHOUGH THE HANDRICH FAMILY'S EXPERIENCE with Johannes occurred almost 150 years earlier, Rapparlie's account felt just as fresh to me as if it had been yesterday. It stirred up memories of my family's tragedy with fresh feelings about an old despair. "[Johannes] then put on his best clothes and a new coat that was the last time we saw him." Was I reading between the lines, to think Johannes had put on these new clothes as if preparing for suicide, to be laid to his final rest in a coffin? "we have already spent all kinds of efforts wanting to find out if he is still alive or dead" sounded especially ominous to me, as if Rapparlie suspected the worst. Such pain and loss, the family presumably never finding out what happened.

I was in my early thirties, five months pregnant with my first child, when my older brother Sandy departed this life. As for my parents, they lost their first son just as they were about to welcome their first grandchild. As survivors, regardless of how torn up we feel, we are forced to find a way through. It was terrible to lose Sandy, but at least someone found him so we knew what had happened. Somehow, we grieved our terrible loss, and kept on living.

I believe there exists in us an insatiable desire to know the truth, to tie up loose ends and learn the fates of those who have gone before. If they survived, how they survived. I wonder if one day I might stumble upon Johannes in my genealogy research, find him having lived out his life in the late 19th century somewhere in Wisconsin, or Texas, or California. Did he marry and find meaningful work? Or give up on life in the U.S. and return to Germany? Or live out his life in a mental institution? Or did he take his own life, his body lying buried in an unmarked grave? The possibilities seem endless. But whether I find him or not, Johannes Handrich isn't just a genealogy record, but a human life, lost to those who loved him with just as much finality as my brother Sandy was lost to us.

Chapter 14

Now that Angela had the letters in hand, she devoted hours and hours to scanning and translating them. Also, when she traveled from Marburg to Freinsheim that fall, she met with several relatives to ask them what they knew of our ancestors.

Curious about the Handrich connection, Angela contacted a woman in Meckenheim who knew something of the Handrich family history in that village. Angela reported to me that according to Irmgard Handrich, the Handrichs who emigrated no longer appeared in the family tree except for Elisabetha who married Johann Philipp Harm in Freinsheim. The Handrichs still in Meckenheim, however, had been training as artisan craft wine-makers for the past five generations.

Angela also visited Gerhard Harm, an old uncle in Freinsheim with whom she had not spoken before. Uncle Gerhard said he remembered when my father, the American Clyde Patterson, had visited Freinsheim for the first time in 1950. He also shared his research about the first Harm to arrive in Freinsheim, a Michael of the 1700s, born several generations before my great-great grandfather. She emailed: "Johann Michael Harm, a blacksmith (4/22/1718) came to Freinsheim and married on September 13, 1746 Anna Elisabetha Reibold (7/28/1724) in Freinsheim. They had three sons who all became blacksmiths and stayed in Freinsheim." I was glad to have this information from her email, which corroborated Dad's family tree.

When Angela shared with Gerhard Harm our finding of the letters, she mentioned how some of them had been written by the Handrichs of Meckenheim. Gerhard told Angela how he'd once been on a hunting trip and met an elderly man from Meckenheim. When Gerhard told the man his last name, the man said: "Harm? Well then, in the end we are related!" meaning that, many generations later in Meckenheim, the Harm-Handrich association was still known.

Angela also met with Tante Gretel, who reminisced again about first meeting my father. Apparently, as a young woman in 1950, Tante Gretel was just returning from the fields when she saw my father Clyde standing in front of the Faber's[1] house. Dad was studying architecture in France that year, and had come to Freinsheim to meet the women with whom his mother Emma had been corresponding in German for decades. Since the Faber family was still out in the fields, Gretel took my father home with her to the Weber's[2] house. She remembered how her grandmother[3] Katherina Kitsch had tears in her eyes when she saw Clyde, because she said she didn't ever expect to see someone from the American family again in her lifetime. It was this visit by Michael Harm's great grandson Clyde, a full 57 years after Michael Harm last visited Freinsheim in 1893 that re-energized the acquaintance for subsequent generations.

For my part, I felt very fortunate to have a German correspondent "in the field" providing the German story. I also was beginning to feel a bit like a conduit. My job as a writer was taking on new dimensions; my role turning out to be one of weaving together perspectives from both sides of the Atlantic into one cohesive narrative.

As the weeks that fall sped by, the topic I'd chosen wasn't getting any easier.

"What's going on with that thesis of yours?" Aunt Elizabeth asked during lunch one Thursday as we shared our weekly outing. She especially liked the Old Spaghetti Factory, which I think reminded her of Clara's Lansing Station restaurant in Michigan, a place she'd taken me once when I'd visited her as a young adult. We didn't talk about my studies all that much, so I was glad to share.

"Angela's doing a lot for me, but we still have many translations to do. My thesis adviser keeps bugging me to write pages, but it's hard." During this confession, my aunt didn't look up at me. Her habit at meals was to focus intently on the plate of food before her. At the moment, she was plowing through bite after bite of mizithra pasta. "Sometimes," I went on, "this whole thing reminds me of that plant in "The Little Shop of Horrors." The more I

---

1   Anna Faber nee Kitsch (1901-1998) was the granddaughter of Philipp Harm, Michael Harm's brother.

2   The Weber house would have been the house of Helene Weber (1903-1996), Angela's grandmother. Anna Faber and Helene Weber were the correspondents with my grandmother, Emma Patterson (1891-1987) for decades. Gretel Kopf nee Weber, the daughter of Helene, was not yet married in 1950.

3   Katherina Kitsch nee Harm (1876-1960), daughter of Michael's brother Philipp. Katherina and her husband had two daughters: Anna Faber nee Kitsch and Helene Weber nee Kitsch.

feed it, the more it threatens to swallow me whole."

She erupted into one of her brief snorts of laughter. "I'd like to read something, once you have a few chapters," she said.

I hesitated, thinking how highly critical Aunt Elizabeth could be. When I was in college, she used to reprimand me sharply for saying "like" and "you know" too often. As far back as I could remember, whenever we met for an outing, she'd look me up and down to assess my outfit. "That looks terrible on you," she'd said more than once. Or, even more bluntly: "You've put on weight." Just the other day, a propos of nothing, she'd come out with: "You're an attorney's wife. You should dress better. People expect that."

When it came to my writing, though, Aunt Elizabeth was strangely loyal. Several years ago, she'd asked to see my first manuscript, the novel I'd written that now languished in the drawer. With some trepidation, I'd printed it out and mailed it to her in East Lansing.

"I passed it around to Louise and Gladys and Eileen," she called to report. "Louise thinks the topic is very marketable."

I'd been thrilled to receive that kind of support, so didn't see the harm now in sharing pages with her.

"When I have something, I'll be sure to give it to you," I promised.

Close on the heels of the translation of the first letter of 1850, Angela emailed me a second translation, written in September of that same year, again by Johann Rapparlie. The thorough address on the front emphasized some of the German history I'd been starting to digest, how in 1850 the Palatinate belonged to Bavaria. The Rhineland-Palatinate region wasn't geographically situated next to Bavaria. In fact, two nation-states—Baden and Württemberg—lay between them. Nevertheless, based on agreements reached among the German monarchies following the fall of Napoleon Bonaparte in 1815, the Palatinate had fallen under Bavarian rule.

H. [Herr] Johann Philipp Harm

Freinsheim bey Dürkheim an dem Hartgebirg [Freinsheim near Dürkheim at the Haardt Mountains]

Königreich Bayern [Kingdom of Bavaria]

Rheinkreis [Rhine province]

Europa [Europe]

8 September 1850

Dearest brother-in-law and sister-in-law,

We have received with great joy your letter from July 4th on September 6th 1850 and have learned from it that you are all still alive. And we were all sorry that your wife is still sick. And I know how it is when the mother is sick in a house (it) is lacking everywhere. What delighted us all is that your older son[4] already writes with such a beautiful handwriting. That is quite a lot for such an age. This is the central point in America when someone is able to count read and write.

Dearest brother-in-law and sister-in-law I have so far never seen you in my life and would surely be happy to see you here in America, because Selzer's[5] brother told us that you have a longing to travel to America if only you would know for sure how it would be. Dear brother-in-law and sister-in-law you are both unknown to me. I also don't know your circumstances how you are positioned with fortune and so on. I want to write you the pure truth and believe what I write you here. As far as the father-in-law[6] has told me, you could bring quite some money into the land so you could buy a property. So I want to write you everything very clearly here the whole circumstances. I believe that if you should come into this land, you might not like it as much as you might think you would. Then second, the language is difficult, because one can't talk with the people, and one who is already 30 years old will never learn it any more.

Even if you or both of you don't like it, for your children it would be better. It is a much easier life than in Germany. We all think that, you can make your living better than in Germany. And if you want to come then just don't be afraid during the journey and if you come, you needn't think that we might just want to lure you here and that we think if you come he's got money so we can also help ourselves and so on. Many are writing like this to their friends: Just come in to us, it is better.

4   Philipp Harm, born 1839.
5   Presumably, this Selzer family referenced in the letter is from Freinsheim. In 1849, Jakob Handrich mentioned in his letter that Selzers (a brother and sister) were in Cleveland that year. Possibly, the Freinsheim Selzer's brother.
6   Philipp Henrich Handrich, born 1783, of Meckenheim

Dear brother-in-law there are more idlers here than in Germany. A man who is poor and is healthy, when he has worked 2 days a week he has money for the whole week and when he is hard working he can always get to own something/be someone. This is surely something you won't need. You can buy yourself a nice farm and you can live quietly.

And if you should come, don't take anything along except for what you have and don't buy new pieces. Don't take more than you need on the journey as you can buy everything here at a low price and then everything here is after a different fashion because the luggage fee costs more than it is worth. Don't take more shoes and boots with you than you need for approximately 3 months, the sea water spoils them. Here they are better, too. Don't take along more than 1 to 2 chests and turn everything into money and take checks /bills of exchange to New York. From there to Cleveland, then none will be stolen from you and won't get lost. And when you come, come only for yourself and don't say my brother-in-law[7] has lured me in. You have to come at your own risk and not accuse anybody and think: "I will now go to America."

Another thing: if you come, don't buy passage in any case to England but go to Havre die Gras [de Grace][8]. It is much more secure. And when you come, write to us that you will want to come and do not think that we need help from you. Thank God both of us are healthy and my brother-in-law Jakob both so far as not to need help any more. And when you come we can receive you in our own home and also have something for you to eat. Now I want to close this. That is all about these things I write to you and can describe to you.

Another thing to Katharina Margaretha[9] a girl has passed away of 1 ½ years of age—on July 10th 1850.

---

7   Johann Rapparlie is referring to himself, here.
8   Le Havre, France, a common port of departure for Palatine Germans, directly west from their region on the Rhine.
9   Presumably, to Katharina Margaretha Scheuermann, sister to Rapparlie's wife.

And when you want to come so write us again then we would like to write to you what you should bring for us. Now I want to close.

We greet you all many times and stay your true ones

John Rapparlie

Jacob Handrich

Jakob Handrich[10]

I savored the wealth of description in this letter. How to travel, what to bring and not to bring for the voyage. This letter also contained evidence that Johann Philipp and Elisabetha Harm had talked about joining the Handrichs in Cleveland. In the end, however, they had not done so. Was it the health of Michael's mother, who according to the April, 1850 letter had been sick for five years? For the purposes of the novel, I thought that supposition was reasonable.

As a next step, I planned to visit the National Archives and Records Administration (NARA), something Kathleen had suggested back in August. Was it too much to hope Michael Harm had followed his Uncle Rapparlie's instructions and sailed on the Atlantic from Le Havre, France to New York City?

---

10 Angela and I are so far unable to distinguish between Jacob Handrich and Jakob Handrich. One came across on the ship Anson with the Handrich family and Johann Rapparlie, presumably Jakob, born in Meckenheim in 1823. The other is perhaps a cousin?

Chapter 15

The first time I entered the National Archives and Records Administration (NARA) on Sand Point Way in Seattle, I signed in and was told to put my belongings in a locker up front. The locker requirement struck me as over-regimented. I'd planned to type data into my laptop as I came across it, but instead was only allowed to bring in a notebook and pencil. In the archives room, beige and gray microfiche reading machines loomed on either side of a dimly lit aisle. After one glance at the set-up, I returned to the front desk.

"I wonder if you can help me?" I asked one of the assistants. "I'm looking for a passenger list from 1857, and one from earlier, too, to see if there's a record of the arrival of my ancestors."

The man stood and led me over to a computer by the front door.

"We have Ancestry here. Why not look up the names first, see what you find?"

Why all the equipment, I wondered, if we just look it up on the computer?

He leaned over the keyboard, fingers poised, waiting. "How's the name spelled?"

I stood by and watched as he typed in Harm and pressed enter. A list of ships appeared, at which point he left me to it and went back to his desk.

I scanned down the arrival dates, but 1857 was not among them. Neither was any Harm with the first name Michael. Giving up, I typed in Rapparlie to see what might show up there, and only one passenger list appeared. The Ship Anson sailed into New York harbor on the 29th of July, 1840. I pulled up the original image and recognized with excitement the names in line right above Rapparlie: Philipp Handrich (56), Catherine Handrich (56), Catherine Handrich (29), John Handrich (27), Catherine Handrich (28), and Jacob Handrich (18).

I felt giddy with hope, but not entirely convinced. Could this really be them? Why were all the women named Catherine? Hadn't one of the Handrich daughter's been named Margaretha? I would not learn until later about the

Tin-type photo of Michael Harm at age 16 in 1857.

naming customs of the region, how first names were saint names and often repeated with each family member. Usually, it was the second, middle name by which they were called— their *Rufnamen*.

With Rapparlie in the mix, I figured it had to be them. The other data fit, too. The *Anson's* point of embarkation had been Le Havre (Havre de Grace), France, the same port Rapparlie had mentioned in both 1847 and 1850. And the year of arrival, 1840, fit too, just one year prior to the first letter dated September, 1841. Their presence in line together seemed to indicate Rapparlie and the Handrichs were acquainted. Because they traveled together from the start? Or had they met on the voyage? Questions that remained unanswered, as villages of origin were not listed. I left the entry on the screen and returned to the front desk.

"No luck?" The assistant asked.

"I found someone else," I said. "But no luck with Michael Harm."

At my request, the NARA assistant came over to help me print out the passenger list for the 1840 *Anson* voyage, then led me over to a long wall of large gray metal file cabinets stocked with microfilm.

"What years are you looking for?" he asked.

"1857."

"What port of entry?"

"New York."

The drawers of microfilm were deep and heavy. The assistant yanked one open and reached in for a New York arrivals microfilm box, the first one of several for the year 1857, but I shook my head no.

"I'd like to start later, sometime around April." I knew Michael Harm's birthday, May 26. Some accounts reported that Michael Harm was fifteen when he came over, but others that he was sixteen, so I hypothesized he might have had a birthday on board the ship. I hoped that starting in April would narrow down the scope of the search.

The assistant handed me the box of microfilm, then led me over to an unoccupied microfiche machine, showed me how to thread it, and left me on my own. Methodically, I began scanning, scrolling, scanning, scrolling. It was rough going. As the pages zipped by, my stomach began to feel queasy.

The handwriting on the lists was uneven, often faded, the film scratchy and flecked with debris.

Gradually, though, I got the hang of it. At the top of each new passenger list, I discerned the port of departure, so decided to breeze over any list that didn't depart from Le Havre. After I'd proceed like this for a while, I grew nervous. So many other ships were arriving in New York harbor during that time, from Bremen, and Hamburg, and Liverpool, from Lisbon, and Glasgow. Could I say for sure Michael left from Le Havre? If he hadn't and I skipped over the other lists, I'd never find him.

In addition to the different types of ships– steamers, three-masted packets, clippers—the manifests noted different classes of passengers—cabin, 2nd class, "between decks." I kept looking for Michael Harm's country of origin— "Palatinate"—but didn't find it listed. As time passed, and I'd seen countless entries for Bavaria, I connected the dots. Back then, I remembered all at once, the Palatinate had been ruled by Bavaria. Was that how they recorded it in the ship registers?

With so many doubts about what, exactly, I was looking for, I slowed to a crawl and began checking the lists for all the ships arriving in New York harbor. Every so often as I went along, I jotted things down—last names that caught my eye, various occupations. Many farmers were listed, but other professions as well: tailor, clerk, butcher, editor, barber, steward, weaver, upholsterer, cabinet maker, cooper, apothecary. These were the professions of Europeans of the 19th century, which broadened my understanding of the kinds of jobs people used to have. I noted large families, couples, many single young men, ships booked with people from Hesse, Baden, Switzerland, France, Belgium. Destinations were sometimes listed, too: Milwaukee, Indiana, New York, Ohio, Illinois, Louisville. The ships were loaded to bursting, many carrying over 300 passengers.

I spent about five hours poring over lists, but found no Michael Harm. Even so, my thesis had broadened and deepened in ways I hadn't anticipated. Growing up, Michael Harm's story had always seemed like an isolated incident. I'd thought his experience was so remarkable in our family because it was unusual. In reality, though, according to these passenger lists, throngs of people were crowding boat after boat to sail from Europe to American shores in 1857. Two, sometimes three ships a day unloaded in New York Harbor alone, not to mention what must have been happening in Baltimore, and New Orleans, and other ports. Michael Harm had been part of a great wave of immigration. But what was it all about? What had happened in Europe to cause such an exodus?

At the end of the afternoon, I reclaimed my belongings from the NARA locker and left with my copy of the Ship *Anson* list in hand, excited to at least have made that find. And now it was clear to me, whether or not I ever found Michael Harm, I wasn't just writing his story, but the story of what appeared to be an unprecedented 19th-century migration out of Western Europe.

Parkinson's isn't a disease from which one recovers, and all along, my father's Parkinson's had been getting steadily worse. Many months had passed since I'd seen Dad, but so much was going on in our family that fall of 2009, with Vivian applying to colleges and Dave moving his law office and my thesis and coursework, that we didn't go to Cincinnati over Thanksgiving.

I dearly wish I had, as it would have been my last opportunity to see my father. During his Thanksgiving meal, Dad aspirated some food, which led to pneumonia. Dad died on December 10. My brother Craig was at his side when he passed, and called to give me the news. Dad would have celebrated his 87th birthday in January of 2010. He'd lived a long and rewarding life.

Among the many email communications I needed to send out with the news of Dad's passing, I sent one right away to Angela.

December 10, 2009

Angela, I am sorry to give you the sad news that Clyde died early this morning. He was doing well until about ten days ago, when he got pneumonia. We will forward other details as we have them. I will be in Cincinnati for the next week.

Love,

Claire

December 10, 2009

Dear Claire,

Our sincere and heartfelt sympathy, also in the name of my mother with whom I just talked on the phone ....

Clyde (and Ruth!) meant a lot to many of us in Freinsheim, as he renewed and kept this precious contact of the families and showed his interest in this side, invited us and supported many different people's interest in your side's culture and ways. My thoughts are with you.

Yours sincerely,

Angela

As I read Angela's condolences, I remembered again about her painful tragedy, how she'd lost her father to diabetes when she was only thirteen years old. She had suffered this loss at such a young age, whereas I had experienced a long relationship with my father well into my adult life.

When I told Aunt Elizabeth, she was very saddened by the news. Although my aunt and Dad didn't get along all the time, I could tell she felt the loss deeply. To give her something to do, I asked her to call her friend Eileen in Columbus, Ohio and tell her, since Eileen also had been very close to my parents. When I told my aunt I'd be away for a week in Cincinnati to help Craig, she was stoic about it.

A few days later, I flew to Ohio to help my brother move Dad's belongings out of his room and storage area at Scarlet Oaks Retirement Community. What we kept went to Craig's home, where he'd go through it over the ensuing months.

But we didn't plan to hold a memorial service right away. Our college-age kids had varying schedules, and the winter weather wasn't convenient for travel, nor for my father's elderly friends in Cleveland where the service would be held. Craig and I decided to schedule Dad's service five months later, in early May of 2010.

Chapter 16

I returned home in time for Christmas with the family, our first with Aunt Elizabeth living in the Pacific Northwest. The holiday was an especially poignant one for me, as I felt keenly the loss of my father.

His death also jogged me into action regarding my aunt, now 88 years old and gradually succumbing to the inevitable fragility of old age. She'd reached the point where she was walking with a cane at Bayview. Whenever she and I went on outings, she used a basic, wheeless walker that was always getting stuck on carpets and door jambs. Dave and I talked it over and decided to give her a Guardian rolling walker with a basket for Christmas. We made it a point to get the one in a racy red color.

"I never thought I'd be excited about getting a new walker, but I'm *really* excited," Aunt Elizabeth said. "I'm up to half-a-mile a day. I walk every day when the weather's nice."

Since moving to Bayview, to try to strengthen her injured knee, Aunt Elizabeth had begun walking outside around the level courtyard. I was pleased she was making an effort to take care of herself. Neither of us remarked on it, but I think we both were aware that, with the passing of Dad, she was the last surviving member of her generation in our immediate family.

AT THE START OF 2010, my schedule for the first half of the year was in place. My brother and I had written the obituary for my father, worked through the post-mortem of his estate, and arranged his memorial service for the coming spring. I'd made plans to go to Cleveland in advance of the memorial to fit in some thesis research. Now it was time to launch into the fourth semester of my MFA program.

In preparation for the impending residency that January on Whidbey Island, I kept writing as often as I could. By the close of the previous semester, I'd advanced from making progress reports to writing scenes from Michael Harm's point of view. Weekly, I posted what I'd written for Kathleen in our thesis advising site.

"I am so pleased to read some chapters from you," she wrote back. "It's happening!"

Despite Kathleen's encouragement, writing chapters was agonizing. At least by this point I'd firmly settled on writing a novel rather than a nonfiction book. Still, the urge to share all the history I'd learned was at times overpowering. Perhaps it's the teacher in me. When I learn something, I want to share it with the world. But in my Craft of Fiction class, I'd been taught that a historical novel should not be a history lesson. Most of all, we were telling a story.

I had trouble with this concept when it came to the Irish immigrants to Cleveland. In the mid-19th century, the population of Cleveland was one-third English, one-third German, and one-third Irish. Knowing this, I experimented with scenes involving Irish characters and conflicts, but the plotline felt like a digression. Michael Harm couldn't speak English when he first arrived, so I imagined he must have relied heavily on the insular German community. Then too, in a historic Cleveland newspaper, I'd happened on a description of Cleveland Germans as being "clannish." In the end, I didn't leave out the Irish entirely, but I didn't devote entire scenes to them, either.

In early 2010, on the ferry ride over to Whidbey Island, I stared out my car window at the shifting waters of the steel-colored Puget Sound and assessed my situation. Not counting the thesis, I was on schedule. I would finish coursework requirements by the end of this semester. But that thesis, oh my. At this residency, I'd finally be turning in the outline, which had taken me an entire semester to devise. As for my manuscript, it needed to be a complete book, of which I'd only written 45 pages. Once I completed the manuscript, approval of it would need to come from two published authors. My thesis adviser would be the first. I'd need a second reader, as well. Graduating that coming August was not looking good.

We met that January at Captain Whidbey Inn on Penn Cove. I always looked forward to the intense, creative kick-off to the MFA semester. I'd only enrolled in one class this time, Craft of Children's/Young Adult writing, the final Craft class I needed. The course aligned neatly with my thesis work. I planned to submit the chapters I'd been writing for my thesis about Michael Harm's early years, to take best advantage of the added editorial eye of my professor, Carmen T. Bernier-Grand, on craft elements like dialogue, point of view, and narrative structure.

During breaks and mealtimes, plenty of my classmates would ask: "Aren't you graduating this August?" to which I had to confess it wasn't going to happen. My deepest unease, though, was that the project had grown into a monster, and I still had no idea what I was doing. But what with my craft of writing class, Profession of Writing sessions, and evening readings, I had plenty to distract me from my morass of self-doubt. I became swept up in the flow, immersing myself in the creative inspiration of coursework and writing friends.

But the "outside world" did exist. Midway through the residency, I received a thrilling email from Angela.

> January 15, 2010
>
> Dear Claire,
>
> I sent you a parcel with a bilingual publication on emigration from the Palatinate. It is the only entirely bilingual one so far, which has been published by a cultural institute in Kaiserslautern. There is much to read ... I was quite surprised about some things e.g. that Cooper's Leatherstocking is supposed to be written with a Palatine emigrant as a role model.
>
> There is so much more I found out, and even more to find out yet ... But really, it would be best if you could spend some weeks here. I have talked to my mother, and as my grandmother's flat is empty right now, there is more than enough space in our house in Freinsheim. You could take Freinsheim as a base and maybe organize some other trips.
>
> Now have a good start onto 2010!
>
> Yours Angela

Once again, Angela had hit on exactly what I needed. Time in Germany, and Freinsheim in particular, would greatly increase my understanding of the place of my main character's childhood. Airfare would be pricey, but with most lodging covered, it was doable. The invitation, and the real possibility that I could go, reinforced for me the idea that I didn't need to be in a rush to graduate, that this novel-writing journey had taken on a life of its own. I needed to trust the process.

That I wouldn't graduate that coming August gave me extra time, the freedom to be more open to creative possibilities. During that residency, students received advice in Profession of Writing sessions about developing a "platform," an approachable Internet presence. About the importance of having a blog as part of that platform, which needed to be up and running well in advance of publishing a book. Hearing this over and over again, an idea began to hatch.

I'd committed to writing the book as historical fiction, but since I loved what I was learning, why not create a blog where I shared my nonfiction discoveries? I could also post about my upcoming travels to Cleveland, and now, hopefully, my travels to Germany. By the end of residency, I actually felt a surge of new energy and hope.

When I returned home, I looked at my schedule, consulted with my husband about costs and the calendar, and emailed Angela my reply.

January 20, 2010

Hallo [hello] Angela,

Your parcel came yesterday, along with your beautiful sympathy card from the whole family. Thank you so much ....

Thank you also for the offer to stay in your grandmother's flat this summer. Actually, I must ask what your schedule is like in October? It looks like that will be the time when I will want to visit Germany.

Here is my schedule right now:

– January-May - Spring MFA semester, writing novel, a chapter a week

– April 16-May 2 - visit Cleveland for research (Clyde's memorial May 1)

– June 10 - Vivian graduates from high school

– August 13-22 - Fall MFA semester begins with residency

– August? Vivian goes to college

– October?? - travel to Germany, part of the time with Dave, part of the time on my own for research

I will tell you more soon,

Claire

As the semester hit full stride, I was submitting assignments for my Children's/Young Adult Craft of Fiction class—scenes in Freinsheim when Michael was a young boy—and also keeping up with my thesis work with Kathleen. All seemed to be going more smoothly. When it came to Kathleen's mentorship, though, I had less time than I thought.

Chapter 17

As soon as I returned from the MFA residency, I registered my domain name—clairegebben.com—and began writing blog posts.

January 18, 2010:

Metal splashes from the Crucible

My great-great grandfather came from Freinsheim to Cleveland in 1857, and apprenticed with his uncle as a blacksmith. He was sixteen years old. I want to explore and write about his experience .... With this blog, I'll share some things I learn along the way.

While I understood the concept of reaching out to the public with a blog, at first I didn't realize it meant the public would also be reaching out to me. Within a few weeks of publishing my first posts, I wrote something about Johann Rapparlie, and quoted a small excerpt of his 1847 letter. A stranger contacted me immediately, someone doing extensive genealogy research on the Rapparlie family. Apparently, she'd set up a "Google Alert" of some kind on that surname. Via email exchange, and with Angela's permission, I shared genealogy information we had on Johann Rapparlie, from a recently translated letter from Rapparlie giving details about his descendants.

Cleveland 8 December 1856

Much loved brother-in-law and sister-in-law,

As we have now such a good opportunity, we will send you a few lines and besides our whole family's and our brother-in-law Jakob's portraits through our friend Jacob

Handrich,[1] who traveled from Cencinardi [Cincinnati] to Cleveland, and in Cleveland he met us and we were cordially happy that we should have such a good opportunity once to send the portrait [not saved with letter] of our whole family to you. And we would have sent it already with Frey who was with you several months ago but he didn't know if he would get to Germany or not when he left. Here are the names of my children as follows. The biggest stands by my right shoulder. His name is John.[2] Sitting on my left is the third or youngest [son], whose name is Wilhelm.[3] My small Sußy [Sussy][4] our daughter, is lying in my wife's lap and sleeping. Further the other one is our brother-in-law Jacob and my son Jacob,[5] our brother-in-law's godchild. Our brother-in-law Scheuermann was also present but he didn't have time to have his family's picture taken but also has two boys and is quite well and further news I don't know as our friend Jacob will tell you everything by mouth how it goes for us.

If you want you can put together for us approximately 80-100 lbs. of dried plums and Jacob will pay for them what they cost and will take them when they come back to America. Put them well into a sack or a box. Don't save costs and buy the best you find so that they don't spoil on the sea. Now I will close this and we stay your faithful brother-in-law and sister until the death and hope that this writing finds you with as good health as it has left us.

John Rapparlie, Katherina Rapparlie[6]

John Rapparlie had signed his name with an elegant, swoopy flourish on the last "e." Katherina Rapparlie's signature, ink-splotched and tentative, lent support to why Johann Rapparlie was the one writing all these letters to his in-laws. Apparently, Katherina Handrich Rapparlie was just marginally literate.

---

1 This Jacob Handrich, differentiated in the letters from the brother-in-law Jakob by spelling his name with a "c," perhaps lived in Cincinnati at this time.
2 Johannes Rapparlie, born 8/30/1849, now eight years old.
3 Wilhelm Rapparlie, born 1854.
4 Katherine Elisabetha ("Sussy") Rapparlie (Bihn), born 8/17/1856.
5 Jacob Rapparlie, born 9/7/1851.
6 Additional scribbled note on this letter: (...) Cleveland—Michael Harm in Freinsheim 1857]

Reading this letter for the first time, I felt cheered to learn the Rapparlies now had three sons and one daughter. After so many infant deaths, it seemed to me the couple had borne enough grief and pain. I sent this information on to the Rapparlie genealogist, who in return sent me a complete Rapparlie family tree and a 40-page history on the Rapparlie family line. The pages contained details such as herbal cold remedies from old family Bibles, and bedside rituals used to ward off evil. Excellent fodder for realistic details, glimpses into how women might have cared for one another, especially when it came to childbirth, a life event historically fraught with potential loss of both mother and child.

As I got into the habit of posting on my blog, my favorite write-ups had to do with my research adventures in the field. For instance, the time I visited a horseshoeing school in Snohomish to learn about blacksmithing.

That trip happened on a cold, gray January day, a few hours when I pushed myself away from the computer and made the drive out to the Mission Farrier School. It turned out the school was not a classroom, as I'd imagined, but a cavernous barn, only slightly warmed by the row of horses and mules lined up to be shod and the propane forges aglow in the center of the room. The instructor listened as I described my errand, his gaze wandering around the room as students assembled at their anvils. When I finished, he turned to me with a shrug.

"Sure, take all the notes and photos you want. But you do know we're not blacksmiths? We're farriers. Sure, blacksmiths could shoe horses, but that wasn't their primary task. Blacksmiths are something else entirely."

I nodded as if I understood. Inwardly, I was unhinged: What?! Blacksmiths didn't shoe horses?! My entire life, I'd assumed my great-great grandfather shoed horses. He was a blacksmith, and later owned a carriage works. Carriages were pulled by horses, right? Horses that needed to be shoed, right? But this guy was telling me those were farriers? If blacksmiths didn't shoe horses, what on earth did they do? How ever would I find out? I'd come to Snohomish attempting to find clarity, but instead landed in an even denser fog.

Back home, totally frustrated, I went online and, after endless browsing, happened to click on the site of the Northwest Blacksmithing Association. By then, I'd learned that modern blacksmithing differed from 19th-century blacksmithing when it came to raw materials. Blacksmiths of old heated wrought iron in coal forges. Blacksmiths of today work with steel and propane burners. If the thesis was going to be authentic, I needed to find an "old school" blacksmithing shop, a place where I could observe a coal forge and old methods in operation. The Northwest Blacksmithing Association website listed a blacksmithing school called Old West Forge. At least the name sounded promising. Following the link, I discovered the school offered classes for a variety of levels, from beginning to advanced. Screwing up my courage, I called to see if someone there could fill me in on what blacksmiths did for a living back in the 19th century.

Tim Middaugh, the owner and teacher, answered the phone. I told him of my interest in older blacksmithing methods and inquired if Old West Forge taught classes using coal forges.

"Nope, we use propane," Tim said. "And steel. Hard to get wrought iron these days. But if you come on out for a session, I'll fill you in on some of the older methods and techniques."

"You mean, like, take a Beginning class?" I'd thought maybe I'd go as an observer. The classes at Old West Forge required four intensive days of blacksmithing, dawn to dusk.

"Yup. Next one's full, but I have one opening left for the June session."

I hesitated, wondering if I had the time, let alone the inclination. Maybe a class, actually trying it out, I reasoned, was the solution. On an impulse, I put my name down for the Beginning Blacksmithing session, which was set for that coming June about a week after my daughter Vivian graduated from high school.

THAT SPRING, I MADE A second visit to NARA for a long session of scanning microfilm. This time, I perused the entire month of May, 1857, which again turned up no Michael Harm. The following week in choir practice, my friend Dave Williams asked how my MFA program was going. I told him about my thesis, and how I'd been spending hours at NARA to no avail.

His eyes lit up. "Your thesis sounds to me like a great genealogy project. I'm taking a class on genealogy taught by an amazing woman named Sarah Thorsen Little. Why don't you join me some Friday morning, and I'll introduce you to the group. It's a fascinating class."

Genealogy project? I thought of my father, of his painstakingly hand-written family tree, its tangled branches of names and dates. I just couldn't see myself starting down that road. When I confessed this to Dave, he was reassuring. A lot of progress had been made with uploading data to the Internet, he told me, and this class showed ways to efficiently access those sites. In the end, I took him up on his offer. The course, offered through the continuing education program of the South Seattle Community College, had a devoted following. Its students were avid genealogists who just couldn't get enough of researching their ancestors.

Using a laptop and projector, the teacher Sarah Thorsen Little guided us online through Heritage Quest and Family Search and Ancestry and GenWeb and a host of other web sites. She logged into Steve Morse and Cyndi's List,

FindAGrave and the Internet Archive, using student inquiries to sleuth out information. After sitting in for only one session, I knew I needed to enroll. Every Friday for the remainder of that spring, Dave and I carpooled to West Seattle for a morning of education on ancestral browsing.

One tip Sarah Little showed us was how to use an "asterisk" where a letter would be, a feature offered in many genealogy search engines. The asterisk worked as a "wild card" so the computer searched the name with every letter of the alphabet, just in case the name had been spelled incorrectly. As I sat listening, I realized the Old German Script would be a common source of misspellings of names. I'd witnessed for myself in the letters how in the Old German Script cursive, the "h" looked like an "f," the "s" like a "t." Except, that is, when "s" occurred at the end of a word. Then it resembled a dashed off loop. Worse, the cursive letters in Old German Script "e" and "n" were practically indistinguishable. No doubt this was a challenge for people of today trying to transcribe old lists into Internet databases. Later, I found the name Scheuermann spelled Schnunuman in a marriage record.

Sarah also showed the class how to access 19th-century digitized newspapers online via our local libraries. Eagerly, I went home, zeroed in on the *Cleveland Daily Herald* newspapers from the 1850s, and typed in the names of my ancestors—Rapparlie, Handrich, Harm, Scheuermann. Not a single article emerged. Except for Harm, but of course, those all had to do with news stories about people who had "come to harm."

Disappointed, I tried again, this time using Sarah's recommended techniques, the asterisk wild card for certain letters, alternate spellings, broadening the date ranges, and still turned up zilch. I tried variant spellings. Nothing. I tried the first search terms a second time, wishfully thinking the computer had simply overlooked the names the first time by accident. Nothing turned up the second time, either.

In fact, if I hadn't had the letters in my possession, I would have begun to wonder if these ancestors were figments of my family's imagination. For instance, where were their obituaries? Why no news item about the opening of the Harm & Schuster Carriage Works? The news article about the Rapparlie shop burning? The accident that caused Katherina Rapparlie to lose her leg?

I found several advertisements for blacksmiths, but none for Rapparlie or Harm or Handrich. I read old accounts of carriage accidents, of the frequent fires plaguing Cleveland's early years, and about the Roman candles men used to light on street corners to draw a crowd to their political speeches. I got a decent glimpse into the *Zeitgeist*, the mindset, of 19th-century Cleveland, a time when newsmen spoke their opinions with no discernible filters, declaiming "Poland Jews" as pickpockets and reporting such minutiae as women's hair-pulling fights and a drunk elderly farmer who nearly got robbed.

While the newspapers were a captivating window into the mid-1800s, I uncovered nothing of substance about my particular ancestors. Hopefully, when I researched in Cleveland come April, I might be able to dig up something more.

Chapter 18

In February, an unexpected email from Germany, written in English, arrived in my inbox from Angela's older brother Matthias.

February 8, 2010

Hi Claire,

Did you have a good start in the new year?

I think Angela told you, that Ina and me want to travel in the US in spring. Now we know the exactly dates:

We start in Frankfurt on March, 24th and fly to Omaha, where Ina's daugter Hannah lives with an American family .... then we'd like to fly to Seattle on April, 6th. Are you there in this time? Perhaps we can visit you?

We also would like to visit Neah Bay, where Angela lived vor(sic) a while.

On April, 13th we are going to fly back to Germany.

I hope, my english is good enough, that you understand everything. I'm looking forward to your answer.

Greetings

Matthias Weber, Freinsheim

Vaguely, I remembered Angela mentioning something about their possible visit. I'd never met her older brother, but I'd been hearing about him for years. Angela had shared with me about Matthias's passion for politics, how in the 1980s, he'd had a job in the German Green Party, which was prominent in those days for its stand against nuclear power. They also advocated for nonviolence and a more ecological approach to the environment. Sometimes, when I asked Angela questions about Freinsheim, she'd reflect for a minute, then shake her head. "I don't really know about that," she'd say, "but Matthias probably does. He's the one who knows all about the history of Freinsheim."

So it seemed a good omen that Matthias and Ina were coming for a visit. I hoped to grill him about Freinsheim, as much as he was willing to share. But would his English skills be as good as Angela's? Would we get along? Really, I knew next to nothing about these relatives.

As Dave and I consulted the calendar, it looked as if the timing of their stay wouldn't be the greatest. Matthias and Ina would be arriving just before our trip to Cleveland for my father's memorial service. I'd made plans to travel from Seattle to Cleveland ahead of Dave, George, Vivian and Aunt Elizabeth to do thesis research. Our family had quite a bit going on just then, Dave with work, Vivian with senior year activities, not to mention my end of semester MFA coursework.

But again and again, experience taught me to be open and flexible when it came to visits with my German relatives. Not once had I ever regretted our times together. The various multicultural exchanges had so far always turned out to be enlightening, entertaining, and inspiring.

February 8, 2010

Hallo Matthias,

Dein Englisch ist ausgezeichnet. Ja, wir werden dann in Seattle sein, und sie konnen bei uns bleiben. (Du sehst, das ich lerne Deutsch, aber wohl kaum so gut.) ... Jetzt ich sage es auch auf Englisch.

[Transl. Your English is excellent. Yes, we will be in Seattle then, and you can stay with us. (You see, that I am learning German, but scarcely very well.) Now I am saying it also in English.]

Your Omaha travel time is interesting, since it is during Easter. I believe you will find many people in Omaha are conservative Christian and make a big deal out of this holiday .... It should also be a good time to observe the "Red State" culture. (Red States are Republican, Blue States are Democrat.)

Herzliche Grusse, [heartfelt greetings]

Claire and Dave Gebben (and George (20) and Vivian (17))

I get a chuckle looking back at this email, one of my first, fledgling attempts at writing in German to the relatives. By February of 2010, what with my sporadic online German studies through the library, I'd managed to build basic skills. Looking back, I can see I hadn't gotten far with the grammar. In the above, in addition to leaving the umlaut off the "u" in Grusse, I did not follow the German grammar rule that the verb always takes second place in a sentence. I'd labored over the wording of this email a long time, and thought I'd done it perfectly, but I should have written, Jetzt sage ich [Now say I], not Jetzt, ich sage [Now, I say]... and so on. Those proficient at German will no doubt catch many more errors in my email above.

As the MFA semester in 2010 progressed, I thought again and again how fortunate I was not to be wrapping up my thesis that spring. I couldn't have done it. I was relieved to have time with my daughter, then finishing up the myriad activities of her senior year. Doctor visits with Aunt Elizabeth had begun, to a rheumatologist, and to find a primary care physician. The first PCP we met with was not a good fit.

"I think we should find someone else," Aunt Elizabeth informed me as we departed the doctor's office. "It wasn't clean there. I'm not comfortable with that."

I tried to remember if it had, indeed, not been very clean. I hadn't noticed. I wondered if maybe Aunt Elizabeth was prejudiced somehow against the woman, and just looking for an excuse? Or if the office had, indeed, been dirty? Regardless, I was able to track down someone else, and this time, as we arrived for the appointment, I had a heightened radar for dirt in the corners and finger marks on the tables. Fortunately, the second PCP received Aunt Elizabeth's stamp of approval. We also found an audiologist, who we visited several times for adjustments to my aunt's hearing aids. The most pressing issue was locating a geriatric dentist. When we went to that first visit, Aunt Elizabeth was in there for hours.

Driving back to Bayview, I asked her how it went.

"O—o—oh," she moaned, a melodramatic wail only half in jest.

I could empathize, especially when I learned she'd had a root canal and they'd put in a temporary bridge. We took care of the real bridge in the end of March. My aunt was trapped in the dentist's chair for hours, which she found distressing. Even more distressing was the $6,000 price tag. Regardless, she kept repeating "thank you" to me after every outing.

Since Aunt Elizabeth was getting less and less mobile, I suggested she might be better off not traveling to Ohio for Dad's memorial service in May. But she wouldn't be denied, and I could hardly blame her. I think she saw it as her last chance to return to Cleveland, to the town of her birth and childhood. Dave and I booked the tickets, but when I informed her I'd be going to Ohio

Matthias Weber and Ina Dörr-Mechenbier visit Seattle.

early, that she'd be traveling instead with Dave, George and Vivian, she glared at me sharply. To my surprise and relief, though, she didn't argue.

MEANWHILE, AS FOR THESIS, IN the midst of everyday demands, and the copious amounts of historical information tangled in my brain, I was beginning to feel scared of it all. Scared of writing about historic times and not getting it right. In the last week of March, I confessed my fears to my thesis advisor. "I'm kind of reeling, not writing at the moment," I posted.

I also felt scared about how little I'd learned of the German language, something I worried I might need very soon, with the arrival of Matthias and Ina. One week into April, they flew into Seattle, and I braced myself for a new challenge. But it wasn't as bad as all that. Not at all. When I picked them up at the airport, I could tell right away that Matthias's fluency in English did not equal Angela's, but he did quite well, and his partner Ina was able to make up for any lack. Her English was very good. I was enchanted by her intelligent dark brown eyes and intent way of listening. Not to mention she laughed at our jokes. Dave and I liked them both immediately.

At first glance, I recognized physical similarities between Angela and Matthias: they both had the same fair skin, light brown hair and large gray-blue eyes. Although Angela and Matthias shared a family resemblance, their personalities were quite different. Matthias was more demonstrative, and he had a deep, rather loud voice and infectious, seal-bark laugh. To Dave's and my delight, Matthias was especially knowledgeable about German wines. One of the first nights of their visit, the four of us had a wine tasting contest to compare Washington wines to German ones, with much teasing and laughter. The wine also helped loosen our tongues. Matthias's English improved rapidly as he adjusted to being with us.

Even better for me, Matthias was well-versed in Freinsheim history. When I shared with him about my thesis project and the time period, he was able to answer many of my questions, backing them up with local lore. An entertaining storyteller, he filled me in on the management of the regional forest, and the water bucket each house had to keep always filled at the ready in case of fires, about local rivalries among the villages nearby, and the unique, deep sounds of the Palatine German dialect. My true appreciation for history in the Palatinate began with the warm enthusiasm in Matthias's voice when he spoke of Freinsheim.

Matthias explained to me about the democratic uprisings of 1848, when Michael would have been just seven years old, how Prince Wilhelm and his troops of Prussia had been invited by the Bavarian king to come to the Bavarian Palatinate to crush the rebel army. Prince Wilhelm had marched his army to Freinsheim. When they'd lined up on the hill above the very medieval-looking gate at the entrance of the stone wall-fortified town, at first, the villagers had wanted to put up a fight. However, a pastor named Pfarrer Bickes (Pfarrer is German for Reverend) talked the villagers out of it. The Pfarrer negotiated a deal with Prince Wilhelm. The Prince could stay in a large, new home outside the village walls during his occupation of the region.

"And that is how," Matthias concluded, "it is now said, the Prussian troops never entered Freinsheim as a conquering army. The Prince did not come inside the fortified wall."

An important distinction. Although Germany is now united under one flag, regional rivalries and differences remain, in cuisine, and in dialect, and in culture, between the Prussians and the Palatines, the Bavarians and Hessians, and so on. Matthias clearly loved Freinsheim, and the Palatinate, the region and its people.

"But … I think," Matthias said, pausing between words, apparently rummaging in his brain for the English. "You and Dave must come to Freinsheim … to see for yourselves."

I was glad he asked. I hadn't forgotten Angela's invitation, but what with everything else, Dave and I hadn't made specific plans. "What about the fall?" I asked. "Would that be a good time of year?"

Matthias sat forward and rested his elbows on his knees. "Okay, yes, I think that is the best time of all. During the *Weinwanderung*." His voice was deep and sincere. He looked around the room with his wide, gray-blue eyes, perhaps thinking through his calendar, or his English vocabulary, or both. "It is the time of the wine … harvest … when all Freinsheim has a … a hike through the vineyards."

Matthias and Ina did their best to explain to us about the Wine Hike, how the vineyards surrounding Freinsheim have paths winding through them. For the Wine Hike each fall Freinsheim wine-makers set up vendor stands along the paths. At each stand, festival goers—wine hikers—can pause to refresh themselves with samples of local wines and cuisine. The full name is the *Kulinarische Weinwanderung*—Culinary Wine Hike. It happens over a three-day weekend.

"Angela thinks I should come for several weeks. Would a month be too long?"

Matthias laughed, I think to encourage me. "That is no problem at all."

"I think you will need that amount of time to see everything," Ina said.

What an opportunity. Dave and I knew then and there we would indeed visit that coming fall. By the time Matthias and Ina were ready to go, their visit felt altogether too short.

FOR MY NEXT THESIS FORUM post, I tried to sneak in a brief progress report without attaching scenes or chapters.

> April 9, 2010
>
> Matthias (Angela's brother), and his girlfriend Ina arrived on Tuesday night. They have been an obliging wealth of information for me. Matthias has lived in Freinsheim his whole life, and has made the decision to do this not unlike Michael's brother Philipp five generations ago. Matthias is involved in the politics of the city, and knows quite a lot about the history ....
>
> So I am taking notes about political history, about the forest nearby, about the village feuds, about the 48er revolution and how it impacted Freinsheim. Michael would have been seven years old when Prince Wilhelm brought the Prussian army to the outskirts of Freinsheim. He would have witnessed this, a scene I can add to the book. Matthias frequents the taverns and the town gatherings— he was at the head of a festival parade and appears on Youtube in costume—so he is always telling me what "the old people in the village say".
>
> Remember when we talked last August about how this was the book I should write next because of the timing? It sure seems to be working out that way. I'm feeling very cheered up over here.

I sent off my report thinking I'd accomplished a good deal even without chapters. Kathleen's reply was not exactly glowing.

> April 12, 2010
>
> Oh excellent. A cousin on Youtube in Freinsheim.

Claire, I think I can live without receiving actual chapters, but I think I need to see actual pages. This is mostly for your own survival.

We have five or six weeks left in the semester, and if you are going to try to finish next semester, you should aim for at least a pile of about 200 pages by then. This gives you something to work with over the summer, and come back in the fall with a draft you can show me. If we work hard, you will pull it together and get it to a reader by the end of the semester.

This means writing on the airplane to and from Cleveland, writing in the shower, writing here and there. Don't get hung up on historical accuracy, except in character development. Think about plot, forward motion, suspense.

I'm taking a leave in Spring 2011 ... so if you lap into that semester, Wayne will be your thesis guru.

My spirits deflated. Kathleen taking a leave? I hadn't seen that coming. If I didn't finish my thesis with her, it meant I'd have to switch advisors. How on earth was I going to cope with that? Kathleen had been with me all along. She knew the ins and outs of my challeenges. If I had to switch to Wayne Ude, fiction professor and MFA program administrator, in a way it would be like starting over.

Not that Wayne was unfamiliar to me. He was an author in his own right. I'd read several of his books. I'd taken Craft of Fiction with him during the first semester of my MFA studies. I had no doubts about his teaching ability or about his willingness to help me with my project. But what if he had different opinions from Kathleen about the story? What if he tried to guide me in a different direction? I had to finish by December, I told myself. I just had to.

Chapter 19

In preparation for my time in Cleveland, I'd begun a list of things I'd need to look for. Perhaps some drawings or old photos of early Cleveland would help me write scene descriptions. Maybe I'd find some newspaper articles about my ancestors that weren't online and locate where the former Rapparlie and Harm & Schuster Carriage Works had stood. I reread the letters looking for clues, a few more of which Angela and I had been translating long distance.

Sometimes, we worked via email, but other times, Angela called me on the phone to jumpstart the process. Since the translations took so much time, she couldn't get to typing them in, too. With the nine-hour time difference, it was usually late at night in Marburg, Angela's family all in bed so she could work without interruption. Apologizing for the roughness of her notes, Angela would read out her English version of a letter, enough for me to get the gist. In the future, we planned to go through the letters in detail. For now, this was all we could manage.

While Angela read the letters to me, I typed down the sentences into a document file, or scribbled notes hastily on a yellow pad. In the 1852 letter below (corrected for this book), Rapparlie gives a good description of his business and house, an establishment clustered together at Michigan and Seneca streets in the heart of downtown Cleveland. Soon, I'd be there in person, at the place where my ancestors began their American lives.

Addressed to: J. Philipp Harm, Freinsheim

14 March 1852

Much loved brother-in-law and sister-in-law,

Now I have such a good opportunity to once again write a few lines to you and also to know why you don't write any letters to us, if you're still alive, and so on. I have now written three letters to you and have not received answers. I don't know if you received those or not or is it too much effort to write a few lines to us. Or maybe I think the cost is too high for you. So much for letters.

You should at least every year once send us an answer for how your family is growing, how many children you have and what happens in Europe with politics and so on because now I don't have any sister or brother or parents in Germany any more. But only you as brother-in-law and sister-in-law. I don't know either one or the other of you face to face[1] still I think much about you as if I see you every day because you are my next friends in Germany.

For God's sake, my family until now is healthy and we have again in August 1851 born a young son[2] who is quite healthy and the two old people are still as healthy as before and our brother-in-law Jakob is still unmarried. He has now purchased for himself a house and a property. The old people are still with him.

Margaretha[3] has also again a few months ago given birth to a young son[4]. Georg Scheuermann has also now gotten hold of a house and a property. They are both quite healthy. We all are now quite healthy and glad that we traveled to America. My brother-in-law Schäfer[5] from Rheingönnheim is now also with us but had a very hard sea journey, but they all arrived alive over the sea.

Furthermore, my business[6] is very strong right now. Last year, from January 1851 to January 1852, I made more than $6000 work. Now I have three fires in the blacksmith

1   Johann Rapparlie emigrated from Rheingönnheim on the same ship as the Handrichs, so it appears he did not know them before that voyage. He was writing on behalf of his wife Katharina Handrich Rapparlie, but had never met his wife's sister and brother-in-law in Freinsheim.
2   Registered date of birth of Johann Jacob Rapparlie is 9/7/1851.
3   K. Margaretha Handrich (Scheuermann), sister to Rapparlie's wife Katherina and to Elisabetha Handrich (Harm) in Freinsheim.
4   John Scheuermann, second son of Georg and K. Margaretha.
5   Possibly Martin Schäfer (born circa 1818 in Rheingönnheim), spouse of Anna Margaretha Rapparlie/Rappalieur of Rheingönnheim who later resided in Cleveland, Ohio
6   John Rapparlie Smith and Wagonmaker on Michigan St. in Cleveland.

shop, four wagon builders. My saddlers and varnishers.

My work is mostly chaises work. My shop has cost me $1200 to build it. The city wanted to buy me out. They offered me $5000 to buy it. I have rented out my other house and have built a new one last year. My house, where my first house stands, they have also offered me $1,400 and I have my business going really well now and the times in America are quite good. Now I want to close this.

Now dear brother-in-law and sister-in-law if you would please send me one barrel of wine and approximately a hundred pounds of dried plums and several pounds of cherries and send a bill what everything costs and Herr Selzer[7] will pay you for that but get good quality the wine explicitly with wine ghosts [Weingeist][8] and put the barrel into a big barrel or box or what I mean a cover and write on it my name and do that very carefully and do it yourself so you'll be sure that it is all right.

Something else, dear brother-in-law. If you want send with Jakob approximately ten cubits[9] of fine cloth for me and him for a coat and Selzer will make it right with you. Buy the best that you can find, even if it is expensive. I don't know any further news. I hope our writing will meet you with as good health as it has left us. We all greet you many thousand times and remain your in-laws.

John Rapparlie[10]

---

7   A family name in Freinsheim.

8   Unsure if this means wine with good alcohol content, or wine with crystals/sediment.

9   The German term used is Elle, an obsolete measure from the elbow to the fingertips of the hand, about 18 inches.

10 [The following text is an additional note in a different handwriting at the end of this letter] You are getting also immediately a banknote with this sending, so one does not have any more debts. Dear brother-in-law today the 12th of October 1852, the date of this letter, Jean Selzer shipped out with family to Mannheim. I take up the quill and have written everything in detail to you, so that Jean Selzer cannot mistake my intention. I believe my letter to you will meet you earlier, dear brother-in-law, than Selzer. Dear brother-in-law, Selzer has taken the wine, plums and cloth with him. I have paid the wine and plums [illegible] Selzer, I think you will immediately ensure that you will reach out

Now Johann Rapparlie was signing his name John, whereas in previous letters he'd written Johannes. Twelve years after arriving in the U.S., Rapparlie was describing himself as a well-to-do business man who could afford fine cloth and a special order of Palatine wine. The hike in real estate prices gave me an inkling, too, of why these immigrants remained in the city and never bought a farm property. Rapparlie, at least, viewed city properties as a strong real estate investment where one could quickly get ahead.

During the phone call with Angela, I shared more good news, how I'd located Michael's immigration record. At least I hoped so.

Driving over to the National Archives and Records Administration for a third time, I'd felt like giving up. I kept asking myself: What was the point? Why even bother? Maybe the record was lost. Maybe I was spending hours and hours searching for something that didn't exist.

Feeling impatient, I arrived at NARA, signed in, and put my belongings in the locker provided. No longer needing assistance, I located the next microfilm on my own, the one for June, 1857, sat down at a machine and loaded it. Scanning through ship arrivals in New York harbor, I paused at the mastheads, then skimmed down the lists.

I'd learned to speed things up by now, scanning the age column first. Since Michael had been fifteen or sixteen, I only double-checked names for passengers listed between the ages of 14 and 20, next checked if they came from Bavaria, etc. Still, it was slow going. Finally, near the end of that third day, on a passenger list dated June 30, 1857, I saw a name that was very close: "Michel Harne, age 16, gender "m," occupation "farmer," country of origin "Bavaria." The hairs prickled on the back of my neck. Scrolling back to that ship list's masthead, I noted it was a passenger manifest for the *Helvetia*, captained by Lewis Higgins, port of departure Le Havre. Could it be? I'd studied French in high school, so knew Michel was the French spelling of Michael. The port of departure matched Rapparlie's instructions. The age of 16 was on target, and the name, Michel Harne, seemed awfully close.

One of the NARA assistants was passing down the aisle, so I tore my gaze from the screen to see what she thought. "I think I found him!" I said. The assistant paused, a sheaf of papers in her hand. "Look, here he is," I pointed. "My great-great grandfather Michael Harm. Michel Harne. It isn't the right spelling, but it sure looks like him."

The assistant squinted at the screen, then shrugged. "Maybe."

I didn't appreciate her skepticism. This had to be him. The oral history said he'd left at age 15 and journeyed for at least 43 days. With a birth date of May 26, 1841, and an arrival date on June 30, 1857, he could have celebrated

for your belongings, as soon as Selzer arrives in Cleveland.

his 16th birthday on board the ship, so age 16 fit. I explained all this to the assistant, eager to convince her.

"You could be right," she said, turning away. Unhappily, I watched her continue down the row. I didn't care for her attitude. Then again, how many people had she watched leap to conclusions based on exactly this kind of wishful thinking?

Now doubting my find, I turned back to the illuminated screen and scrutinized the flowery handwriting, wishing Michael Harm could magically arise from the image. I checked above and below Michel Harne's name for parents or siblings, but he appeared in line without family members, just several other passengers around his age. That fit, too, how he'd come alone. Then, I spotted something else. Six names above Michel Harne, on the previous page, the name Philipp Haenderich was listed, age 24, gender male, a United States citizen. Haenderich looked to me like a variant spelling of Handrich, the name of Michael's grandparents in Cleveland. Could it be? Had Michael been brought across the Atlantic to America by a relative?

This idea caused a major shift in my understanding. Not only did I feel certain I'd found my great-great grandfather. I was now convinced I'd hit on a plot twist in the oft-told oral history. Michael Harm hadn't traveled entirely alone, after all. He'd been brought by a relative. This story was getting better all the time. Taking deep breaths to contain my excitement, I went to the front desk and requested a photocopy of the entire passenger list for that June 30, 1857 voyage of the *Helvetia*.

I emailed Angela about my discovery, and she in turn shared the news of her visit to a research center in Kaiserslautern, where she'd learned that the Leises and the Ümbstadters mentioned in the first letter were well-known Mennonite families in Cleveland. Whenever I had a question, I fired it off to Angela, and she would look into it and reply. With both Angela and Matthias helping me so much, in some ways it felt as if the bar was rising ever higher. It was intimidating. I was doing my best to wring chapters out of my overtaxed brain, for Angela, for Matthias, for Kathleen, but I couldn't shake the nagging feeling I was only scratching the surface. I had so far to go. For all of them, and myself, too, I wanted badly to do this right.

Chapter 20

Just five days after Matthias and Ina departed, in mid-April I said farewell to Dave and the kids and Aunt Elizabeth and flew to Cleveland on my own. Dad's memorial service wouldn't happen until May 1 on the southeast side of Cleveland at the Presbyterian Church of the Western Reserve. My brother Craig and I had each done our part in making arrangements in advance, allowing me to carve out the last two weeks of April to research on site in Cleveland, to dig up whatever I could find about the German immigrant ancestors in my thesis.

A thesis that had taken on a life of its own. By the middle of that semester of 2010, I'd at last come up with a working title: *Something to Tell About.* The idea emerged out of research into the Romantic era of literature, from a quote by the German poet Matthias Claudius.

"*Wenn jemand eine Reise tut, so kann er was erzählen.*" ["When someone goes on a trip, he has something to tell about."]

I liked the sound of that. *Something to Tell About.* It echoed the tone of the letters, how the relatives communicated news back to the Old Country without effusive adjectives. Certainly, after emigrating from Freinsheim, my great-great grandfather had something to tell about, a story that had been handed down through the generations, the story I was now trying to shape into a novel. I liked the awkward phrasing. It sounded like something an immigrant might say, someone for whom English was their second language. Kathleen thought it was okay, at least better than previous, clichéd ideas of mine, like "Veins of Iron" and "From the Crucible."

WHEN I ARRIVED AT CLEVELAND Hopkins International Airport, I couldn't help but heave a sigh of relief. At last, I could focus on thesis alone. As in the Matthias Claudius saying, I was going on a trip. Would I have something to tell about?

On the shuttle ride to the rental car lot, I spotted the sign: Welcome to Cleveland, The Forest City. I must have seen that motto dozens of times in

My childhood home at 38400 Chagrin Blvd, Moreland Hills, Ohio, Circa 1965.

my life. In the past, I'd always assumed "Forest City" referred to the extensive Metroparks ringing the Cleveland area, a loosely strung chain of parks nicknamed the "Emerald Necklace." This time, I saw it in a new light.

In a book called *The Heartland* by Walter Havighurst, I'd read how the first settlers to arrive in Ohio and other states "out west" were a miniature presence under a canopy of ancient, towering trees. Havighurst described sycamores so huge, farmers hollowed out the trunks to use them as granaries and hog pens. Vines in the deep woods measured sixteen-feet in diameter. But by the early 1800s, Ohio's landscape along Lake Erie and its rivers had been denuded of its old-growth forest, of its maples, oaks, hickory, sycamore, beech, and white pine. The trees were felled for shipbuilding, house- and barn- building, lumber exports, and fuel. By the mid-1800s, the landscape of Cleveland had become so devoid of trees, city leaders chose the motto "The Forest City" to inspire citizens to replant them. It worked. Within a few years, most of Cleveland's avenues and streets were lined with graceful elms, broad-leaved sycamores, and sturdy maples and oaks. Downtown Cleveland today is not particularly forested, but beyond the industrial areas, amid the meandering neighborhoods on the east and west sides, many streets are lined with deciduous hardwoods arching majestically overhead.

Once I picked up my rental car, my ultimate destination was our Patterson family property located a 45-minute drive across Cleveland from the airport, all the way from the far west side to the southeast suburb of Moreland Hills.

Driving away from the airport, I merged into rush-hour traffic feeling a bit like a homing pigeon, my radar set to the same property I'd returned to now for forty years, since I left it as my permanent residence at age 18. No one was living there at the moment. Realizing the house wouldn't have a stocked frig, on my way, I stopped at a Panera for dinner. Using their WiFi access, I logged in and posted a blog about my arrival. As often as I could, I planned to share my travel discoveries in real time. My first entry that evening had to do with how Cleveland got the motto, "The Forest City."

I spent so long at Panera, as I continued on to Moreland Hills it was starting to get dark. The properties out here were not as urban as in downtown Cleveland, the lots zoned at two acres, many with large homes and sprawling, well-kept lawns.

Two houses stood on our family's ravined and wooded property. The house in the back where I'd grown up was then being rented out. The other, smaller house closer to the street had once been my grandparents' home. At the moment, it was between renters due to a much-needed replacement of the decks at the front and back.

In his career, my father had been a residential architect and professor of architecture at Kent State University. He'd designed both homes. True to the mid-century Frank Lloyd Wright era in which they'd been built, their low-slung, wood-toned facades melted naturally into the forest as if they'd grown there. The front house was the second to be built, constructed for Dad's parents in 1967, ten years after we moved into the one at the back of

Backyard view of Grandmother's house at 38380 Chagrin Blvd., Moreland Hills, Ohio, with completed deck. Both homes were designed by my father, Clyde Patterson, Jr., and stood in ten acres of forest.

the property. Grandpa died soon after my grandparents moved into their new home. My grandmother, Emma Patterson, the granddaughter of Michael Harm, had lived in the front house alone from 1967 until her death in 1986 at age 96.

As a young girl, on walks home from school, it was my habit to stop in every so often to visit Grandmother. When I had a little time, she and I would sit across from each other at her kitchen table sharing news and stories, or she'd call me over to the stove to show me how to cook whatever she was preparing—pork chops, or macaroni and cheese, or apple sauce. Other times, she'd pull out her photo albums, or her collection of hand-tatted laces. During those visits we'd sit together on the couch while she reminisced over the items. This continued until I went away to college in Michigan in 1976.

That time seemed so long ago now. For the next two weeks of my Cleveland research, this front house would be my jumping-off place for traveling back 150 years to the days of my grandmother's parents and grandparents.

My brother Craig had been the one to suggest I stay at the front house. He'd even gone so far as to warn me there was no furniture at the moment, not even a bed, so in my luggage I'd packed a sleeping bag. As I turned off Chagrin Blvd onto the narrow, paved driveway at twilight I noticed the trees had grown taller, completely taking over the front meadow. When I arrived at the circular drive in front of the house, the exterior driftwood-gray siding gave the house a ghostly glow in the growing darkness.

I had not visited the property for five years, not since I helped Craig move Dad to Cincinnati. As I approached the entranceway, memories flooded in. I caught a whiff of my grandmother, a mixture of talcum powder, baked rolls, pork chops and gravy, a memory smell, not a real one. Emma Patterson hadn't inhabited this house for over twenty-two years. Dad had lived here later, once Mom was gone, but Grandmother's presence was the overriding one. Behind the unlocked door to the garage, in the very dim light, I felt for the key that always hung on the nail and there it was. The door opened with the same stiffness, forcing me to push extra hard.

I crossed the threshold into the utility room, into an unbelievable mess. Skill saws, toolboxes, rolls of brown paper, paint spattered rollers and roller trays, sanders and drills, hoses and electrical cords, and a thin sheen of dust clung to every surface. I continued into the kitchen to a similar chaos, the white Formica counters clogged with tool boxes, rags, and rolls of tape. In the living room, paint cans, rolls of plastic sheeting, ladders and wood-handled brushes and brooms leaned on walls and against the brick fireplace in the center of the room.

All this just to replace the decks? It looked as if an army of workmen had been called home in the rapture, leaving me behind in tool shed hell. Feeling uneasy—would a crew of workmen be appearing at any moment?—I pulled out my cell phone to call my brother. No bars. I roamed through the house in search of service. Finally, in a corner of the living room where two windows met, a signature design feature my dad used in his houses, two cell bars registered. I wedged myself against the windows and dialed. My brother picked up right away.

"Hi Craig, I made it to Cleveland. Can you give me Dale Duheid's number?" Dale Duheid was our Cleveland handyman, the guy we relied on for fix-it projects on the rentals.

"How come?"

"I'm at thirty-eight three-eighty," I said, using our habitual way of distinguishing the two houses on the property by street number. "It's empty, just like you said, but not exactly. I need to reach Dale about some tools he's left around here."

"Really?" My brother was not impressed. "That's because he's replacing our decks."

"I know, but ..." I stared around helplessly. "You'd have to see it to believe it." I didn't want to upset Craig. What could he do about it?

"Huh. Okay, well, I need to talk to Dale anyway about his progress," Craig said. "Sorry I forgot to tell him you were coming."

"That's okay. I didn't think of it either."

I stared out the window at the half-built deck and railing jutting into the backyard. The trees out back were taller, too, their branches arcing high above the house. In the twilight, oaks, maples and black cherry trees, just leafing out, laced the fading sky. My grandmother, and then my father after her, had probably stood at this very spot peering up at a similar twilit sky.

"Tell him not to come tonight," I said. "Tell Dale I'll be gone most of tomorrow, so he can come by then to put his stuff away. And let him know I'll be here for the next two weeks. "

After we hung up, I scanned the room for a place to sleep. Despite all the tools, like Craig said, the house had not a stick of furniture in it, no table or bed or chair. Tired, and with no place to sit anyhow, I unrolled my "bed" next to those same corner windows. The floor was carpeted, but firmer than any mattress I'd slept on in a long while. Shifting to get comfortable, I told myself I was roughing it like Michael Harm, maybe in a way similar to how he'd slept coming over on the boat. Did they have mattresses at sea? Or sleep in hammocks? Questions for another day. First thing in the morning, I'd be off on my first Cleveland research errand. I cracked a window to let in the April air, and dropped off to sleep.

Chapter 21

I awoke early, eager to make the most of my limited time. By 7 a.m. at Panera, over hot breakfast and coffee, both of which were severely lacking back at the tool-cluttered house, I had logged into my online classes and read the week's lectures and assignments to get them out of the way.

Next, I pulled out the brief list of research questions I'd brought with me.

- Did records exist of the John Rapparlie blacksmith shop?
- Where was Champlain Street, the first location of Michael Harm's carriage works? (I hadn't been able to locate Champlain Street on any Cleveland maps.)
- Were there any libraries with holdings specifically addressing German Clevelanders?

That was about it. Other than a brief list of questions, I planned not to have a plan. I wanted to play it by ear. The Matthias Claudius quote came to mind: I was going on a journey, so I'd have something to tell about. In the spirit of a novelist more than a historian, I was looking for sights and sounds and smells and historic intersections, real places that might work like portals transporting me into the past, anything to clue me in about how, more than a century and a half ago, my German immigrant ancestors to Cleveland had subsisted and thrived. I felt open to discovery, and welcomed it.

The first stop on my adventure, I decided, would be Public Square, to try to find the former location of the Rapparlie Shop where my great-great grandfather Michael Harm had begun his apprenticeship as a blacksmith in 1857. From the return address of the old letters, I knew where it once stood, at the corner of Michigan and Seneca Streets. Rapparlie's 1847 letter had instructed the Harm family, once they arrived in Cleveland, to "just ask for John Rapparlie." I interpreted his statement to mean the Rapparlie shop had been right downtown by the shipping docks, in a Cleveland that had once been a very small town.

Leaving Panera, I drove downtown and parked my rental car near the Browns Stadium along the latte-colored waters of the Cuyahoga River. I got out and started walking, but instead of heading south to Public Square, I headed north toward the lakeshore. Back home in the Northwest, I'd pictured arriving at Lake Erie for many months now, pictured gazing out across the flat silver horizon, now nearly absent of boats, where so many steam and sailing ships had once clogged the waters. I imagined feeling the wet spray on my cheeks from cold waves breaking against a rocky shore.

In reality, though, the closest I could get was a chain-link fence, hundreds of feet from the lakeshore. The fence protected a large, empty parking lot and several cinderblock

Cleveland's Tower City (Terminal Tower) on Public Square.

buildings. In the distance, Lake Erie's green-brown waters shifted and swelled, almost as intangible as they'd been on the internet webcam back home.

Turning around, I plodded toward Public Square, walking up along W. 3rd Street snapping photos of the present-day skyscrapers and the signature building of my childhood: Tower City. What year had Tower City entered the picture? I wondered. Before Michael Harm died in 1910? After? Growing up in Cleveland, I knew Tower City as the Terminal Tower, our family's jumping off point for almost everything we did downtown. Similar to Union Station in New York City, Tower City is an inter-connected, several-block stretch of buildings with offices, shopping, hotels, and restaurants, all built over a rail terminus of train and rapid transit stations.

Entering the main lobby of Tower City via brass-framed glass doors, I scanned the area for historical information and spotted an interpretive sign along one wall. "Cleveland's Union Terminal" had started with a hotel and been constructed gradually between the mid-1910s and 1934. The complex today covered a remarkable seventeen acres. So, not my great-great grandfather's era. Mentally, I scratched Tower City off the list of potential scenes in the book.

Regardless, I stood there under the arched ceiling of the lobby, memories of my childhood flooding in. Each year at Christmas, my family used to take the Green Road Rapid Transit to downtown Cleveland, to shop, and to gape in wonder at wintry, North Pole window displays. On our first steps out of the Terminal Tower and into the streets, we were assaulted by city air thick with the roasted nut aroma wafting from Morrow's Nut House. Our family would head toward Higbee's and Halle's department stores, the Salvation Army bells ringing and ringing. I remembered watching my young girl feet in their plush-lined boots as I concentrated hard on skipping over deep puddles and piles of cinder-slushed snow.

But I'd come here to research an even earlier era, so I shook myself out of my 20th-century reverie. Spotting a lobby kiosk of brochures, I went over to browse it for sites of historical interest and picked up a map of downtown Cleveland to unfold and examine. I spotted Michigan Street right away, but Seneca was nowhere to be found.

Outside, the only snow on Public Square that April of 2010 drifted from the pink tree blossoms surrounding the Soldiers and Sailors Monument in the middle of the square. To reach the monument, I had to cross a bus- and car-crowded Euclid Avenue. Climbing the monument's stairs for a better view, my skin was both bitten by a chill lake wind, and teased by a thin April sunshine. A plaque informed me the Soldiers and Sailors Monument had been built in 1896. All around the Public Square from this vantage point, the buildings were tall and imposing, not at all like what a young blacksmith apprentice would have seen on arrival in 1857. In its earliest days, well before my ancestor's arrival, Public Square had been lined with tree stumps and featured a clapboard courthouse and jail. Already by the time Michael Harm arrived, the Courthouse had been moved to southwest of the square.

The Old Stone Church (1820) on the north edge appeared to be the only building my ancestors would have seen when they first arrived in town. I noted its mismatched towers and remembered reading in an old Cleveland Daily newspaper about the fiery inferno in 1856, when one of the church spires caught fire and toppled into the street.

I left the monument and headed back to W. 3rd, where I spotted German-sounding street names like "Hamburg" and "Frankfort," hints of a former German influence. Continuing west, I made my way down to The Flats, a paved-over bank of the Cuyahoga River located near its mouth, where the river linked up with Lake Erie. Passing an old warehouse, I noticed what looked like carriage doors on a rose-colored brick building. The original doors, I imagined, probably swung wide enough for a horse and carriage to pull through. I stepped inside the entryway hoping to get a feel for the smell, the quality of the daylight through the windows, the heavy beams and interior brick walls. It turned out the building housed an architectural firm.

The person at the front desk said it would be okay if I took a few photos of the original wide-planked flooring and exposed masonry. As I did so, all around the large open room employees remained fixated on their computers and drawings, barely noticing me at all.

Back outside, I continued along the east bank of the Cuyahoga River, the natural dividing line between the East and West sides of Cleveland. Looking across the river to the West Side, I thought of an 1893 letter in our possession written by Michael Höhn, a West-Sider of Berea, the same area where the Lindsey family lived. It was the only letter in our possession from that decade. As far as we knew, Michael Höhn[1] was not related to the Harm/Handrich family, but he seemed to have emigrated from the village of Freinsheim just like my great-great grandfather.

Michael Höhn's letter was addressed to the Harm family in Freinsheim. It was apparently written just after he and Michael Harm made a trip back to their homeland.

> Berea, November 9, 1893
>
> Dear Friends,
>
> I think Michael[2] would have written you already, that we have arrived back in Cleveland happily. I have re-encountered my mother[3] and all of my brothers and sisters[4] healthy and in good spirits. My mother did not recognize me anymore until I told her who I was. Then, she was very happy and could remember a lot of the old Freinsheimer [people]. You can imagine that her eyes are becoming weak but apart from that she is getting around well for her age because she will soon be 83 years old. In New York, we saw a lot of Freinsheimers and we also have found John Aul[5]. He works in a furniture factory. I think he is an industrious man but now you really have to be industrious if you want to keep your job because it is bad everywhere you go.[6] I will see if I cannot find

---

1   Höhn, Michael, born 8/25/1843.
2   Presumably, Michael Harm.
3   Gertraud Hissgen (Höhn).
4   In the Tabellarische Übersicht der Auswanderungen der Gemeinde Freinsheim 1853 and following, two Höhn families emigrated, in 1854 (6 family members) and in 1858/1859 the Michael Höhn family (7 members)
5   Possibly, a Johannes Aul born 7/3/1825 in Freinsheim.
6   The U.S. suffered a severe economic depression in the latter half of 1893.

him a better position close to us because in New York everything is very expensive and the rent is eternally high. We have arrived at Cleveland on Sunday morning at 4 o'clock and half an hour later I was already standing at the bed where my son Frank slept. He had not thought of me in this moment because he slept very soundly so I called to him once and when he heard my voice he was out of the bed with one jump and clasped me around the neck and said "Papa, you are here!" and that was all that he could say. He had always thought that he would not see me again because, as you know, I have written him that we left the 12th of October, but then we left the 19th of October. This he didn't know so he was counting the days from the 12th of O[ctober] on and then he said every day "I will not see my father again. They must have been drowned." My son is pretty healthy and strong and he has not lost an hour of time while I was gone. He often regretted that he didn't go with me to Germany because he said such an opportunity I won't be getting anymore. As far as I am concerned, I am pretty healthy and think about traveling further next week to the west. I would like to see once how it is there. And so I hope that these few lines will reach you as healthy as they leave me.

Your true friend,

Michael Höhn

A greeting from both of us to all of you and also to Grätchen[Gretchen] and her husband. Also from me (to) the mayor Pirman. We hope for quick reply. My address is

Mr. Michael Höhn, Berea, Cuyahoga County, Ohio, North America, Box 454

Angela and I surmised that the "we" in the letter must have referred to Michael Harm and Michael Höhn. Based in part on this letter, in my thesis, I'd settled on the year 1893 as the time when Michael Harm would return at last to Freinsheim to see his brother. As to the reference about the bad economic times, a financial crisis that year had again spurred bank closures. Perhaps, I speculated, the economic downturn signaled the beginning of the end of my great-great grandfather's carriage works business?

Standing along the Cuyahoga River beneath concrete and steel bridges that partially blocked out the sky, I reflected on the possibility of looking for German immigrant communities on the West Side of Cleveland, too, but decided against it. It was more than I could manage for this project. Instead, I'd confine my explorations to the East Side where the shops of Rapparlie and Harm had been located.

After snapping a few photos of the waterfront, I continued along the east bank of the river looking for Michigan Street, which the brochure map showed would pick up and run along the river. But I soon gave up. I doubted I'd stumble across Seneca Street, after all, which I couldn't locate on the map. Instead, chilled and footsore, I made my way up from the Flats to the other side of Public Square, and a little farther beyond to the Cleveland Public Library. I'd intended to first visit the history and genealogy collection, but the elevator directory listed a map department, so I pushed the button for the sixth floor instead.

"I'm looking for Seneca Street," I told the librarian at the map desk, holding out my brochure, "but it doesn't seem to be on this map."

The woman gazed at me with a bored expression, like she'd fielded this inquiry many times. "They renamed the streets to numbers back in 1906," she said. She pointed to the counter, where a couple of large printouts of early maps were spread open. "Today, Seneca Street is called W. 3rd."

W. 3rd? I'd been walking on, and criss-crossing, W. 3rd all morning. Excited now, I stared down at an 1868 map and traced the route I'd walked from my parking spot to Tower City. The intersection of Seneca and Michigan, now W. 3rd and Michigan, occurred at a curve of the Cuyahoga, at what looked to be the start of the Ohio and Erie Canal. That canal system, I knew by now, had opened in 1832, creating a water passage from Lake Erie to the Ohio River.

"What stands there now?" I asked.

The maps librarian looked at where I pointed on the map.

"Those are parking lots now," she said, "along the river there."

"Have you ever heard of Champlain Street? Is that right downtown?"

The librarian shook her head. "No, but you can look it up on this street index."

I bent over the tiny print and eventually pinpointed Champlain Street in the central map quadrant, right in the heart of downtown.

"What's here now?" I asked, the tip of my index finger now resting on Champlain Street, just a few blocks toward Public Square from the Rapparlie Shop.

"Tower City. That there's Tower City."

Wonderment prickled the back of my neck. What were the odds? Michael Harm's first carriage works had stood at the present-day site of Tower City? My great-great grandfather had established a 19th-century horse-and-buggy business right at the heart of Cleveland's 20th-century hub of transportation? How had I not known this? Every time I'd taken the Rapid Transit downtown, I'd been landing at the origins of my immigrant ancestor's American life. With all the talk about Michael Harm in my grandmother's reminiscences, to my recollection she had never mentioned this detail. On reflection, though, maybe she'd had no idea. By 1891, the year of Grandmother's birth, the Harm & Schuster Carriage Works had moved to 811 Woodland Avenue, 50 blocks east of Tower City, the only carriage works she'd ever known.

To the librarian, I must have seemed over the top, the way I gaped at those old maps. I leaned over her counter studying them for a very long time, long enough that she volunteered to let me have them.

"They're just copies we were going to recycle," she told me.

Before she could change her mind, I hastily scrolled them together, maps of Cleveland in 1835, 1861 and 1868, plus 1874 Sanford maps of downtown. Precious maps with details about old marketplaces and stagecoach roads heading to Buffalo, Pittsburgh, Columbus and Detroit. So many immigrants had traveled not only to Cleveland in those days, but through Cleveland on their way someplace else.

THAT FIRST EVENING IN CLEVELAND, I ate dinner at another restaurant with WiFi, then returned to Moreland Hills and the pitch dark house after nine o'clock, a bit worried about what I'd find. When I flipped on the utility room light, much to my relief, all evidence of tools had been removed, the dust and grit swept away. I wandered through the empty kitchen to the empty living room and settled on my sleeping bag with a sigh.

I'd made so much progress in a single day, my disordered image of Cleveland now more tidily in perspective, swept clean almost as neatly as Dale Duheid spiffed up these rooms. The deck project wasn't complete, he had plenty of work yet to do. But in another couple of weeks, no doubt he'd have the boards sanded, stained, and nailed into place. If things kept going this well for me, I mused, perhaps I could pull off something similar, make sense out of the confused jumble of my imagination and produce an ordered, compelling story of my great-great grandfather's life. I sure hoped so.

Chapter 22

Everywhere I went in Cleveland, I took my camera. Initially, I'd planned to use it for visuals when I made blog posts, but I came to rely on it heavily as a research-gathering tool. I took photos of old city directories. I took photos of museum interpretive displays and artifacts, of 19th-century artwork and tax records, old photographs, and living history exhibits.

As for resurrecting the look and feel of Cleveland in its early days, though, I'd run into trouble. The downtown area was radically different from what it once had been. Almost everything that once stood there had been torn down and replaced with glass and steel skyscrapers, structures that dramatically changed the cityscape. Back in Michael Harm's day, the elevator hadn't been invented, so buildings generally stood no higher than five stories. High rises were out of the question. In an effort to travel back in time to a more 1800s environment, therefore, I drove south to Hale Farm & Village, an outdoor living history museum intended to replicate the pioneer era circa 1825. Located in Cuyahoga Valley National Park, the place is a portal into a bucolic time, a town rebuilt with homes, barns, fields, and authentic artifacts in order to recreate the way of life of early settlers to northeastern Ohio.

The day was gray and misty. The summer season hadn't started yet, so the grounds were deserted. I wandered around peering into the windows of homes from the early 19th century, with their pot-bellied stoves and rustic furniture and crockery. I poked my head into a barn, not sure I was even allowed inside, and to my amazement spotted sleighs, toys, and barrels stored there, all items once made by German craftsmen. In the 1841 letter, my 4x great grandfather had mentioned barrel-making as the first work his sons found when they arrived in Cleveland.

On another day, I drove downtown past the Cleveland Orchestra's Severance Hall and continued along the gracefully curving road through Rockefeller Park toward Lake Erie. It was a gorgeous day, the buds of leaves just popping out on the towering, thick-trunked oaks and basswoods, some

*Sleighs in the barn loft at Hale
Village & Farm, Ohio.*

trees more than a hundred years old. I drove under the historic stone bridge and onward to Gordon Park on Lake Erie. At last at this park, I was able to climb out of the car and stand at Lake Erie's shore. The wind pressed against me, waves slapped against the rocks and the odors of lake bracken tickled my nose. I remembered how deathly afraid my grandmother had been of the water, a fear originating from a boat trip she'd taken as a child, when a sudden, vicious storm made her believe she was about to die. I'd read many newspaper accounts of deadly storms on the lake. Now not a single boat dotted the horizon.

Returning to my car, I headed back up the Rockefeller Park greenway. In 1897, John D. Rockefeller, Sr., that iconic American oil baron, had donated over 270 acres of land to the City of Cleveland. That same man had been a contemporary of my great-great grandfather, just two years older than Michael Harm, and getting his start in Cleveland at the very same time. In 1855, Rockefeller's father had abandoned his family, so the young man took it on himself to support his mother and siblings. He wore out the soles of his shoes on Cleveland's streets looking for work, until finally, Rockefeller landed a job as an assistant bookkeeper for Hewitt & Tuttle, a Cleveland company that bought and sold trade goods from and to Ohio's interior. Two years after Rockefeller landed his first job, in 1857, Michael Harm got his start as a blacksmith apprentice. Amazingly, the two young men had spent their formative years just a few blocks from each other along the Cuyahoga River.

Did they ever meet? It's likely Rockefeller and Harm passed each other on the street. My Grandmother claimed in the heyday of the Harm & Schuster Carriage Works, her grandfather's company sold carriages to the Rockefellers, Severances, and other wealthy Clevelanders. Still, I doubted the two men's lives intersected in any significant way. To concoct a relationship between them struck me as false, as well as tangential to the theme of the untold story of Cleveland's Germans. Rockefeller was American born. The English-speaking Clevelanders and German-speaking Clevelanders mostly kept to their own communities.

Today, Rockefeller Park is home to the Cultural Gardens, a collection of over thirty gardens representing distinct immigrant cultures: Irish, Hebrew, Lithuanian, Greek, Chinese, Armenian, and so on. One of the earliest to be established was the German Garden along East Boulevard. I visited there next.

Locating it after a bit of trial and error, I entered the iron-trellised gate with no particular expectations. Mostly, the monuments were heads, bronze busts of famous men affixed to pedestals. On first impression, the solemn graveyard character of the garden confused me. The centerpiece—full figure bronze statues of Goethe and Schiller—made some sense, based on what I'd learned about these lionized Germans. Goethe and Schiller were influential writers and playwrights in what historian Peter Watson has called Europe's "Third Renaissance," a time when German scientists, musicians, philosophers, naturalists and artists were at the forefront, leading the search for truth and meaning in life and human existence. On the gray granite pedestal of the statue, several phrases had been engraved and painted gilt-gold. Only later would I be able to decipher them, my favorite the one by Johann Wolfgang von Goethe.

Nur der verdient sich Freiheit wie das Leben,
Der Täglich sie erobern muß.

—Goethe: Faust

(One only earns his freedom in this life who daily conquers it anew.)

Apparently, having escaped European monarchies and oppression in their old homelands, the Cleveland German Americans who established this garden felt passionate about maintaining freedom in their new land. In addition to that impressive centerpiece statue, a replica of one that stands in Weimar, Germany, the German garden features busts of other famous men sprinkled throughout the grounds, for instance the composer J.S. Bach, the philosopher Gotthold Lessing, and the painter Albrecht Dürer.

I also spotted Heinrich Heine, "Romantic Poet." Seeing him so honored reinforced my growing conviction that 19th-century Cleveland German Americans were romantics at heart, men who believed in the primacy of individual experience, and in the importance of literature and music as sources of inspiration. I especially liked a verse Heine is known for: "When words leave off, music begins." I imagined my great-great grandfather as a lover of music based on the story I'd heard often that he "followed a music band to Cleveland." In the chapters I'd written so far, I'd characterized Michael Harm as having a love of music. Seeing Heine in the German Cultural Garden reinforced that inspiration.

One figure I recognized, well-loved in the 19th century but less well-known today, was "The Great Naturalist" Alexander von Humboldt. Humboldt was a

German scientist and explorer: the Carl Sagan of his day. In the early 1800s, he sailed the globe, then wrote about his discoveries in the widely-read volumes titled *Kosmos*. Nineteenth-century Germans absorbed Humboldt's accounts, and his theories of the interconnections of the natural world and Earth's place in the universe, with amazement and reverence.

Standing among these monuments, my initial confusion evaporated. German immigrants of earlier times had planted these statues and busts of influential men to express their culture, to make certain that, with the permanence of bronze and stone, future generations wouldn't forget their origins. To those who knew their history, who understood the code, the Cultural Garden worked as a time capsule into the passions and beliefs of an era.

DURING THE SUBSEQUENT DAYS, I stumbled across more and more evidence of the active German American community in the Cleveland of the past. At the City of Cleveland Records Department, Martin Hauserman, Chief Archivist, obligingly helped me look for traces of the Harm & Schuster Carriage Works, the family business my great-great grandfather eventually owned.

As I leafed through the large old ledgers of carriage tax records (taxes were levied on city carriages just as they are on cars today), Hauserman disappeared into his office, then returned a short time later with a brief history of Harm & Schuster in the 1870s.

"The company did an annual business of $10,000 and hired twelve employees," Hauserman reported as he handed over the printout, a hint of new respect in his voice. "You know, right around 1874, Germans were at the height of their power in Cleveland."

Their influence remained significant through the turn of the 20th century. In the 1900 census, citizens of German heritage numbered over 131,000 in a total population of 382,000. But in 1918, the visibility of German Americans in Cleveland dropped off dramatically, almost overnight. As reports of war atrocities in Europe created anti-German hysteria across the U.S., Clevelanders reacted in fury, banning the practice of teaching German in schools and staging a public burning of German books. As a result, many Germans anglicized their names and stopped mentioning their German heritage, even in the home, forbidding their children to speak of it. To this day some Clevelanders don't realize they have German ancestry.

Growing up, I'd heard how Cincinnati and Columbus originally had large German immigrant communities, but somehow I had not understood Cleveland had a similar history. I'd thought my grandmother's stories about her German American roots were somehow unique. But as I dug deeper beneath the rubble of 20th-century wars, the presence of German Americans was cropping up everywhere.

At my next stop, the Western Reserve Historical Society (WRHS), I hoped to look into the German newspapers in their archives. The WRHS library was open only certain days of the week, so I planned ahead and arrived early. I spoke first with Ann Sindelar, Reference Supervisor. She suggested I look through the *Annals of Cleveland*, condensed volumes of Cleveland's English newspapers dating back to 1818. I followed her lead and found a few scattered references. One about how German immigrants were "friends, with characteristics of industry and honesty" (1844), and how, by 1858, Germans were presenting Italian opera at the Bank Street Theater.

I took a few notes, then wandered back to the reference desk.

"What about German newspapers, how do I see old issues of those?" I asked.

"We're cautious about bringing them out," Ann said. "They're very old and fragile. We try to minimize the damage."

"I'd love to see some early issues."

She looked doubtful. "Do you speak German? They're in the old German font, it's really hard to read."

"I don't." I felt the warmth of embarrassment creeping up my cheeks. "But I should be able to make out some of it. I've looked at Cleveland's English newspapers online, and what I'm looking for just isn't there."

Thankfully, Ann decided in my favor and helped me fill out a request to bring out some newspapers from the back archives. Soon an elderly man wheeled out a cart that held large, yellowed issues of newspapers dating back to 1860 and 1861, the closest years in the collection to when my ancestor Michael Harm arrived in Cleveland. Ann handed me white gloves and stood by as I put them on.

"Well, I'll leave you to it," she said. "We can't make copies of these, you know."

"May I take photos?"

She reflected before answering. "In this case, I think it would be all right, as long as you don't use a flash."

I had to stand, not sit, in order to get a full view of the large pages. Ann had been right, I could hardly decipher a word. Even so, the newspapers were rich with clues. I took photos of advertisements with drawings of stoves, classified listings for saloons that sold German lager (Lagerbier) and stores carrying German wine imports. News items covered local, national, and international events. In 1860 newspapers, I was surprised to learn, the German Americans had loved Abraham Lincoln. The *Wächter am Erie* [Watch on the Erie] heartily endorsed the Lincoln ticket. The idea that Germans leaned heavily toward Lincoln had never occurred to me, nor had I come across it in my research so far.

Later, I would learn that in 1860, of the 265 German newspapers in the U.S., only three supported secession. All the rest supported the Union. German Americans, it appeared, had an avid interest and strong influence in that historic election.

As I browsed through the old newspapers, I finally got it. Of course, news of my German ancestors would not be in the English newspapers. They'd be here, in the German ones. As the afternoon came to a close, on my way out, I stopped in at the WRHS museum gift shop and happened upon three treasures. Seminal 19th-century Cleveland German publications: *Memories of a Forty-Eighter*, *Cleveland and Its Germans*, and *The Jubilee Edition of the Cleveland Wächter Und Anzeiger 1902*. Originally published only in German, these books had all been translated into English by WRHS in 1996. The large, hardbound books were even discounted. They'd take up a chunk of room in my suitcase, but I scooped them up anyhow.

Memories of a Forty-Eighter was written by Jacob Müller, a Cleveland immigrant who arrived in town about seven years ahead of Michael Harm, a political exile of the 1848 rebellion for democracy in the Palatinate. In his picaresque-style memoir, Müller describes colorful stories of German immigrants to Cleveland and his first experiences there.

Cleveland and Its Germans [1897-1898 Edition] chronicled the lives of many German Clevelanders of influence. In the table of contents, Michael Harm was not listed, but I found my great grandfather W. F. Hoppensack, the father of my grandmother Emma Patterson. I am not sure of the author of these biographies, but the write-up had a strongly reminiscent character, that of a German immigrant who saw the culture slipping away in subsequent generations.

> W. F. Hoppensack—It is a frequent pattern here that when an old German pioneer dies, his American-born descendents have nothing better to do than to get rid of everything that reminds them of their German origins, most of all the language, then German customs and practices, and often even the honorable old German name itself is ejected or Anglicized in an ugly manner ....

The voice of immediacy in this account served as a poignant reminder of the common immigrant experience. In 1898 when the book was published, first generation immigrants were watching their children and children's children forget their German heritage in favor of becoming Americans.

According to the "biography" of W. F. Hoppensack, my grandmother's father, he was of the second generation, but had "remained German to the core." Something noted as unusual.

In the Hoppensack biography, his father-in-law was mentioned as "… respected fellow citizen Michael Harm, a German through and through." As I found this reference, I wondered why Michael Harm did not have his own entry in the book. Perhaps there was a class system at play? My great-grandfather W. F. Hoppensack had been a banker, whereas perhaps blacksmiths and carriage-makers were considered laborers? I didn't find a biography for any other blacksmiths or carriage-makers in the book. I'd also heard that during this era people sometimes paid to be included in books such as this one. That would have been just like my great-grandfather Hoppensack, a very political man who ran for election as Bank Commissioner several times.

In any event, the book was full of bios of other Germans, great material for characters. I also lucked out with the *Jubilee Edition* annals, a fat tome offering a compilation of articles that had appeared in the German *Waechter und Anzeiger* newspaper. That book became my resource for everything from the advent of the Bessemer steel process in Cleveland to what kind of automobiles were first manufactured there. Here were German books by German Americans, all translated into English as if just for me.

In my update that week to my thesis adviser, I again had very few pages to upload.

April 23, 2010

Hi Kathleen,

Um, now please don't get upset with me. There are not as many pages here as you would like. Or as I blithely promised late last week.

But what I'd really like around now is for you to celebrate with me. I mean, this journey to Cleveland has been amazing. There's such a wealth of material here: a special collection at Cleveland Public Library, a special collection at Case Western Reserve University, a Western Reserve Historical Society library that covers three floors of archives, and a special collection at Cleveland State University. I've been poring over maps and photos and fragile German newspapers and talking to people and seeing lots of historic sites. I've been up and out of the house by 7 a.m. every morning and am not back until 9 at night, which is when I type up whatever I've written during the day.

And I don't have to guess anymore about Cleveland, which I was doing before in so many ways. I'm becoming familiar enough with my subject, finally, that I'm going to have a good summer of productive writing. After the blacksmith class in June, I'll really have immersed myself and know whereof I speak.

Kathleen replied: "Thanks for the pages to read. My job is to encourage you to explore the topic while driving you mercilessly towards finishing a thesis. Only you can know which is more helpful."

Her understanding came as a great relief.

DURING MY TIME IN CLEVELAND, I'd put off focusing on my father's memorial, but not entirely. Life unspools in a constant tension, that of looking ahead and thinking back, of experiencing new, sometimes marvelous encounters even amidst times of mourning and loss. To cope, our minds may have to push one thing momentarily to the background in order to give our attention more fully to another, but the pull of that undercurrent is ever-present.

I thought of Dad often during those weeks, not only about who he was, but about how I often feel like I take after him. Dad had a habit of pushing himself just as I was doing, of being busy with some project or another every spare moment. Dad had similar personality traits and values to his mother and hence, I presume, to his German ancestors, especially in his meticulous attention to schedules and details, also similar to my modus operandi. And he and I shared a love of music. Dad used to sing in the church choir and inspired me to do the same. I don't remember him telling me, but Dad may have known Michael Harm was a long-time member of his German Lodge's Harmonie Choir, something I only now was finding out.

Those two weeks that I stayed in the home he'd designed for his parents, I appreciated again Dad's eye for balance and perspective. While not everything in our relationship was sweetness and light, my memories of him that week were especially meaningful to me. With increasing clarity, I saw that I had my father, and my mother, too, to thank for so many opportunities in my life. As I learned more about Michael Harm, I realized the same was true for him. He may have left his brother and parents behind, but his family had his back. He'd been set up to apprentice in his uncle's shop. It appeared he'd not even traveled entirely alone, but had a relative, Philipp Haenderich of the USA, to escort him across.

Such realizations clued me in that the concept of rugged individualism in America is largely a myth. A person who succeeds entirely on their own is an anomaly. Michael Harm stood on the shoulders of his parents and grandparents, just as I stood on the shoulders of mine.

In any case, I'd done all the research for the moment that I could possibly fit in. It was time to set the thesis aside and rejoin the rest of my family.

It had been an ambitious plan, I knew, to expect Dave and the kids to accompany Aunt Elizabeth on the long plane flight from Seattle to Cleveland, almost six hours in the air, not to mention the wheelchair logistics at the airports. But I should have been accompanying her. I was the one most familiar with helping her, with managing her walker, and dealing with her hardness of hearing. So when the rest of my family arrived in Ohio, it didn't surprise me that they all looked a bit frazzled.

"How'd it go?" I asked Dave once we'd settled Aunt Elizabeth in her hotel room and checked into ours.

"Not good," Dave said. "You should have seen Elizabeth. At the airport, she kept plowing ahead of everyone trying to get on the plane. They weren't even boarding yet. The kids had gone to a shop and Elizabeth kept saying, 'It's time to board. It's time to board.' Elizabeth stood up, except I knew they weren't boarding yet. I told her, 'you wait here, I'll be right back.' I was gone probably two minutes, but when I got back with the kids, Elizabeth was pushing her way to the front. The airline people were telling her it wasn't time, but she acted like she hadn't heard. Or maybe she hadn't. Anyhow, when I got up to her, I said, 'Elizabeth, I told you to wait.' The airline people looked at me like I was an ogre or something. They were like, 'now, we'll get everyone boarded just as soon as possible, sir.' Like I was the problem."

I felt bad, for Dave and for Aunt Elizabeth. In any case, the time had come to say a final farewell to Dad. It was time to gather with family and friends to celebrate the long, full life of Clyde Patterson (1923-2009).

While I felt closure in paying tribute to my father, my sense of guilt toward my aunt only increased as the weekend progressed. The schedule was jam-packed with funeral and burial arrangements. In addition, Dave's parents had driven from Michigan to attend the service and were staying at our same hotel. My high school friend Laura and her family all were gathered in Cleveland for Laura's mother's memorial. Of course we took advantage of these rare opportunities to spend time with family and longtime friends.

Although Aunt Elizabeth never said so, I had an inkling she would have liked to experience it all differently. She would have liked to spend time on the West Side of Cleveland, in Berea, to be driven past the house where she grew up on Daisy Avenue. No doubt she would have liked to see the first library where she worked as a young woman, and to visit the cemetery where her parents and sister were buried. But none of that happened.

The closest Aunt Elizabeth came to visiting a familiar haunt happened when, on a sunny spring afternoon, we all drove over to the property on Chagrin Blvd. where I'd been staying for those two weeks. Aunt Elizabeth used to visit us here, her sister's family, about twice a year. She had not asked to come see it. We all went there because my kids and the nieces had expressed an interest in spending time at their grandparents' old place.

When we arrived, Aunt Elizabeth had trouble getting up the one step it took to enter the house. Once inside, she pushed her red walker to the middle of the living room and, amid the hubbub of everyone talking and exploring, plopped down on the seat of her walker and looked all around with a reflective gaze.

It would be the last meaningful visit there for all of us. My brother Craig would continue to try valiantly to maintain the property, to keep the two houses rented and the 300-yard driveway plowed all winter. But within two years' time it would become too difficult to manage things from afar. Craig and I would agree to sell the family property to the neighbors. Grandmother's house would remain standing, but the house of my childhood on the back lot would be leveled, replaced by a mansion with a four-car garage.

Throughout that prolonged stay on Chagrin Blvd., I felt an ongoing push and pull, the precarious life balance of being both full of joy and the desolation of loss. Of needing to be there for loved ones, while needing to strive to meet personal goals and look ahead to the future. My thesis project only heightened this sense, reminding me of a saying from a Lennon song lyric that Mom and I used to quote often. "Life is what happens while you're busy making other plans."

Chapter 23

After returning to the Pacific Northwest that May, I plugged along on my thesis, trying to get Michael out of Germany and into Cleveland. To get there, I'd have to write about his voyage across the Atlantic to New York harbor. When it came to writing about New York City, so far I only had Michael Harm's obituary in my grandmother's scrapbook, which stated "After a short rest in the port city Harm continued to Cleveland and started an apprenticeship."

I needed to find a pithy news item or two on or near his date of arrival, some event I could draw from to write a scene. I typed in his date of arrival, June 30, 1857, and location, New York City, expecting not to find much. Instead, those simple key words elicited browser results for historic events much wilder than anything I could have dreamed up on my own.

During that first weekend of July, 1857, some of the worst rioting ever occurred in New York City, caused by a squabble between the New York City mayor and the New York State governor. The 19th-century newspaper accounts from that alarming, chaotic weekend were sensational. Two separate police forces—the Old (the mayor's) and the New (the governor's)—stood off against each other in New York City's streets. With no one in charge, gangs of the notorious Five Points Slum had free reign to loot, rob, and settle grudges with rival gangs.

The obituary description of Michael Harm's "short rest in the port city" did not even hint at the damage and fatalities described in the newspapers during those few days. And what were these "Five Points" repeated so often in the articles? As I dove deeper, a book by Tyler Anbinder called *Five Points* surfaced, a book that tells the history of that infamous Lower Manhattan slum.

Somehow, as I explored that tumultuous time, I stumbled across a 1981 thesis called *Kleindeutschland* [Little Germany], about a neighborhood in lower Manhattan near Tompkins Square Park. Nadel wrote: "German New York was the first of the great urban foreign language speaking communities in the United States, growing from thirty-three thousand people in 1845 to over three hundred-fifty thousand in 1880 .... Between 1855 and 1880, Vienna and Berlin were the only cities with a larger German population than New York."

Wow. I hadn't pictured that at all. From the write-up, Kleindeutschland sounded like a city within a city. If Michael Harm took a "short rest" in the port city, he must have stayed with immigrants from Freinsheim who were most likely living in Little Germany—"Dutch Town," as the English New Yorkers referred to it. Where else would he have gone? Perusing old maps, I located Kleindeutschland just north of the Five Points Slum. Leaving the Castle Garden Immigrant Center at the southern tip of Manhattan Island, if Michael had walked up Broadway, he would have passed directly through the Five Points Slum on the weekend of some of the worst rioting in New York City's history.

This amazing plotline was simply handed to me, hardly requiring any imagination at all. Other plotlines came much less easily. Take blacksmithing, for instance. I was so desperate to figure that out, I'd signed up for a "Beginning Blacksmithing I" class. As the time drew near for me to take the class, I wondered if I'd made the right decision. Would it give me any real insights? Could I even do it? My growing anxiety was evident in a blog post from that time.

May 14, 2010

The art of blacksmithing

For my MFA thesis, I'm writing about my great-great grandfather, who apprenticed as a blacksmith in Cleveland, Ohio in the mid-nineteenth century.

Unfortunately, as a 20th/21st century woman, I don't come across the blacksmithing craft very often. So, my plan is to take a class this June at Old West Forge.

I know a metalworker named Pia, of B32 Metal Fabrications and the other day I was talking with her, nervously, about my upcoming class at Old West Forge.

"How should I prepare?" I asked her. "Lift weights? Walk on my hands?"

"I'd practice my aim," Pia said. "If you can hit the mark with your sledgehammer, it'll be a lot less frustrating."

> I don't have an anvil at home, but I do have a large cedar log. Hence, for Mother's Day I requested from my husband and kids a set of large wood-carving tools, specifically a straight chisel, a gouge, and a small sledgehammer to pound with ... and got them!
>
> I couldn't be more delighted. Already, I've been practicing my aim, and so far, I haven't done injury to myself. Somehow, though, I think it's going to take more than this to measure up come June.

Never mind how I misused my brand new wood-carving tools in the process. In retrospect, I should have been hacking at that cedar log with a small hatchet or an ax, not my new, expensive gouge. But the pounding and aiming helped me get familiar with holding a hammer in my hand, I reasoned, and helped steel my nerves for what lay ahead. At least I was doing something to prepare.

That spring, Michele Genthon, a woman with whom I'd formed a writing group several years before, emailed me to suggest an arrangement that turned out to be a godsend.

> May 23, 2010
>
> Claire,
>
> I was scribbling away about how rigor leads to rigor mortis and I realized that, since lunch with you on Monday, I have written every day this week (in addition to editing my manuscript) ....
>
> You said you had written the next morning after we had lunch as well, so I was wondering—What would you think if we checked in with each other once a week? Just a short Monday morning update about what we have accomplished and what our goals are for the week. I think this might be helpful to me—at least for a while. Just let me know if you think this might help you as well. We could always try it and abandon it if it loses its usefulness.
>
> Peace,
>
> Michele

It sounded fine to me. Michele and I had become good friends, and I could definitely use her weekly support, not to mention someone to moan to when things got tough.

> May 31, 2010
>
> Dear Michele,
>
> Guess I'll kick off the "writing update" exchange. Are we counting today, since it's Memorial Day and all? I sincerely hope you're out enjoying the late afternoon sunshine. I have a touch of bursitis in my hip or something, which is keeping me in.
>
> I can't believe tomorrow is already June 1. I was a good student today—I hunkered down and finished *Elective Affinities* (Goethe) this morning, and read about blacksmithing tools, and tried to write a little. I'm stymied by my plotline—I'm spending way too long on the transatlantic crossing and I'm afraid I'll have to toss most of it. But it all feels like formative stuff, and I'd rather decide later what to get rid of ....
>
> My plan for the week is to get Michael to NYC, plow through those gangs of New York riots, and move on from there.
>
> Blessings,
>
> Claire

COME JUNE, MY FAMILY CELEBRATED another milestone: daughter Vivian's graduation from high school, a week-long series of ceremonies for which I was most willing to set aside the thesis. Vivian had been accepted at Willamette University in Salem, Oregon, where she'd begin her studies in August.

Next up was my trip to White Salmon, Washington, to spend four days hammering away at Old West Forge. Dave had agreed to manage the home front in my absence. When it came to that, he was consistently supportive of my research adventures.

All that remained was a visit with Aunt Elizabeth, in part to remind her I'd be gone for a few days.

"You're late," she greeted me as I came around to her side of the van. As soon as I pulled up, she'd already hustled her way from the Bayview lobby down the sidewalk ramp and now stood waiting for me to open the passenger door.

"Only by two minutes," I said, yanking the door open. "You're always early."

She smirked at the truth of this as I helped her into the car. I'd been early to pick up Aunt Elizabeth on several occasions, but never early enough to arrive ahead of her. She was always down in the lobby, coat on, purse in her lap, watching out the windows.

When I climbed back in the driver's seat, she handed me pages I'd given her, a print-out of the early chapters of my thesis. I had to make a hard copy because my aunt never went near a computer.

"Things get very exciting when the Prussians come to Freinsheim," she said.

I took the pages and nodded gratefully. Maybe my aunt had found something positive to say out of loyalty, but even so, her words meant a lot.

That noon hour, I took Aunt Elizabeth out to lunch as was our habit. Usually, I visited her twice a week, on Thursdays for lunch outings and shopping errands, and on Sundays when I picked up laundry and helped her with apartment needs.

Aunt Elizabeth waited until we were on the drive back from lunch to bring up my blacksmithing class.

"I don't think you have to blacksmith to write about it," she said.

I suspected she really meant she didn't want me to go away. Or was she nervous on my behalf? "It's only five days," I said, hoping to reassure her.

I parked at the retirement community, unloaded her walker and brought it around to the passenger side to give her something to lean on as she climbed stiffly out. There on the sidewalk, I kissed her on the cheek by way of farewell.

"Thank you," she said. "I hope for your sake it goes well, and they're not too … boorish."

Aunt Elizabeth turned and pushed her way slowly up the sidewalk to the sliding glass doors that opened automatically.

I watched her go, my brain racing with new concerns. Boorish? I hadn't pictured boorish blacksmiths. Maybe I wouldn't get along with the other students? They'd all be surly and boorish?

It was too late to back out now regardless. I'd set the days aside and even posted a blog about my plans. Feeling off balance, I went home to pack: a few old t-shirts, a pair of work boots and two pairs of work gloves, my hammer and my camera, and early the next morning hit the road for the other side of the Cascade Mountains.

During the long drive from Seattle to eastern Washington, then south toward the Columbia River through wide-open plains dotted with white, spinning wind turbines, my thoughts ran in circles. What had I been thinking? Did I really have to pound hot metal for four days to get into the psyche of my

Tim Middaugh, master blacksmith at Old West Forge in White Salmon, Washington.

protagonist? Couldn't I just take photos and notes? I was a writer, after all, not a he-woman.

Too late to back out now. Five hours later, I arrived in the town of White Salmon along the Columbia River, where I checked into the Inn of the White Salmon. I set my alarm for 7:15 a.m., then tossed and turned all night in anticipation of the first day of class.

Bright and early at 8:30 a.m. I arrived at Old West Forge, stepping from the sunny meadow into the dark, warm workshop and a tangle of tools. The walls were crammed with tools, floor to ceiling, every conceivable variety of hammer, tongs, and what have you. My heart pounded heavily and my breathing was shallow. I wasn't only worried, I was terrified. I couldn't believe I'd signed on for this.

The owner and teacher of Old West Forge, Tim Middaugh, greeted me and asked to examine the hammer I'd brought along. I tried to look strong and confident as I handed it over, as if my being here in this jungle of metal was the most normal thing in the world. Without a word, Tim set my hammer down, pulled one of his own hammers off a rack, gave it to me, and pointed at an anvil up front, closest to his own. Clearly, I required supervision. I wanted to know why his hammer was good, and mine woefully inadequate, but I didn't want to look like a complete idiot from the get-go. Even though I already had.

The class started with students introducing themselves. We numbered six in all: a retiree, a research scientist, a gardener, a boatyard manager, an English teacher, and me, a self-proclaimed writer. The propane forges were already roaring as we six "apprentices" perched on folding chairs amid vises, slack tubs, buckets of tools, and anvils, ready for the first lesson of the day. Our teacher—the "master"—stood before us at his anvil.

"Today, there are very few blacksmiths left," Tim Middaugh began. He was a serious but kind-looking man, a bit stout around the middle, clean shaven, with soft wavy brown hair. He wore a light blue t-shirt and blue jeans held up by suspenders. His skin bore no visible scars or tattoos. "I traveled all over the country to learn from the ten or twelve blacksmiths who were keeping the craft alive all these years. I learned what I could from them, and now I'm passing that knowledge along. Blacksmithing used to be an everyday kind of activity. Kids would stop by the forge to watch the blacksmiths. The craft was intuitive to them, a part of daily life."

I practice the technique of "striking" with fellow student Roselie Rasmussen.

The first task of the day, he told us, would be to make a chisel. "Every blacksmith used to make his own set of tools. A blacksmith is always making tools for this and that job, as the need arises."

Using what he called "tool steel," he started the first demonstration, heating the round metal rod to a bright yellow glow, pounding it with deft, swift blows, then quenching the now red-orange tip in oil. It burst into angry flame. .

"We quench the business end in oil due to the hardness of this type of steel, to avoid cracking," he told us, swishing the rod until the fire subsided. He pulled out the rod and examined it, now flattened at one end and cooled back to its original color. "This here is called a walking chisel. Now you give it a try."

I didn't leap right up with the other students. Instead, I sat stunned, mulling over my first key insight. Of course, books and illustrations didn't teach what blacksmithing was all about. Blacksmithing couldn't be learned by reading. It was learned by demonstration. Hence, the apprenticeship system. For as long as there was the artisan craft system, blacksmith apprentices devoted countless days to hauling water and coal, pumping the bellows, sweeping the floors, pedaling the grinding wheel, and more, all while observing skilled blacksmiths plying their trade.

But the others were getting started. With trepidation, I rose from my folding chair and went to my anvil. The bar of tool steel rested on top of it. Cautiously, I gripped it with a tongs and set one end into my previously lit, now red-hot propane forge. My brain felt tied in knots, my limbs thick and clumsy. Desperately, I rifled through memory trying to remember what Tim had just shown us. What I now had to do myself. Take my hammer and wail the bejesus out of hot metal.

From the start, I was terrible at it, further cluing me in that one learned blacksmithing by demonstration, and by actually doing it. With each new project I felt less and less coordinated. I needed practice. Lots of it. Tim often came by to help. We students made tools all day: a walking chisel, a fuller, a punch, and a hot cutter to slice through hot steel. These tools would be ours, Tim told us, which we'd use for the next three days, then take home for future projects. As I heated and hammered, heated and hammered, a paraphernalia of equipment amassed around my anvil—a pile of cast-off tongs, a small can of water for cooling tools when they got too hot to handle, and a growing collection of finished product.

By 4:30 p.m., my brain vibrated with roaring forges and banging and pounding and grinding and sparks flying and metal in various shades of heat: shiny silver to yellow-orange to cherry-red to blue to straw. Tim Middaugh taught us about the SOR method of hammering (Square, Octagonal, Round). Add an E and you've got SORE, as in Egads! my forearm was killing me. That first night at dinner, my hammering arm hurt so much I had to drink my beer left-handed. I saw Tim with his family in the restaurant that evening. It turned out he wasn't a blacksmith for a day job—he was the town dentist.

First thing the next morning, the blacksmith master fired up the forges an hour earlier, at 7:30 a.m. As I started in, groggy and aching, everything went wrong. Tim showed us how to use the punch we'd made the day before to punch a hole in a metal bar. When I tried, I took too long to make the hole. I worked through so many heats, the heat crept up the steel and singed my bare arm. The next half hour found me outside, my elbow stuck in the cold water of a slack tub while I waited for the burning sting to subside. When I tried to fit a rivet into the 3/8-inch punched hole, I spilled the can of water that held my punch and chisels, plus the rivet and the metal bar. Hot metal clattered all over the place on the dirt-coated cement. Finally, I managed to hammer the glowing hot rivet into place, only to discover I'd fit the pieces together backwards. Tim kept an eye on me and came over to help me cut the thing apart so I could start over.

At the hardest moments, Tim tried to lighten my mood by saying things like, "Since I gave up hope, I feel a lot better," (quoting a Steve Taylor lyric) or "Lord make me the person my dog thinks I am." But his encouragements did little to ease my embarrassment and humiliation. That night, I posted a blog in which I confessed: "Thank God Tim turned off the forges when he did or I would have started to weep."

Horror stories aside, I was learning what I needed to know. At last, I was living into my protagonist, following in his footsteps, experiencing first hand a hint of the things Michael Harm possibly endured. In those few short days, I learned blacksmiths had to be quick, patient, stalwart, and constantly alert for danger. I felt like I possessed none of those qualities, but somehow, I kept at it. By the end of the fourth day, I'd forged a set of tools, two fireplace pokers, a wreath hanger and a sign bracket. I even teamed up with a fellow student to practice smithing and striking (hammering with a sledge).

From then on, whenever I sat down to write blacksmithing scenes, I had sights and sounds and smells and physical and emotional agony to draw from. In addition, I had Tim Middaugh's insights and sayings to characterize the profession. And, the language used in the smithy struck me as metaphorical, terms like "upset," "temper," "quench," and "rivet," which kept my brain churning with ideas.

I especially loved Tim's comments about the golden mean or golden ratio, the ideal distance in proportions. It occurs in nature, for instance in the spiral of a sea shell. Sometimes called the Fibonacci sequence, the golden ratio is pervasive in art and music, too. It influences our human perception of beauty and balance. In modern times, accurate dimensions are spit out of calibrated machines and computer programs. In former times, the artisan developed an eye for the "rightness" of things. In music, I thought about how one wrong note is instantly noticed, and of writing, how we work each word and phrase and sentence until it sounds just right.

The biggest lesson I learned in the field was the power dynamics at play between a master blacksmith and his apprentices. Tim had to keep a vigilant eye on all of us, or we'd inadvertently inflict harm on ourselves and one another. His manner was a bit abrupt and demanding, some might even say "boorish," because he had to be. If we apprentices deviated from Tim's instructions, we did so at our peril. By the end of the four days, the art of blacksmithing, and the challenges and muscle aches therein, I understood at last from firsthand experience.

Chapter 24

During the last months of spring, Dave and I were gearing up for our trip to Germany. I wrote a couple of emails to several cousins of my generation—to Matthias and Angela, and to their cousin Manfred—to make plans. I wrote in German to try to do my part. Besides, I needed to practice the language whenever possible.

May 4, 2010

Subject: Deutschland Reise

Hallo Matthias, Angela, und Manfred,

Bitte, ich hoffe nach Deutschland (Frankfurt) am 19 Sept. ankommen, und am 17 Oct. ausgehen. Was wollt ihr alle denken? Sind diesen Daten ausgezeichnet, oder nicht so gut? Ich glaube, Dave wird auch für einer Woche nach Deutschland besuchen, aber ich weiß nicht genau in welcher Kalendarwoche. Ich warte für Ihre Antworten. Ich müsse eine Reservierung bald machen. Viele liebe Grüße aus Seattle, Claire. Es tut mir leid für mein schlectes Deutsch.

[Transl.] Please, I hope to come to Germany (Frankfurt) from Sept. 19 to October 17. What do you all think? Are these dates excellent, or not so good? I believe Dave will also visit for a week, but I'm not sure exactly which week … I wait for your answer, I must make a reservation soon. Many loving greetings from Seattle, Claire I am sorry for my bad German.

That same day, English responses began arriving in my inbox.

Email from Matthias Weber, May 4, 2010

> Hey Claire,
>
> You chose a great time: it's a mixture of "Altweibersommer" (=old women summer) and "Goldener Herbst (=golden autumn)! If you arrive on Sunday, 19. Sept. you're even able to visit the "*Wurstmarkt*" (=Sausage Market) in Bad Duerkheim, that's the biggest wine festival of the world!
>
> For your explorations I propose you start with visiting a few places which show German and European history in the Palatinate, and I suggest a hike following in the footsteps of James F. Cooper. Also you'll meet the Palatine relatives. The next weekend (25./26. Sept.) is the Freinsheim Weinwanderung, the Wine-Hike in the vineyards - I'm sure you remember, that we talked about it.
>
> The following weeks you're going to visit several local museums and you're going to meet several local history researchers. Perhaps there will be also time for some more sightseeing: for example the Speyer Cathedral and the Worms Cathedral. So we're looking forward to have you with us! —Matthias

Email reply from Manfred Weber May 5, 2010

> Hallo Claire and Dave,
>
> You have chosen a good time to come to Germany / Palatinate.
>
> We all are looking forward to have you with us.
>
> Love and "viele Grüße"[many greetings] from Freinsheim
>
> Manfred and family
>
> Your "Deutsch" is not "schlecht", but it will be much better after your visit, I'm sure :-)

In hindsight, once I'd learned more German, I better understood Manfred's joke about my bad German—in my email I'd spelled schlecht wrong—schlect without the second "h." That really is pretty bad. No doubt my relatives found enjoyment in my fumbling attempts. I didn't mind at all if they did.

Angela also chimed in from Marburg:

> May 5, 2010
>
> Hallo Claire,
>
> I am the last one to add: *Gute Reisezeit* [Good traveltimes]!
> I hope I can come to Freinsheim more frequently in this
> time, even on weekdays, if it fits Christoph's schedule. Bis
> bald! [See you soon]
>
> Angela

Before long, we'd firmed up our plans: Dave would accompany me to Germany for the first week, then leave me on my own to research for about three weeks. Since I felt I needed to be able to converse reasonably well with the elder relatives who spoke next to no English in Freinsheim—Tante Gretel and Onkel Otto Kopf, Tante Inge Faber, Tante Marliese Weber, and Tante Bärbel Weber, the mother of Angela and Matthias, I grew even more desperate to tackle the language. When I'd visited Freinsheim in 1988, the hospitality of the relatives had been generous indeed. I felt certain Dave and I would get a similar reception, and I wanted to be worthy of their kindness.

I searched for a local German class, rather than just the online library programs, but in the end had better luck with another online venue: The Goethe Institute. First, their mandatory test assessed my skill level. I scored just one peg above the beginning level. I got started right away, working on reading, writing, and conversation, for which I had to get a headset with a mouthpiece to practice pronunciation. The class even came with a tutor, a German teacher named Katrin who lived in Köln [Cologne]. Via the Goethe forum and Skype, she graded my homework and checked in with me from time to time.

All that summer, I struggled to balance German language learning, thesis writing, and a hiking trip with our family and Craig and his family to Washington State's Alpine Lakes wilderness. Time was galloping along when Angela called out of the blue one afternoon to talk.

"When you come to Germany, I have something exciting for you," she said.

"Great. What is it?" I was sitting at my kitchen table, the summer afternoon sun slanting through the window. Outside, a bicyclist pedaled up the steep slope of Mercerwood Drive. With the time difference, I knew it must be very late for Angela in Marburg.

"I've spoken with the curator of the *Heimatmuseum* Bad Dürkheim about the book you are writing," she said. "We are talking about a time when you're here, when we could give a presentation about the letters. That way we have a chance to discuss our findings and possibly get further clues."

"Wait, *Heimatmuseum*? I don't know what that is."

"It's the local history and culture museum here. They have a history club."

I did not like the sound of that at all. A local history club based out of a museum?

"What kind of presentation?" What could I possibly tell them, I wondered, that they didn't already know?

"About what we found out from the letters. It would be interesting for them."

"You mean you would give the presentation."

"Both of us would give it. You should also tell them about what you are learning in your research."

"Angela, I can't do that. I can't speak German."

"You can give it in English. Most of the younger generation understand that anyhow. And I can translate for you."

"But I'm not far enough along to know what I'm talking about. I need to be in Germany to do research."

"But we already learned things people do not know."

I found that hard to believe. "I don't know, Angela ..."

Angela gave a sing song "hmm hmm," followed by a little giggle. "And there's something else I thought of. It's a great idea. Before we give the talk at the *Heimatmuseum*, we should give it to the family. We could put something together, and while you are here, we can invite all the relatives to my mother's house. I think before we talk about our family in public, it is better to let them know about the contents of the letters. And maybe it will start conversations, to see what further knowledge they have and which memories are triggered."

How could I say no, with all the help Angela was giving me? Not to mention how much her brother Matthias and the rest of the relatives were doing for me.

"Maybe we could do some kind of PowerPoint," I said, thinking of all the photos I'd been taking. We also had the letter scans, and from Dad's things I'd even come across old tintypes, an early form of photography, of Michael Harm's family through the years. "When I was in Cleveland, I found some pretty cool historic pictures of German immigrants."

Angela said she liked that idea. I still felt full of doubts, but she sounded so excited. By the end of the call, I'd agreed to put some kind of PowerPoint together.

MEANWHILE, I WAS STILL STRUGGLING to bring my outline under control, an outline Kathleen had accepted, but called "longish." My desire to be true to my ancestors' historic record continually complicated my decisions regarding what to keep and what to let go. Even with big gaps in time between letters, wherever possible I resisted fictionalizing events. For the 1860s, I had one letter written by Michael Harm, well after the Civil War in 1869, badly faded and nearly illegible.

> Cleveland, 24 June 1869
>
> Most loved brother and sister-in-law.
>
> ...[1] and has immediately handed us the portraits intact. I found the photography better than expected [he] should stay fit, so that he will still [illegible] be in good shape. When I will knock on your door once again, your two dear girls[2] call me, as it seems to embarrass me, with their dolls in their hands[3] [saying] Christ child has not forgotten us, even if you, uncle and aunt have forgotten us.
>
> [Illegible] ... Jacob Dieringer came to see you without a sign of gratitude from me, has only happened because he went to Europe without letting me know anything in time.
>
> The first knowledge I got by accident at an unexpected meeting with him Saturday afternoon at 4 o'clock on the street he said then, I will start traveling on Monday morning at 5 o'clock to Germany. I was so upset about it that I didn't answer more than happy travel and then went on my way.
>
> When I went to Europe 5 years ago[4] I let him know 14 days in advance and have done a lot of errands for him,

1   Due to damage, the first part of this letter is illegible.
2   Philipp Harm and Susannah Margaretha Harm (Hisgen) had two daughters at this time, Elizabetha (3/25/1864) and Margaretha (3/19/1865)
3   The Philipp Harm family had a portrait taken, the two young daughters holding dolls in their hands. Perhaps Michael was gazing at the portrait as he wrote the letter?
4   M. Harm traveled in 1864 to Germany, presumably on the death of his mother Elisabetha Handrich Harm in October of 1864 aboard the ship *Hansa*, Bremen, Germany and Southampton, England to New York, arriving on 10 Oct 1864. Year: 1864; Arrival: New York, United States; Microfilm serial M237; Microfilm roll: M237_246; Line: 43; List number 1022.

but he secretly went away in order to be released from such a commission. But I will sure remember that of him.

Like I have further learned from your writing you thought to have received the New Yorker Stadtzeitung through (the) Oberholz[5], that is not the case dear brother, but the newspaper comes from me, and is being sent to you on my account. You will also find the stamp Cleveland and not Akron.

As far as my family is concerned we are all quite healthy the children grow and advance and Ph Heinrich[6] is already going to Sunday school now.

Uncle Jakob[7] has been living in his house over in town but left last week again for Columbus to work. We have spent time together oftentimes. And I shall greet you many times from him, his wife and his child[8] are still here, I think he will be coming back soon.

As far as business is concerned times aren't as brilliant as we once had because money is lacking everywhere.

My partner Ernst Butler[9] asks you through me if you might possibly soon after receiving these few lines pick 1/2 Schoppenglas [half liter glass] of unripe beech nuts, dry these but not in the sun but in the air and occasionally send them in here (into the country).

Now I want to close in hope of receiving an answer soon. I greet you all many 1000 times and remain Yours

M.Harm

[Note from Elisabetha Harm]

Many greetings from me [and] from my parents to all of

5   Oberholz is a common surname in Freinsheim
6   Philipp Heinrich "Henry" Harm (1864), eldest child of Michael and Elizabeth Harm.
7   Presumably, Jakob Handrich (1849 letter writer).
8   A Jacob Handrich, boilermaker, and Mary Platt (Handrich) had a one-year-old daughter Anna in the 1870 census.
9   Ernst Butler was part owner of the original carriage works on Champlain, in partnership with Beach and Harm. (per Thomas A. Kinney)

you. Elisabetha Harm.[10]

Address: M.Harm 102 Champlain Str. Cleveland O. America

"let us have pice of ouer Contry."

Chronologically, this 1869 letter was the first in our possession written by Michael Harm. After 1858, Rapparlie had written no others, and Michael did not seem to be as prolific a letter writer as his uncle. In the 1869 letter, I wondered about Michael's statement that he "went to Europe 5 years ago." Angela suggested perhaps he had returned to Freinsheim because his mother, Elisabetha Handrich Harm, had died in 1864, the year of death listed in Dad's family tree. Maybe so, but for the novel, adding an ocean journey during the Civil War, I feared, would dilute the power of the story. Michael had just up and left while the war was raging? That didn't fit my outline at all. Not to mention yet another ocean journey would exacerbate the "longish" nature of the book. It may have happened, but I resisted including it

This clue did support the idea Michael Harm had not enlisted. None of the oral history ever mentioned he had, nor was his involvement mentioned in his obituary. For the moment, I decided to set the factual story aside and stick with my fictional one, that he hadn't served in the war, but also had not returned to Germany as a consequence of it.

What I did value highly in the 1869 letter was the closing statement, written in English no less: "let us have pice of ouer Contry." "Let us have peace" was the campaign slogan of Ulysses S. Grant, who served as president from 1869-1877. Since Michael added this quote in his letter to Freinsheim, it seemed possible he supported President Grant. And, whatever else the phrase revealed, it indicated that my great-great grandfather appeared to be learning at least few phrases of the language of his new homeland, however misspelled.

The letter also spilled the beans about Uncle Jakob Handrich getting married, although, if it didn't happen until the late 1860s, he had to have been over forty years old. I planned to definitely make something out of this new detail.

Despite these breakthroughs, I felt frustrated by all the things this letter did not contain. No mention of what happened to Johann Rapparlie and his wife Katherina of the wooden leg. Nothing about how Michael Harm managed to travel to Germany during the Civil War, a time when travel was

---

10 [Michael added below his signature:] Many greetings to all good friends and acquaintances such as Richard Pirmann and family, John Fuhrmann, (female) cousin Harm and families Philipp Prettinger and T. (?) Reibold, Philipp Aul and his young wife, Ann Maria Gumbinger and her family.

greatly restricted for men of conscription age. I still hoped to get closer to the real story, but it looked like the better of part of the later chapters would be sheer invention.

By that next residency, held in August of 2010, I estimated I was one-fifth of the way done. I'd divided the book into five sections, mirroring the five stanzas of Goethe's poem "Primal Words, Orphic": Destiny, Chance, Love, Necessity, Hope. In my outline, those five parts amounted to a daunting forty-four chapters. All I'd managed to write so far were 125 rough draft pages.

Residency was held that fall semester at Camp Casey on Whidbey Island. The gorgeous setting instantly re-energized me, as well as seeing fellow students and faculty in person. As we greeted each other and caught up on writing progress, I had to admit to my classmates I wasn't as far along as I'd hoped to be by now. I squirmed inwardly at the thought that, when I'd started thesis last fall, I'd expected to be graduating this August. Now it appeared that even a whole extra year might not be enough time to tackle this monster of a project.

At least I had blacksmith bragging rights. When it came time to present my student reading, I trotted out the fireplace pokers and sign bracket I'd made at Old West Forge that past June. First, I passed around the objects, explaining how I'd immersed myself in a beginning blacksmithing class in order to get inside my protagonist. Next, I held up the pale underside of my arm, with its lingering burn scar, as evidence of my travails. I concluded with a very brief reading, a few paragraphs I'd written shortly after I'd taken the class.

As I read the passage out loud, I felt my voice change, almost as if it was Michael's voice, not mine, doing the narrating. I could hear him speaking through me. It felt strange, and wonderfully right at the same time.

Afterwards, one of my professors came over to me. "I really think you have something there," she said, handing back my metal sign bracket.

I accepted the heavy bracket, and the praise, with an inner glow. Whatever creative muse was beginning to guide me through this process, I hoped it would continue.

At lunch early on during residency, I sat with fiction faculty member Bruce Holland Rogers, who had teased me about learning German the year before. He asked me how my thesis was going. Although he was not a priest, Bruce wore a priest's collar, just one of his many charming idiosyncrasies. Perhaps it was the clerical collar that, subconsciously, prompted me to confess my anxieties. I told Bruce about Angela's plans for our presentation at the cultural museum in Bad Dürkheim, and how nervous that made me.

Bruce gave me an amused smile, his gray eyes twinkling behind wire-framed glasses. "You know, I thought learning to blacksmith was impressive. Now you're giving talks in a foreign country."

He chuckled, almost gleefully it seemed to me, and my weighty task felt just slightly lighter. If anyone could appreciate the immensity of my undertaking, it was Bruce. Recently, he'd returned from teaching for a semester at Eötvös Loránd University in Budapest on a Fulbright grant. For fun, in our online school forum last semester, he'd been posting phrases in Hungarian. Previously, he'd taught writing seminars in Finland, and in Greece.

While I realized I'd never match his brilliance with languages, I had a sudden inspiration.

"Maybe you could give me some pointers?" I said.

Bruce agreed to help.

Later that week, he and I sat outdoors on the steps of one of the Camp Casey buildings, and I explained how my progress with my Goethe Institute course had only gotten me far enough to know my German was doomed to remain at entry level. Numbers, letters of the alphabet, greetings, asking directions, commenting on the weather, I could do. But giving a learned historical presentation for German scholars? Such a prospect felt way beyond my abilities.

I asked Bruce if I should go with Angela's suggestion and give the talk in English.

"If at all possible, you should give the talk in German," he told me. "You can read from a script, can't you?"

When it came to that, I supposed I could. I'd been practicing pronunciation with my Goethe Institute course, and my rate of success there was passable. I told Bruce this, and he nodded.

"Well then, it sounds like you can." He proceeded to relate, in his usual soft-spoken manner, the essential points I needed to know: be genuine, honest, and confident, even if you might be making serious errors. Oh, and have a sense of humor about it all.

Chapter 25

Come mid-September, all the arrangements were in place for our trip. Son George and daughter Vivian were both beginning their university semesters. I'd found a neighbor to look after our cat and packed and made lists and gathered necessary equipment: a camera, audio recorder, and laptop, notebooks for writing longhand and small gifts for each of the families.

The only important item remaining was saying good-bye to Aunt Elizabeth. I knew my absence for a whole month would be hard for her to deal with. I'd been visiting her religiously every Thursday and Sunday since my return from the MFA residency, hoping that might hold her over during my long time away.

The final week before our departure, I went over to pick her up at Bayview for our lunch outing.

"It's not for that long," I assured her as I settled her into the van, then folded and loaded her walker in the back.

"I'll need to stock up," she said as I climbed in the driver's seat.

Aunt Elizabeth and I often made stops at Bartell's drugstore for one thing or another, sundries she'd run out of, like face powder and Tums. Today would be no exception.

At Bartell's, the cashiers at the front saw us enter but didn't respond to my friendly nod. Their eyes were riveted on Aunt Elizabeth, hunched over her walker and plodding forward, her hair flaming red, her dark burgundy lips pressed in a grim line.

As she plowed ahead down the aisles, I followed behind her, grabbing a few travel-size items for myself: mouthwash, contact solution, a packet of Tylenol. Up ahead, my aunt reached out, grabbed a tube of toothpaste and dropped it in her shopping cart. I remembered she'd bought a huge tube just two weeks before, but didn't say anything. No doubt she was nervous about getting by without me.

"I have a surprise for you," I said once we'd returned to the van. "I talked

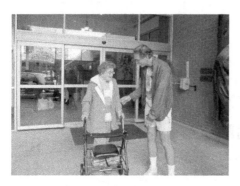

Aunt Elizabeth and Craig Patterson outside Bayview during my brother and family's summer, 2010 visit to Seattle.

to Sue Donovan. She and I both feel bad that you don't have a computer and aren't going to be able to read my blog. Sue says she'll print my blogs out and put them in your mailbox."

"That's too much trouble." Aunt Elizabeth really hated to depend on anyone for anything.

"No, Sue is excited about it." Did my aunt not realize people liked her? At least, they told me they did. The intake officer at Bayview, Sue Donovan, kept telling me she really liked Aunt Elizabeth a lot. "She says she wants to read my blog anyhow."

"She tells you that."

Clearly, glib reassurances weren't going to appease Aunt Elizabeth today.

"Well, anyway, it'll just take a second. All Sue does is call up the website and click print. She said she really doesn't mind."

Aunt Elizabeth didn't reply, so we left it at that.

Wanting to make this visit special somehow, before stopping for lunch, I drove over to Alki Beach. It was a crisp, breezy September day, the Seattle skyline at its most stunning across the glistening bay. The tide was out, and people wandered the beach and bicycle trails with dogs and children. As I drove along I wondered why I hadn't taken her over here before. Aunt Elizabeth had been living in Seattle now for more than a year, and this vista of Seattle was amazing.

Circling back, I took her to lunch at Luna Park Café, the hamburger diner under the West Seattle Bridge, where the food was reminiscent of the 1950s. Luna Park's booths and stools shone with chrome. The walls and corners, even the ceiling, were loaded with 20th-century amusement park memorabilia. My aunt seemed to enjoy the decor, and dug into her hamburger with a healthy appetite.

Afterwards, as I pulled back up in front of Bayview, Elizabeth pulled her purse firmly into her lap and looked over at me. "Now, where did we go again?"

"Luna Park Café."

"Where is that?"

"That's Alki Beach. In West Seattle."

Aunt Elizabeth nodded, as if committing the names to memory. All at once, I pictured her tonight, seated with her dinner companions, telling them

Matthias Weber gives Dave and me a tour of Freinsheim on the first day of our visit, 2010.

about her outing with her niece, the places we'd gone.

"I enjoyed that," she said. "Thank you."

I told her you're welcome and hopped out of the van to help her out. She descended gingerly, pulling her walker toward her with a determined grip. I arranged the Bartell's purchases and her purse in the front basket and leaned down to give her a hug. She offered her right cheek for a kiss, which I delivered.

"I'll only be gone a month, and I'll try to blog every day," I said. I hoped I didn't let on how guilty I felt about deserting her. I wanted to convey confidence, especially in her ability to get along during my absence.

"Have a good time," she said. "I hope you get what you're going for."

"Me, too," I said. I sure did.

I stepped aside and watched my aunt plod inside.

My days had been hectic getting ready to leave, but I was glad I'd carved out the time to see her. I didn't have Dad or Mom to tell about my plans, or to be excited for me regarding things that were happening in my life. I knew Aunt Elizabeth really did care for and love me. Even though it would be hard for her, I'd be back in no time.

DAVE AND I LANDED IN Frankfurt, Germany at sunrise. Out of the window,

A wall encircles the old section of Freinsheim. The front gate, called the Eisentor, was built in 1514. The steeple of the Evangelical Protestant Church, at the center of town, is visible in the background.

pale hints of daylight peeked through dark gray clouds along the horizon. By email, we'd been told Matthias would meet us at the airport. Angela was living in Marburg north of Frankfurt and wouldn't be coming to Freinsheim until later that week. It was a Tuesday morning, so Matthias had arranged to get away from work, but we wouldn't see Ina until the evening. I felt honored by all the plans they were making on our behalf, and grateful.

Once we connected with Matthias, within an hour or so we were in Freinsheim at the Weber family home located just on the outskirts of the *Altstadt*—the historic "old town" of Freinsheim ringed by the medieval wall. The house has been passed down in the Weber family for several generations. Most structures in and around the old town date from the 1700's, so the Weber home is considered one of the newer ones, built at the turn of the 20th century. Bärbel lived on the second floor. Dave and I would stay in the first floor apartment where Bärbel's parents had lived out their old age.

But first things first, before unpacking, we sat down to breakfast, a German breakfast artfully set before us by Bärbel—cold cuts, fresh rolls, cheeses, fruits and coffee.

I had met Bärbel back in the 1990s when she'd visited Angela at Neah Bay in the Pacific Northwest. Bärbel's hair was in the same pageboy style as back then. She'd aged gracefully, not looking much older than she had fifteen years before. As the sunlight poured through the dining room windows, we began to get reacquainted. Bärbel's English was about as rudimentary as my German, so there were many pauses as we searched for the right words.

It was Dave's first trip to Germany. Years ago he and I had traveled in South America for several months, a time when he'd picked up a bit of Spanish. As we were enjoying the meal, Bärbel stood up and asked Dave in very careful English: "Would—you—like—more—bread, Dave?"

"*Ja, mas pan, por favor,*" he said in German-Spanish, giving us all a good laugh.

Once we'd eaten, Matthias and his mother sat across from us and Matthias pulled out a notebook and paper.

"So now," he said, "we make a schedule. We are German, you know, so we always make a schedule."

"We're fine with whatever," Dave said.

"Yes, but it is important that

Inside the fortified wall, it is possible to walk around the village via an inner ring walkway.

we make plans. There are many relatives here, and they all want to see you, and they all want to meet Dave. They will want to know everything that you are doing."

"I thought tonight we were going to that wine festival," I said. "Isn't it the last night?"

"That's right," Matthias said with a twinkle in his eye. "It's the last night of the *Dürkheimer Wurstmarkt*. There will be wine-drinking, and fireworks. Unless you are too tired, after your flight?"

"It's okay," Dave said. "We slept some on the plane. It's much later in the day for you than for us."

"Okay, good then, tonight, the *Wurstmarkt*." Matthias looked down at his list. "And, during the week, there are times I have to work, and times you will eat a meal with Tante Inge, have *Kuchen* and coffee with Tante Gretel and Onkel Otto. And at night, we have things, too. But no matter what happens, next Saturday we have a special treat. It only happens once a month, and it is happening next Saturday, and you can't miss it. We go to see the *Schmiede*."

I nodded as if I understood. Actually, I had no idea, but I was too embarrassed to say so. As we continued to review the schedule, Matthias checked over each activity, often pausing to discuss things in German with his mother.

"And now, unless you want to take a nap or a shower or something, I have the day off, and can give you a tour of Freinsheim. Would you like to do that?" Matthias asked.

Dave and I said we would.

September 21, 2010

Blog Post—Seattle nach Freinsheim

In 1857, Michael Harm traveled from Freinsheim, Germany to New York on the packet ship *Helvetia* with 297 passengers on board. The journey took 43 days. In 2010, Dave and I flew from Seattle to Freinsheim on a Boeing 777, packed to capacity at 440 passengers, in 9 hours and 20 minutes. We flew over the Atlantic under the beacon of a full moon. We arrived at dawn.

My cousin first gave us a walking tour of Freinsheim, and what I've written for my thesis so far has instantly eroded to sandstone rubble. Knowing a place through books is like knowing the German language through an online computer class—sketchy at best. Along the Freinsheim wall walk, we encountered some narrow passagways, one nicknamed "stink alley." Once upon a time there were only two gates in and out of the village, and no houses outside the fortified wall.

I've learned the wine farmer carried a *Logel* on his back, a special barrel backpack for lugging around harvested grapes. Did I mention it's harvest time? I may get to harvest grapes while I'm here—I'm definitely going to sample the vintages.

In the evening we went to the last day of the *Wurstmarkt* in Bad Dürkheim, the oldest and largest wine festival in the world. I'm told the *Wurstmarkt* is celebrating its 570th year. (Official mention of the festival dates to 1830.) Back at the start, farmers wheeled casks of wine to the town in wheelbarrows, set up tents and served food and drink. My cousin tells me the whole point is to cram together, to drink and to laugh and to meet people.

Willkommen auf Deutschland.

The "sandstone rubble" of my thesis had to do with the 1988 trip I'd made to Freinsheim, how my memories collided with the realities of what my eyes beheld twenty-two years later. I had not pictured the Harm family home correctly—the *Hof*, the Freinsheim word for farmhouse—with its walled-in courtyard abutting similar farmhouses lining the narrow streets of the village. This arrangement was so different from American farmhouses, homesteads planted at great distances from one another with acres, sometimes miles, of fields between.

That first day, I also got a glimpse of the hard work and uncertainty of peasant life.

"This keystone in the wall was dug out of a field," Matthias said. "It's called a *Grenzstein*. The K and Z stand for *KirchenZehnt*, church tax. The farmers worked on their own land, but also had to share the work of this land to grow food for the church." I knew the farmers had to pay a portion of their crops to the political rulers, but a church tax, too? It seemed an onerous obligation when they could barely feed their own families.

In my early chapters about Michael's childhood, I had not pictured the caps the men wore and the headscarves and aprons of the women, the four-spigots well for clothes washing, the sulfurous *Gute Brunnen*, a natural well said to have healing properties. As Matthias, Dave and I walked through Freinsheim that first day, my brain worked frantically to revise scenes, embellishing some and abandoning others.

Chapter 26

Somehow, I managed to post a blog entry on my very first day in Germany, and just about every day thereafter. I composed them at the Weber house at the end of each day in an attic room with a sloped ceiling, working beside an old computer Matthias had given his mother. In the days of Ethernet cables, I could easily unplug the Ethernet from Bärbel's desktop, plug it into my laptop, log on and make my posts. My digital camera came with a removable memory card that fit into a card slot in my laptop. Amazingly, everything worked the moment I fired it up.

Writing blog posts also served as a journal for me, and kept me ever alert for what adventure I might share next.

September 22, 2010

Timeless Autumn

We are on our way to Berwartstein, a magnificent castle, apparently one of many in the Wasgau mountains. My pen bumps and dives along the page as I try to take notes from the back seat of an Opel going 140 kilometers per hour.

"There is Hambach Castle, you will go there another day," Matthias shouts back at me above the road noise. "See it on the hill? In 1832, the whole region made a protest, not just Germans, but Poles and Czechs, too, a protest for a parliament with elections, and for a free press." My cousin Matthias Weber is our guide again today, as he was yesterday when we made the wall walk in Freinsheim. Dave is in the front passenger seat, his eyes glued to the *Autobahn* as Matthias barrels us along. "What is that word, for the thing you put the baby in when you put him to sleep at night?"

"A crib?" I shout back.

"That's right. *Gut.* A crib. So then, Hambach is called the crib of Democracy."

I burst into laughter until I have to hold my stomach from the ache. Matthias is mystified. At last I regain enough composure to explain how it sounds funny, because we call it a cradle of Democracy, and "crib" conjures such a strange image. He laughs along.

Later, as we wind along mountain roads, Matthias squeals the car to a stop at the sight of a *"Leiterwagen"*—a ladder wagon—on display in the middle of a field. It's special to this region, Matthias tells me, and of very clever design, since it is made up of two ladders and two sets of wheels. Farmers would arrange the lightweight wagon in various ways for different uses. Because it is collapsible, it is easier to store.

For my part, I'm captivated as much by the wagon as I am by the crocuses all around us—in late autumn! Beautiful purple crocuses sprinkled among the thick green grass— they're called *Herbst-Zeitlose*, Matthias tells me. I've never seen crocuses that bloom in autumn before. I learn the translation later, back at the house—Timeless Autumn.

Ach ja, the food. The well-set *Pfälzer* table. Merrily, we feast. At an afternoon meal, the food is cooked to perfection by Manfred's mother Marliese. We're enjoying *Saumagen* (stuffed sow's stomach), *Leberknödel* (liver meatballs) and Bratwurst, all served with mashed potatoes and sauerkraut. *Und naturlich*, Riesling *Schorles* (wine mixed with mineral water). The weather has been beautiful. We ate in the courtyard of my cousin Manfred Weber's home.

For my daily posts, I had plenty of adventures to recount, including Dave and my train journey to Cologne and a photo collage of the many relatives who invited us to their homes. On the second weekend, Angela arrived from Marburg with her daughters just in time for the annual Freinsheim Wine Hike, an event the whole family took part in. And to solve the mystery of what exactly Matthias's *Schmiede* outing would entail. *Schmiede*, it turned out, meant "blacksmiths" in German. I guess I should have known that already.

September 26, 2010

Friedelsheim Blacksmiths

When my relatives take me to see a historic working blacksmith shop in Friedelsheim (a village not far from Freinsheim), it feels like I'm seeing ghosts of my deceased ancestors. Albeit stalwart ghosts.

When these men laugh, the whole room rumbles. Matthias tells me they are speaking a very heavy Palatine dialect, the kind that booms like a subwoofer from the back of the throat. It's the most authentic blacksmithing I've witnessed to date. Note the coal forge, and the enormous bellows hanging from the ceiling.

"I asked the guy about that," Dave said to me after I'd roamed the shop taking photos of everything in sight. "He said the bellows are just for show. One of these guys had their oven vent fan replaced at home, so they brought the old one down and installed it here. That's what they're really using."

Close enough. After the visit to the *Schmiede*, I study 19th-century relics in a side room— a machine to form iron wheel casings, a drill press, and a leather-punch. When I finally tear myself away, we walk over to a bakery for a peasant "treat"—bread spread with lard, then topped with salt and radishes.

As I posted blogs along my journey, only rarely did I share bad news, like the time I lost my camera. And I only reported that sad tale once I'd found it again. I was filtering my blog posts in part for the sake of my Aunt Elizabeth, not wanting to worry her about things that might not be going so well.

I think it's a natural instinct, not only to keep from revealing our imperfect selves, but also born of a desire not to worry others. The Cleveland letter writers of long ago seemed to have done the same self-filtering. There's so much they didn't say, I'm guessing, about their struggles and challenges and tragedies.

For my blog, I wanted to give news and entertain those reading along, and as I did so, most often I had my Aunt Elizabeth in mind. That second weekend, the last weekend before Dave flew back home, I titled a post "Two Churches" and led off with a line I knew Aunt Elizabeth would appreciate: "Sunday I visited two churches—the Church of my Ancestors, and the Church of German Soccer."

The visit to the church of my ancestors had been especially meaningful for me. The Freinsheim Evangelical Reformed Protestant Church dated back to the 1500s and stood in its sandstone glory in the open, cobblestoned center of town by the Community Hall. The church's slate roof featured a frame for a stork nest, and its round bell tower rose above the other rooftops, its steeple and cross visible from just about anywhere in the surrounding countryside. The bells still rang on Sundays to call people to church, but in former times, they rang every day, to mark when it was time for the farmers to go to the fields, and when to return, and to mark when a person had died in the night, or to sound an alarm. The pealing of the bells was deafening when you were right up close, deep and sonorous, loud enough to be heard for miles.

Actually, I went to church twice that weekend. We fit a visit in on Saturday, too, at the invitation of Tante Inge Faber. Some Saturdays, Tante Inge sat in the church pews as a volunteer to greet tourists who might drop in to admire the 16th-century high, arched ceilings of pink and gray sandstone, or sit in the lustrous dark wood pews. When Dave and Matthias and I arrived, Tante Inge was waiting for me with a gift, a book called *Kleiner Führer Durch Die Protestantische Kirche In Freinsheim* [A Brief Guide to the Protestant Church in Freinsheim], in German and English, which had key information in it relevant to Michael Harm's era.

- 1852: Fiftytwo (sic) people from the parish of Freinsheim emigrate to North America

- 1853: In this year sixtysix (sic) people emigrate

- 1854: The number of emigrants to North America is seventy-nine

What an exodus that must have been, an exodus my great-great grandfather witnessed in his own small village when he was just a boy. It must have seemed as if families disappeared forever almost every week. These numbers added support to the massive emigration of the 1850s I'd learned about at NARA, the boatloads of European peasants arriving daily on American shores.

Sunday morning, I returned for the worship service and sat with the elder relatives—Tante Gretel, Tante Inge, and Bärbel. As I sang the German hymns and listened to the German prayers, of which I understood very little, I felt a deep connection to my ancestors and to the women sitting beside me in the pews.

The Church of German Soccer, on the other hand, was an outing mainly for Dave. Manfred's brother Hans-Günter drove us across the Haardt Mountains to attend the game in Kaiserslautern. It was Dave's last big event before returning home.

It had been fun travelling with my spouse, fun seeing the sights and introducing him to the relatives he'd never met, relatives of both the elder and more recent generations. Then too, at this point, time was pressing in. I couldn't help worrying whether I'd be able to gain access to the Freinsheim historic archives, and when Angela and I would find time to translate my PowerPoint script into German, something I'd pulled together at the last minute before departure.

But most of all, I wanted to live on my own in Freinsheim and build a stronger sense of place in order to write realistic scenes. In an approach similar to my research time in Cleveland, I wanted to absorb sensory imagery—not just visuals, but smells and sounds and tastes. Not as a tourist, but as a young boy might have experienced life in Freinsheim a century and a half ago.

Chapter 27

On the morning of Dave's departure, Angela drove us from Freinsheim to the Frankfurt Airport, where we said good-bye to Dave. Then, she and I continued north to her home town of Marburg.

I'll finally get to work on my thesis, I was thinking as Angela drove us at high speeds on the *Autobahn*. Even as I thought it, I knew I was kidding myself. Close on the heels of my stay with Angela, I'd be making a two-day side trip to Berlin, something I'd planned in advance in order to see my longtime friend Wolf Bielstein. Wolf was not a relative, but a German exchange student who'd lived with my family in 1976, during my final year in high school.

I'd visited Wolf on my trip to Europe in 1988, which was the last time I'd seen him. Trips to Germany happened so rarely, I couldn't resist making plans to see him while here. But I had no need to research the history of Berlin; it really didn't figure into the novel. This side trip would be another few days when I'd have to set aside the thesis. *Too late now*, I thought, inwardly kicking myself for trying to do too much. *At least during these few days, Angela and I will have time to work on translating my talk.*

About an hour after we left Dave at the airport, we pulled into Marburg, a town with an impressive medieval aura. The City of Marburg, located on the Lahn River, has long been the seat of the German region of Hesse. Ancient cobbled streets wind up and around a steep hillside to the city's centerpiece, Marburg's famous Landgrave Castle, formerly the home of the royal family who ruled Hesse for centuries, now a museum of history and culture for the region. The buildings and homes in the old town are pressed against one another along the narrow streets and alleys, their white-washed faces checkerboarded with dark-framed windows and criss-crossed with thick half-timbers.

The apartment where Angela and her family lived was part of a more recent complex, a compound-style structure built in the 20th century. The Otterbeck/Weber apartment looked out over a courtyard of lawns and a

Visit to Schmiede *(blacksmithing) demonstration in Friedelsheim, Germany in 2010.*

playground, a perfect spot for their girls and other children in the area to run and play.

I received a warm welcome from Christoph and the girls Carlotta and Luzi (11 and 6 years old in 2010) and we enjoyed a pleasant, sociable evening. The next morning, as soon as the girls had gone off to school and Christoph to work on a museum exhibit he was curating, I suggested to Angela that she and I work together on the PowerPoint. At least she could see what I'd come up with so far.

But Angela had many things to show me, she pointed out, and we also had errands to run. First things first, we took a long hike through the town to see some sights, then stopped by an Internet café for me to make a blog post, and then to a travel bureau to get my train ticket to Berlin. We shopped for food at the market and returned home to prepare dinner. In the evening, Angela took me to the University of Marburg, where there had been a lecture given by a French scholar on the subject of South American Indigenous cultures.

Angela and I didn't attend the talk, only the champagne reception afterward, as Angela had a friend in particular she wanted to meet up with. I learned that night that when there is an international audience in Europe for a university lecture, say, or a business meeting with several countries represented, English is the language spoken. The students at the reception all spoke fluent English, and the French scholar had given her talk in English. More than one student complained to me about the scholar's presentation, saying her English was poor and difficult to understand. Their English was impeccable.

At the reception, champagne and snacks were served in a dim hallway that gleamed with dark polished wood, arched stone pillars and lead glass windows through which nighttime Marburg gleamed. Angela took me into a room off the hallway to show me large murals on the walls, paintings featuring Luther and Zwingli and other Protestant reformers debating at the Marburg Colloquy. Angela filled me in on some of that history, but I admit I didn't listen all that attentively. It wasn't just the champagne. I was fixated on Palatine history of the 1800s. The argument between Luther and Zwingli at the Marburg Colloquy occurred in 1529 in Hesse. Michael Harm probably had no inkling of it. I felt overcome that evening by a kind of tunnel vision, a desperation to narrow down the subject matter, which was beginning to feel incredibly overwhelming.

Out of politeness, I took photos of the wall murals. By contrast, what really grabbed my interest was the elaborate ironwork of the University of Marburg building's iron railings, scrolled and ornamented, and no doubt forged by blacksmiths centuries ago during the artisan craft era of the guilds. I'm not sure anyone at the reception noticed, but if they had, they might have wondered at the American taking copious photographs of wrought iron balcony railings.

The following day, once everyone else was out of the apartment, Angela suggested we bicycle over to the Waldorf School where her daughters Carlotta and Luzi were in junior high and elementary school. The day was sunny, and we took a pleasant trail along the Lahn River to get there. At the school grounds Angela showed me the mosaic art she had designed and helped the students construct. I'd known for years art was among Angela's many talents, and I admired her creative handiwork.

That afternoon, though, I was feeling distracted and anxious about not having enough time for my research, and about my untranslated script for the presentation. Angela was sharing with me what she'd learned about American contact history during the French-dominated fur trade, which started in the 1600s and 1700s. She guessed there might have also been Palatine fur traders among those French who wintered in Native communities. In some cases, the fur traders had intermarried with the Natives forming trading alliances, which would provide a different background yet to the 19th-century German immigrant experience.

It was only natural Angela would talk to me about this—since the 1990s when she'd first visited me in Seattle she'd been interested in the history of Northwest Native peoples. That afternoon, she offered to look more closely into the contact history in Ohio also, to be sure I didn't rely on stereotypes for my book. As generous as the offer was, it didn't seem like it would help that much. By this point, I'd found out about the Indian Removal Act of 1829, which meant the removal of all Native tribes from Ohio by early 1850. While the MFA faculty member David Wagoner had mentioned to me once about Natives remaining behind and continuing to live in the forests, I hadn't found evidence of that in the Cleveland urban environment, where the thesis story was centered. In the end, I'd veered away from including much about Native Americans in the narrative.

At some point, I confessed to Angela I couldn't assimilate all the things she was telling me. I was just too distracted. I'm not sure she understood, as she continued ahead. As we roamed the garden at the Waldorf School walking beside our bicycles, I tried to follow the thread of her interest in a historical person from the Palatinate named Prince Rupert, who had been involved in the fur trade somehow back in the 1600s.

I was trying to listen, but my brain felt overloaded. Prince Rupert? I had not come across that name in my research, and I felt reluctant to go there. In fact, I was beginning to feel overwhelmed and desperate. If I didn't limit my learning to the 1800s, I'd never get this thesis written.

A queasy sensation came over me that things were growing ever more scattered, that I was losing ground on my thesis instead of gaining it. During my visit to Marburg, I'd been drifting ever farther from the original plan. Sure, the research and history were important, as well as taking the time to consider all the various influences on what happened back then. The irony was not lost on me, how Angela was researching Indigenous cultures of North America, and I was researching the story of white Europeans who ended up eradicating their way of life. But I just didn't see how I could work stuff about the 1600s into the novel. While I appreciated Angela's perspective, her interest lay in a different time period and different population altogether.

I longed just then to write, to reflect, to envision potential scenes and dig deeper for the story. So far on this research adventure, I'd been having great experiences, but every spare minute had been taken up with visiting and touring amid a deluge of new information. There'd been little opportunity to process any of it, and time was ticking away. Next up I'd be whisked off on the train to Berlin to see Wolf, another stretch of days when I wouldn't find a chance to sort out this jumble of new material. As each day succeeded the next, I felt more and more out of my depth.

I don't think Angela could tell how hard I was struggling just then to keep my wits about me, and I doubt I could have articulated it if I'd tried. Regardless of my internal anxiety, the sun beamed down on us as if nothing at all were amiss. Soon enough, we were bicycling back to her apartment. Take it easy, I coached myself as we pedaled along. Stop being so single-minded. I resolved to do my best to chill, to not get so tied up in knots. I needed to trust Angela, and the process.

THE FOLLOWING DAY, WE VISITED more spots in Marburg—among them an ancient Lutheran Church and the home where the Grimms brothers had lived and collected fairy tales in 1802-1803. The sun had disappeared, and a drizzle descended, coating the town in a wet mist, but all the same, as we walked the winding streets and stairways among the gorgeously preserved half-timbered houses, I saw much to admire in Marburg.

At one point as we descended an ancient stone staircase I heard a small, gentle birdsong, and came to a halt. There on a tree branch at eye level perched a small black bird.

"What kind of bird is that?" I asked Angela in a hushed voice.

"We call that an *Amsel*, it's a common bird here."

The *Amsel* didn't fly away, which allowed me to stand rapt listening to its soft, sweet warble. The moment gave me a sense of awe and served as a reminder to me to soak up the impressions and inspirations all around me while I had the chance.

Chapter 28

Perhaps it's the writer in me, but I've never minded traveling alone. The solitude provides me with uninterrupted time to think and write down impressions and experiences in my travel journal, as well as to organize my notes for what's to come.

Once Angela put me on the train to Berlin, though, instead of setting to work, I fell into a funk, regretting how I'd not engaged fully in the Marburg visit. I wished I'd been more appreciative of all Angela wanted to share with me. We'd done the tours of Marburg's key historic sites, but mainly, I'd had the chance to spend time with her family, to share meals and conversation. Her daughters and I had begun collecting words that sounded the same in German and English, but meant different things. An especially amusing word was the German word *Fahrt*. "*Gute Fahrt*," Germans say, meaning "Have a good trip." When I told them what the word fart means in English, we all got a good laugh.

The last night of my visit, Angela's and Christoph's younger daughter, Luzi, was invited to a birthday party for a friend. The parents were invited too, and Angela and Christoph brought me along. The party didn't strike me as much different from an American one, with balloons and decorations, presents, cake and activities, the adults talking together while the children played in their midst. Out in the side yard, the hosts had lit a fire to warm the brisk October air. I was sitting inside talking with Christoph and some of the other parents when Angela rushed inside.

"Claire, where's your camera?" she asked. "You won't believe what they're playing."

I handed Angela my camera and followed her outside. It turned out Luzi had invented a game she called "*Schmiede*," modeling for her friends the method of poking a stick into the fire, waiting for the point to turn red hot, then "forging" it by pounding the red tip with a hammer over on the sidewalk.

"I came to see, because the mother asked me what Luzi wanted with a hammer," Angela said, snapping photos.

Luzi, I realized, was doing just what she'd seen the blacksmiths do in Friedelsheim. I was amazed and impressed.

During the Marburg visit, I'd also been able to see Christoph in his own element, surrounded by his large collection of art books, and to hear about the museum exhibit he was then curating. I spent some one-on-one time with Angela's older daughter Carlotta, now almost 12 years old. We went out for cake at a *Konditorei* (cake and coffee house) on my last afternoon in town. Carlotta was very patient with my bad German, telling me the words for different kinds of cake, and helping me find the right phrases for ordering and paying the bill. Angela and I shopped at the market and prepared meals together and told stories.

I only wished I hadn't felt quite so stressed about the upcoming PowerPoint talk the whole time. Angela and I had never really gotten a chance to work on it. "I'll email you my part in the next few days," she told me, and we left it at that.

The trains in Germany run with efficiency. The seats are roomy, the ride smooth. Some cars even have tables to use as a work space, and I was lucky enough to have one on that leg of the journey. Tearing my gaze away from the ever flatter landscape of northern Germany, I jotted down impressions of the past few days. I read over some notes I'd made and thought about what research still needed to be done. Too much. And the more I learned, the less I knew. I was beginning to suspect everything I'd written so far was wrong. But I couldn't let myself think about that. It was just too frightening.

Not in a good frame of mind to write, not wanting to even think about writing, I flipped open my laptop and began reviewing, slide by slide, the PowerPoint I'd pulled together back in Seattle. Seeing it again for the first time in several weeks, the talk appeared in better shape than I remembered. Back home, I'd found images to go with the history I wanted to share. In addition to the personal family story of Michael and Philipp Harm, I wanted to cover two broader themes: what German immigrants had experienced as they arrived in a foreign land, and what influence German immigrants had on American culture, politics, education and religion. A surprising amount, actually, which I hoped told a compelling story.

I opened the presentation with photos of Whidbey Island, the inspiring, Puget Sound setting where my MFA residencies were held, then switched to old photos of the two brothers, Michael and Philipp Harm, side by side. Angela and I had talked about what letter excerpts to include, which she'd promised me she was going to email while I was in Bremerhaven. While she read the excerpt, I'd show a slide with the digital image of the letter as a place marker. Next it would be my turn again, to talk about German Romanticism

*Chistoph Otterbeck and Angela
Weber at their flat in Marburg,
2010*

and the fascination of 19th-century Germans with America in part inspired by the James Fenimore Cooper novels. Then came a bit of history about the 1848 revolutions, a time when German political activists longed for democracy and pressed for a unified Germany. We planned to talk about the immigrant journey, so I'd added in images of sailing and steam ships on the Atlantic crossing, of the Castle Garden Immigrant Center, and the crowded German immigrant neighborhood called *Kleindeutschland*—Little Germany—in New York City.

For the part about Cleveland, I'd added black-and-white photographs showing German immigrants in the early days: delivering pianos, drinking in beer gardens, playing in brass bands, and putting on physical fitness demonstrations, to show how 19th-century Germans had brought not only themselves to America, but their culture along with them. They'd even introduced the holiday tradition of the Christmas tree.

That was the good news on what I'd accomplished. Now for the bad. The script I'd written was in English, and way too long. As slate-roofed villages and stubble-fields whisked by out my train window, I considered my predicament. My German was too rudimentary to translate the talk on my own. But what if I made a start on it? I only had my German-English pocket dictionary to work with, but still, I had several more hours before the Berlin arrival. *It'll be good practice*, I told myself. *If nothing else, I'll be learning more German.* I pulled out my dictionary and set to work.

DISEMBARKING AT THE MAIN TRAIN station in Berlin, I took another train to the Berlin *Nordbahnhof* [North Train Station] where Wolf and I had arranged to meet. The last time I'd seen Wolf, back in 1988, the Berlin Wall had still been standing. As I exited the train station, now two decades later, I happened upon the Berlin Wall Memorial, located where a small Wall remnant had not been torn down.

It was good indeed to see my old friend, and especially poignant to meet Wolf at that location. He'd told me back in 1988 the Berlin Wall was obsolete and should come down. Twenty-two years later, he and I were able to wander together through the Memorial to what once was. I was deeply moved by the memory of 1989 when East and West Germany were reunited, a historic event that played out dramatically on our TVs in the U.S.

Afterwards, Wolf and I stopped for coffee and started to catch up on many years. Thankfully, Wolf's English was still very good, if not better than when I'd seen him last. He'd become a traditional Freudian Psychoanalyst, he told me, a method not very common in 21st-century times. Wolf wanted to show me his office, so next we went there to see the room where he treated his patients.

His office building had formerly been on the East Berlin side of the Wall, but blended into the cityscape as if there had never been a divide. Upstairs, the room was daylit and uncluttered, the main feature being the ubiquitous couch and chair used for his Freudian psychoanalysis.

We stayed there just a few moments, then headed back down to the street.

"I thought about taking photos," I said to Wolf as we were leaving, "but the room felt like a private space for your patients. I didn't think I should post a blog about it or anything."

Wolf thought for a moment. "I think people like it when you write about them," he said.

His words struck me as very wise.

Wolf drove me to his apartment to meet his wife Katrin and teenage daughter Luiza, and my short two-day stopover in Berlin was off to a pleasant start.

I HADN'T COUNTED ON GETTING any research done in Berlin, but I did all the same. In Wolf's music library, he owned a collection of Schumann's music, including the *Wanderlied*, a 19th-century "wandering song" that captured the homesick sentiments of German emigrants. I took photos of several songs in the book to take home with me for future reference. In the National Gallery (*Nationalgalerie*), we admired paintings of realistic scenes from the 1800s, of people in peasant villages at work and at play, of men toiling in an ironworks factory, and of indoor salons that provided details of period furnishings. The museum guards let me take photos *ohne Blitz* [without flash].

"Look at that lamp," I commented to Wolf as we peered at a Hasenclever oil painting called *The Reading Room*. "It looks more modern than I would have thought."

"Perhaps," Wolf said with an amused smile, "we could pick one up at IKEA."

The second and last day of my visit happened to be October 3, 2010, German Unity Day, an annual celebration of the reunification of East and West Germany. All of Berlin seemed to turn out for the holiday; the streets were packed with festival-goers.

I had not planned to visit Wolf on Reunification Day, it just worked out that way, and felt strangely synchronistic. I looked at things more historically these days, and found myself reflecting on how, until the 19th century, Germany had been separated into many different feudal nation-states. A main goal of the 1848 revolutions had been the desire for a unified Germany, but that had not occurred until 1871. Then, disunity struck again following WWII, the country being divided into East Germany and West Germany, only to be reunified 1989. In more recent times, European nations were joining together, economically, to form the European Union, but that effort was already showing cracks in its veneer with a growing debt crisis.

These ongoing tides of history reminded me of something Angela once mentioned in an email, how the letters from the 19th century reminded us that "good times and years of crisis can follow each other so fast." No wonder German immigrants had inscribed that Goethe quote in the Cleveland Cultural Garden: "One only earns his freedom in this life who daily conquers it anew." They understood from their own experience the fleeting nature of progress.

ALL TOO SOON, I WAS back on the train. I spent the night of October 4, in Bremen at the house of a friend of Angela's. The friend was out of town, but left instructions saying I could use her computer, so I even managed to post a blog for Aunt Elizabeth that evening. I hoped she was reading them. It was hard for me not to know how my aunt was doing. Hard to trust she was fine, although I knew Dave would email if she wasn't. I hoped time was zipping by for her as it was for me.

Then, on October 5, 2010, with two weeks remaining of my twenty-eight day research trip, I arrived early in Bremerhaven, a seaport on the edge of the Atlantic in northern Germany. Not the port from where Michael Harm or my ancestors shipped out. They'd traveled overland through France and left from the port at Le Havre. Nonetheless, Bremerhaven had been the debarkation point for millions, and was the present-day site of the state-of-the-art German Emigration Museum (*Deutsches Auswandererhaus*). Angela had been to the museum a few years earlier and encouraged me to go.

As I made my way out of the train station in Bremerhaven, a cultural detail caught my eye, a line of young men standing at stiff attention, each beside a duffle bag. A uniformed military officer paced back and forth before them. Instantly, the scene reminded me of how military service was still compulsory for German young men. When we'd been teenagers, Wolf and I had talked from time to time about how he'd have to serve in the German military for at least one year. Either that, or work at some compulsory community service. He'd opted for the latter. By 2010, the conscription term had been reduced to six months. (In 2011, mandatory conscription in Germany was fazed out altogether.)

Luzi Weber tries out blacksmithing.

While the oral history of Michael Harm's emigration didn't support it, a plausible theory for his departure at age fifteen could have been draft dodging. In the mid-19th century, all young men were liable to serve in the Bavarian military. In Bremerhaven that morning, my heart went out to these young men arriving for duty, for their lack of choice in the matter.

At the Emigration Museum, I had just one day to seek answers to so many questions. Writing scenes of the transatlantic crossing, I'd had trouble grasping what conditions had been like. I'd been on an ocean cruise liner once, but never a three-masted sailing ship. I had been able to find out that a three-masted "packet" ship in those days operated on a regular schedule and carried mail "packets" from continent to continent. On the journey from east to west, the ship's cargo was mostly mail and emigrants. On the journey from west to east, ship carried mail and U.S. exports, mainly cotton, tobacco, sugar and grain. All well and good, but not enough for me to imagine scenes on board.

The museum that morning was crowded with what looked to be students on a high school field trip. In an early part of the tour, weaving among chattering young people, I learned about the various waves of emigration and the main reasons people had left in each time period. On a plaque on the wall, I scanned the number of emigrants who left between 1850 and 1860; the total came to a little over one million. The figure was humbling, driving home how in that decade, my ancestor Michael Harm had been just one of a million other emigrant souls.

In the next rooms I entered a living history exhibit of life at sea. The interiors of ships from three different eras were on display. I dwelled the longest on the ship from the year 1854, a type of boat very similar to the one on which Michael Harm had sailed. I worked my way slowly passed the dark, cramped wooden platform bunks of steerage. All along, I'd been picturing hammocks; it turned out those had been used by the crew in their quarters. I examined the wash rooms and cook area and cabins. The emigrants brought with them their own tin plates and cups and stored them in racks along the wall. Travelers had to supply their own mattresses, which consisted of cloth bags stuffed with straw purchased just prior to departure.

Another exhibit showed the quarters on a steamship quite similar to the one Michael Harm traveled on during his return to Germany in 1893. Being able to wander around in life-sized replicas gave me just what I needed to write those scenes.

In the final room, computers lined the walls, allowing visitors the opportunity to search the German Emigrants Database of all European emigrants to North America between 1820 and 1939. I typed in Michael Harm and his name showed up, departing Bremen on the ship *Hansa*, arriving in New York on October 10, 1864.

This data confirmed the 1869 letter reference to a journey Michael Harm had made to Freinsheim five years before, possibly just after the death of his mother. I was glad to have the information, but knew I wouldn't include it in the thesis. One day, I knew, I'd need to write the true genealogical narrative of Michael Harm, to set the record straight for future generations.

Chapter 29

On Wednesday, October 6, I took the eight-plus hour train journey from the northern flatlands back down to the rolling hills of the Rhineland-Palatinate, back to Freinsheim. The long hours on the train afforded me the opportunity to translate the rest of my presentation script. All that remained was Angela's scrutinizing eye for grammar. While I'd been away in Bremen and Bremerhaven, I did receive an email with her notes about the contents of her talk, and adjusted slides accordingly. We'd give our first presentation, the one to the relatives, that coming Sunday.

I only had ten days left in Germany. For the duration, I'd be staying in Freinsheim in the flat at Bärbel's, an arrangement I looked forward to. Bärbel's English was as basic as my German, so we did not have the easiest time communicating, but we got along. Most of the time, she resided in the large house on Hauptstrasse by herself. Back in 1984, her husband Rudi Weber had died from complications of diabetes. As a widow, after raising Matthias and Angela through their remaining teenage years, she'd worked as a kindergarten teacher in a children's hospital and looked after her elderly parents. Now that her parents had passed away, Bärbel spent her days doing church work and maintaining the large house and gardens. Each morning, she woke early and walked across the street to the baker and butcher to pick up fresh foods for her table. In the evenings, she enjoyed attending talks and concerts.

As I arrived back in Freinsheim among the now-familiar sandstone houses with their orange tiled roofs, I hoped I could spend the next several days mentally traveling back in time, to come as close as I could to what it might have been like to "be Michael Harm."

My first morning back, Bärbel and I talked about my schedule. She and Angela and Matthias had made several plans for me: a visit to a local history museum in the neighboring town of Bad Dürkheim, a meeting with the retired Evangelical Protestant pastor of Freinsheim, a bicycle tour with Matthias and Ina, and so on. She explained it all with carefully enunciated German,

Anna Kitsch Faber and Helene Kitsch Weber, Freinsheim sisters who wrote to my grandmother, Emma Hoppensack Patterson.

attempting English words whenever I frowned or looked confused.

"*Aber ist dieser Morgen frei?*" I asked, wanting to know if that morning was free, with no immediate plans.

Bärbel looked around and shrugged. "*Der Besuch mit Herrn Walter ist um zehn Uhr, danach is der Mittag frei.*" After a visit with the Protestant pastor Herr Walter, Bärbel assured me, the noon hour would be free.

Unsure what I'd learn from the retired minister, I felt reluctant to lose valuable time visiting him. However, like so many other experiences I'd had, when I arrived at his home, my doubts were once again unfounded. The kind, elderly Herr Walter spoke English with a charming British accent, and was a passionate scholar of history. In particular, Freinsheim history.

First, Herr Walter told me the story of Pfarrer Bickes, who had been the Evangelical Protestant pastor in 1849 when Michael Harm was a boy in the village. It was Pfarrer Bickes who had convinced the Freinsheim villagers not to fight the Prussian Prince Wilhelm and his troops, because the Prince was known for harsh repression of rebels. Prince Wilhelm had come to the Palatinate at the invitation of the Bavarian King to crush the "Free Corps" movement for democracy then fomenting. I'd heard a similar account from Matthias earlier that spring, and was glad to have more details.

Next, Herr Walter launched into an account of a peasant rebellion in 1525 in the Freinsheim region, a year when peasant bondsmen revolted, burning castles and killing some knights. The authority of the region in those days was the Prince-Elector of Heidelberg, who ordered the beheading of the rebels in the Freinsheim marketplace and forced all the citizens to be present to witness the executions. Herr Walter concluded his account by saying: "Some things are burned into the memories of the people, especially bitter things."

I scribbled down what I could in my notebook. Listening to the pastor narrate history, I wished he was the one writing this book, not me. I needed to capture that quality, the voice of a first person narrator. But so far, I'd written the whole thesis in third person, and it sounded nothing like this. What it sounded like, if I was truly honest with myself, was an American narrator living in modern times. It sounded remote from anything real and lacked the ring of truth.

With crushing clarity, I realized that after all this time and effort, I still had no idea what I was doing. I was an MFA candidate just shy of 53 years old. It wasn't like I'd actually earned a graduate-level degree. I'd never

Three generations of Cleveland correspondents: Elizabeth Harm, Emma Patterson, and Lucy Hoppensack.

published a book. Yet here I was, traipsing all over Germany claiming to be a writer. I had some kind of nerve, and all at once it looked to me like this could end very badly. Who did I think I was?

After my visit with Herr Walter, instead of going back to Bärbel's, I took a detour through the old town's main *Eisentor* gate and out into the countryside to gather my thoughts. The rural town of Freinsheim, with a population of approximately 5,000, is small enough that it takes less than an hour to walk from one end to the other. Just outside the main gate of the ancient, crumbling wall, I passed by the house where Prince Wilhelm was said to have stayed in 1849. Since that one brief moment in Freinsheim history, the house has ever after been called the *Kaiserhaus*. Thinking back to what I'd written in those early scenes, I shuddered at how little I captured. I was in way over my head.

Continuing onward, I strolled through the vineyards and along a dirt track beside a brook, listening to bird song and to farmers hailing one another from their tractors. I inhaled the acrid smoke drifting from a pile of burning grapevines and noted snails feasting on roadside weeds. I knew the landscape had altered since the 1840s and 1850s when Michael was a boy, but tried to picture childhood scenes in this setting—boys playing under the massive branches of a willow tree, or lining up armies of horse chestnuts for battle on a cleared patch of ground.

I wished Dave was with me. These days when I posted my daily blogs, I thought not only of Aunt Elizabeth, but also of Dave. I imagined my husband following my adventures from afar, and, during my long absence, feeding our cat Gracie and commuting daily to his office in Seattle.

From time to time in the past weeks, Dave had emailed me cheerful notes, about how he'd talked to the next door neighbor Chuck about the length of

View of Freinsheim from the cemetery gate.

our grass, and Chuck had suggested maybe Dave could bring in a couple of cows to avoid having to mow it. About how our son George went to Salem, Oregon with Dave to see Vivian, then in her freshman year at Willamette University, for Parents' weekend, an event I was disappointed to have missed.

Wandering aimlessly around the outskirts of Freinsheim, I came eventually upon the cemetery, which I'd not yet visited during this stay. My parents had been here, long ago. I knew this because I recognized the front gate, which Dad had photographed and enlarged. On my wall at home, I had the framed photo, the view looking from inside the cemetery gate out to the surrounding countryside, in the direction of the village of Freinsheim nestled among vineyards and hills.

I stepped through the entrance and took in the array of gravestones. Encircled by a stone wall, the graveyard lay in the shadow of the ruin of a chapel tower built in the 11th century. That structure was there centuries before my Harm ancestors first arrived from Stuttgart in the mid-1700s. Around the tower, each grave plot closely abutted the next, seemingly in an effort to conserve space. On the headstones of many different sizes, shapes and styles, I spotted familiar names: Harm, Weber, Faber, Kitsch.

If these dead souls somehow knew what I was up to, what would they think? Could they see me plainly for who I was? I was being treated so graciously by their descendants. I had been offered so many insights, so much friendship and trust. Yet I didn't have a single decent page to show for my efforts, nor for theirs. How on earth had things gotten so out of control? I went around saying I was a writer, but that didn't make it so. I'd made a bad start, and seriously doubted I'd ever be able to fix what I'd done, let alone turn it into a book.

Regardless, I had to go through the motions. I had to keep pretending. Angela would be arriving in Freinsheim again that coming weekend. Our presentation for the relatives, our "trial run" before we gave our talk for the Bad Dürkheim history club, would take place that coming Sunday. Whatever else happened, for the moment the talk took precedence, which, when it came to that, was another mess crying out for attention.

But I didn't have time to work on the presentation, either. Matthias and Ina had arranged a bicycle tour for me tomorrow, which I'd been looking forward to with anticipation all week. I couldn't say no. I didn't want to say no.

I sighed in frustration. Maybe I just wasn't cut out for this. For a while longer, I stood in the dappled shade of the graveyard, visiting the graves of my ancestors, in particular those of the two women, Helene Weber and Anna Faber, who'd written letters to my grandmother all those years. Though they'd never had the chance to meet my grandmother in person, even so, the original love between two brothers had endured, lasting five generations. Inwardly, I said a special thanks to them. Then, time was up. Bärbel was waiting for me back at the house. Turning to leave, I exited back out through the iron gate and headed toward town.

Saturday morning dawned sunny and warm, perfect weather for a bike ride.

October 10, 2010

Fahrrad Tour [bicycle tour]

Today is Saturday, and Matthias and Ina have invited me along on several outings. First, we purchase wine at Lebenshilfe, which produces them organically. It is a work cooperative for people with special needs. The grapes are grown on hillsides not accessible by machine. Matthias has the responsibility of buying wine for several family members. To buy wine, of course, one must first taste it.

Next, lunch (including a healthy dose of water to recover my senses), and after that, a *Fahrrad* (bicycle) tour. We cruise the vineyards—there are many paths among them—and stop at a restored Roman ruin (a winery operating from 100 A.D. to 350 A.D.). Matthias tells me how the Romans brought peaches and figs and certain kinds of grapes and apples to the region.

In Forst, we drink new wine at a roadside stand. (The red one has a hint of cherry and goes down like sweet juice.) Oh happy day.

"It seems to me that the Palatinate is like the California of Germany," I say to Matthias.

> He sits up straighter. "Or it could be," he says, "California
> is the Palatinate of the United States."

FINALLY, THE LONG-ANTICIPATED SUNDAY OF the family presentation
arrived. Angela and I were both staying at her mother's house. That morning,
immediately after breakfast, we hunkered down to work in the downstairs
living room where the talk would take place. For some reason, perhaps
because the dining room table had been moved to make room for the chairs,
I remember Angela working on her laptop spread out on the floor, trying
in haste to correct my German translation of my script, which I'd proudly
emailed to her. The effort I'd put in, however, did not appear to have saved her
any work.

"I can't tell what you're trying to say here," she said more than once, staring
at her screen with obvious exasperation. "So much has to be corrected. Show
me your English version so I have something to compare."

My German must be worse than I imagined, I thought ruefully.

To add to the challenges, Angela and I did not have the luxury of
uninterrupted concentration. Both of her daughters, Carlotta and Luzi, played
in the same room with us and often demanded her attention. Angela's mother
also needed to know what Angela thought about refreshments for the guests,
and how many to expect. Angela kept her face glued to her computer screen
trying to work as she called out replies to her mom and her kids, clearly under
terrific pressure. I realized once again how much I relied on her, how much
I needed her help for this project of mine. And her children needed her, too.

I wished I could do something to alleviate the stress, maybe help Bärbel
set out the plates and coffee cups and wine glasses, but I also needed time
to practice pronouncing the German words in my part of the script. We'd
titled our talk "Tracing 19th-century Emigrants," which in German was:
Spurensuche Auswanderer aus dem Neunzehnjahrhundert. A mouthful in
itself. I kept tripping over the words, especially *Neunzehnjahrhundert* [19th
century], which I had to repeat many times throughout the talk.

Plus, I was suffering from nerves. Honestly, I couldn't imagine how anyone
would choose to spend a gorgeous sunny afternoon listening to me, the nosy
American, presenting herself as a pseudo-historian. An American telling
Germans about German history. It was almost laughable.

As we worked through my script sentence by sentence amidst the hubbub,
I could tell my German was sketchy enough that I didn't understand half of
what I'd be reading. However, I did pick up on a spot where Angela had added
a phrase.

"Angela, what's this part in here, am I reading it right? About how the wars in the 20th century erased all the good things that happened before?"

"Yes, I thought that should be in there."

"But I'm not talking about the 20th century and the wars. This is before any of that happened."

"We talked about that, though, about how no one talks about the emigration, about how the wars took over our history, so we don't even realize how it used to be."

"That's one interpretation. People listening to our talk might come to that conclusion. Or they might not. I'd like them to draw their own conclusions. I'm going to take that part out."

I didn't like to argue, but felt strongly about it. When it came to my thesis, the wars were not the point. Not the wars of the 19th century, nor of the 20th century. I was writing about the stuff of everyday lives, about the little guy, the everyman forever forced to adapt and survive come what may.

I drew a line through that part, and then we had to call it done. The guests were beginning to arrive. We'd shaped it up enough, I hoped, to make it worth their while. I hadn't imagined it would be a big crowd, but was pleasantly surprised. Tante Inge Faber brought her son Wolf, who'd made a long drive from his home to Freinsheim to be there, and whom I'd never met before. Tante Gretel and Onkel Otto Kopf and their daughter Sigrid Steil attended. Manfred Weber and his family came, his brother Hans-Günter and Stephanie Weber as well, plus Tante Marliese Weber, Bärbel's sister Sybille, and Matthias and Ina. All the chairs—almost twenty—were filled.

Despite the beautiful Sunday outside, my relatives arrived to sit in a darkened room. After the greetings, I went to my place by the PowerPoint and watched everyone settle loyally into their chairs. As they gazed toward Angela and me, waiting for us to begin, their expressions were a bit uncertain, it seemed to me, as if they weren't quite sure what they'd gotten themselves into. Angela made some opening remarks, all in German, about the letters we'd found. Then, I clicked on the PowerPoint showing pictures of Whidbey Island, began to read from my script, and off we went.

Angela and I alternated, taking turns explaining about the emigrant experience, and she read excerpts of the letters. We talked about the bank failures and rapid industrialization in the 19th century. I especially enjoyed being able to share what I'd learned about the influence of German immigrants to America: how they'd introduced singing clubs and physical fitness clubs to a pioneer culture; how they'd brought better gardening methods and skilled artisan crafts; and helped elect Abraham Lincoln to the presidency. I talked about the temperance movement, and the English Protestant campaigns at that time against alcohol that included Bible-toting Women's Christian Temperance Union groups praying on their knees inside German saloons.

When I talked about the English efforts to shut the German wine import trade down, some frowned with disapproval. Wine was still an important export business for their region today.

Later, I talked to Angela about my impressions of the talk, especially when people first arrived. "They looked a bit guarded, like they were worried about what they might hear."

"Germans are always like that when they attend a talk," Angela said. "The mood is very serious. We were all looking forward to it. Actually, I thought then, in the living room before our talk, how the relatives had an openness to you because you were your parents' daughter. They remembered Clyde and Ruth, and seeing you was like an extension of their relationships with them. Actually, they were more open than usual."

Angela told me how some of the family members only saw each other or socialized to such an extent when the Americans came, first when it had been my father and mother, and in later years with my brothers and me.

When we talked about the whirlwind preparations just before the gathering, Angela admitted to me that she was often doing things last minute, which was usually stressful for everybody involved. She thought probably she should have warned me about that.

After the presentation, the family all migrated to the glass-paned garden room for wine, treats, and conversation. The mood was upbeat, congratulatory, and full of laughter. I couldn't understand everything, but Angela told me later people had really appreciated my perspective and learning more about the life circumstances of emigrants once they'd left Germany. They had also appreciated Angela's and my common effort to bring both sides of the story together.

The lighter mood, and the sense of relief I felt, brought to mind the admonition of my professor to keep my sense of humor. I regretted taking the whole thing way too seriously. As we sat together and shared stories, I enjoyed being among all the generations, the elders, those of my own age and the youngest, Carlotta and Luzi, who were playing with their Uncle Matthias, giggling and basking in his attention. The reception of these relatives felt like an embrace. Somewhere along the way, they'd become more than just the relatives, they'd become family.

Chapter 30

That following week in and around Freinsheim, a trail of insights drew me ever closer to the childhood experiences of my great-great grandfather. As my relatives took me on tours of local farms and history museums, I learned more about agriculture, peasant lifestyles, clothing, politics, and military conflicts. Through all the insights gained, it became more and more obvious to me how, in my thesis draft so far, I hadn't gotten it right. I'd been imagining peasants had some power over their lives, but they weren't free. A tradesman could not cross state lines, or even go from village to village without a special passport called a *Wanderbuch*. A man had to prove he had property in order to marry. Taxes were onerous, and all men liable for military conscription.

The oral history of Michael Harm made no mention of any of this. I had no idea where his parents stood concerning politics, for instance. Did they stand with the Free Corps rebels, or with the Catholic government in Bavaria? Or did they not have the means to do more than eke out a meager existence? Inheritance laws stipulated that land was to be divided equally among the children, male and female alike. Perhaps the Harm family had enough farmland to sustain only one family? Or perhaps they wanted at least one son to escape military conscription? Whatever the reasons for Michael Harm's departure, it was quite clear Angela had been right all along. Michael Harm could not have run away. He was either sent, or departed with his parents' blessing.

And there remained yet another mystery in the oral history. Dad had written it down in our family tree, just in case we forgot. "Michael Harm hated farm work, followed a music band, blacksmith apprentice, Cleveland."

Followed a music band? What did that mean? The reference had always intrigued me. I had learned by then that music was an important part of Michael Harm's life. But "followed a music band"? How did that work?

At some point, I mentioned the music band reference to Bärbel. Her eyes lit up. She and Angela talked in German for a while, and then Angela turned to me.

"My mother suggests we go to the *Pfälzer Musikantenland Museum*. They talk all about the music bands there. We can go when we have our meeting with Dr. Paul in Kaiserslautern."

Bärbel and Angela's daughter Luzi wanted to go along. We agreed to make a day of it.

The *Musikantenland Museum*, housed in an old medieval castle called the *Burg Lichtenburg* in the western Palatinate, unveiled for me another historical trend in the 19th century. The Palatinate is divided by the Haardt Mountains. To the east is rich farmland in the Rhine Valley. West of the mountains, the soil is less arable. In the hope of making money to feed their families, men of the western Palatinate began forming music bands. During the long, mostly idle winters, they would rehearse, and during the summers, take their shows on the road.

At first, the bands travelled locally, but as the railroads became more prevalent and the popularity of the music bands increased, they ranged ever farther, performing in Russia and Scandinavia and eventually, in North America. By the late 19th and early 20th century, Machenbacher was the common U.S. term for this type of music. Several of these bands achieved international acclaim and drew large crowds. They might have continued entertaining for longer than they did, if not for the onset of the Great War in 1914, an era when anti-German sentiment grew strong around the world and the bands were no longer in demand.

As we toured the museum exhibits, I wondered how these traveling bands played a part in Michael Harm's emigration story. The details were compelling, the displays showing elaborate bandwagons, the musical instruments and uniforms and maps of where they traveled. But if Michael Harm didn't run away, how did the music band story fit?

After we quit the museum, our next stop was in Kaiserslautern, where Angela had arranged for us an appointment with Dr. Roland Paul, a renowned scholar and head of the Institute of Palatine History and Culture. He'd co-written *300 Jahre Pfälzers in Amerika* with Karl Scherer and also published immigration letters and diaries. As I understood it, we'd come to talk with him about the value of our letters, but as we waited in the lobby, I picked up a brochure and discovered this Institute held some 300,000 emigration records going back 300 years. The full weight of the honor of this meeting hit me full force. How I wished I'd prepared a list of names and dates of family ancestors to trace.

As we entered Dr. Paul's office and engaged in cordial introductions, it was obvious he spoke English fluently. Roland Paul wore his brown hair cropped close to his head, his neat appearance as tidy as his language ability. The three of us sat down and there was an uncertain pause. Then, Angela asked Dr. Paul in English about Palatine emigration in the 1700s, which they discussed for a while. As I listened, the arrival of my ancestors in 1840 began to seem recent by comparison. Michael Harm, I realized, had been not at the forefront, but at the tail end of the wave of migration from the Palatinate.

Next, Angela asked Dr. Paul about the possibilities for publishing our letters. Dr. Paul agreed our collection was valuable and rare, and would have been even more valuable if we also had the letters of reply written from the German relatives writing to America. Angela added I'd come along with questions about my thesis. They both turned to me and I launched into how, based on these nonfiction letters, I was writing historical fiction to capture the more universal emigration story of that era. Casting about for a way to convey my theme, I explained I'd decided the thesis title should be "Something To Tell About" based on the quote by Matthias Claudius.

"When someone goes on a journey, he has something to tell about," I said, to clarify the reference.

Dr. Paul nodded, almost dismissively. "Yes, it is a common quote here: *Wenn jemand eine Reise tut, so kann er was erzählen.*" The phrase rolled effortlessy off his tongue.

I was impressed. "I'm afraid most Americans aren't familiar with the saying," I said, "or Matthias Claudius, so the title might not work for an American audience."

Dr. Paul made a "pff" sound, similar to the way the French react to ridiculous notions. "We are very familiar with Claudius here, and also the songs of Krenz."

I felt a jolt of surprise. "Really? You know about Krenz? Most Americans don't know of Krenz, or the emigration songs. I wouldn't either, except I came across the songs in the back of a book called *Cleveland and Its Germans*. When it comes to that, most Americans don't even know about *Die Lorelei.*"

Dr. Paul didn't seem to know how to respond to this, perhaps because the legend of Lorelei is so well-known among Germans. I'd learned by then that Lorelei is a slate rock on the Rhine River said to look like a bewitching woman who has lured many sailors to shipwreck. The Romantic poet Heinrich Heine wrote a poem called "*Die Lorelei,*" later set to music by composers Clara Schumann, Liszt and Strauss. Although Americans might not recognize its origins, Lorelei exists in modern lore, too: in a song by The Pogues, in an episode of Star Trek, and as a trainer in the Elite Four class of Pokémon.

Angela said something to Dr. Paul in German. I concentrated hard trying to understand what she'd asked, and what Dr. Paul said in reply, but I couldn't make it out. Even after these several weeks in Germany, I couldn't understand much of anything being said. I found it impressive how courteous Germans generally were, how they'd willingly speak English to allow me to be part of the conversation.

"Really?" Angela turned to me, her expression one of amused amazement. "I asked about Michael going with a music band. He says this is not unusual, this story."

"Yes," Dr. Paul said in English, "it's what many Germans say about those who emigrated, an explanation of how the people who left were not serious, they didn't want to do the work. A metaphor."

I sat back, stunned. What a revelation. Dad had proudly recorded this history on our tree, the gist of which was that our ancestor Michael Harm was a *Luftikus*, an idler. All along, Dad had understood this account to be a real story about an actual incident. But maybe it wasn't? Who among our family had talked of Michael Harm this way? Did it truly reflect something about his character? Or did it reveal more about those who remained behind, who needed a rationalization for the choice they'd made to remain? True or not true to Michael Harm's life, I reveled in the complexities of it. A traveling music band, I decided, had to be included in the thesis, regardless.

"Of course, the singing societies in the Palatinate were very important," Dr. Paul added. "But not for the reason you might think. Political gatherings were forbidden, so the men met in singing clubs, but they were also meeting to secretly talk politics."

Another surprising revelation. Somehow, I'd not come across this key detail in anything I'd been reading so far. It was a gift, offering me important nuances about what life had truly been like back then.

Chapter 31

Angela remained with me for the week in Freinsheim. One thing she especially wanted to show me was her plum field, a grove of trees growing wild amid acres and acres of vineyards.

"It is hard to keep the blackberries from taking over," she told me as we wandered through the tall grasses under the trees.

I took in her overgrown orchard, and the plowed and planted vineyard rows stretching all around. I'd learned so many things by then about the farmland here, how in Michael Harm's time the crops had been diverse. In addition to grapevines, which most families cultivated on a small scale, crops ranged from wheat to currants, from flax to cabbages to asparagus. In the 1700s, tobacco had been a crop, until the American production made that unprofitable. By the late 19th century, orchards had supplanted many fields, mainly apples, plums and cherries. Now, most of the orchards had ceded to grapevines and asparagus. Wine harvesting methods had changed, as well. Grapevines used be grown much closer to the ground, forcing the farmers to stoop over to harvest the grapes. I'd seen old oil paintings at museums depicting the low grape rows, the farmers stooped over them. These days, vineyards were trained to grow much higher, not to spare people's backs, but for harvesting grapes by machine. All historical details I would not have known, had I not come to Germany.

On October 13, 2010, just four days before I headed home, it was time for Angela and me to give our long-anticipated talk for the history club in Bad Dürkheim. The rehearsal with family had gone well enough, but I still felt nervous and apprehensive about speaking German in front of a public audience.

At the presentation venue, a room in an upper floor of the building that housed the *Bad Dürkheim Heimatmuseum*, Angela did all the initial talking with the club leader regarding the PowerPoint set up and what to say for introductions. As the hour for the presentation neared, I sat by the laptop and projector while people filed in singly or in pairs, perhaps a dozen in all. Mostly they were casually dressed, only one or two among them wearing business attire as if just coming from work.

Angela introduced us, and then I clicked on the first slides and began reading from my German script. While Angela talked, I clicked slides from time to time, and otherwise took in the room and the people. As she read a letter excerpt, I watched one white-haired, white-bearded man leaning back with hands folded across his belly listening intently, chuckling now again, apparently at various turns of phrase. A tanned, tweed-jacketed man cocked one ear, every so often nodding in appreciation.

Afterwards, Angela asked club members questions that might help with our research, for instance if anyone knew of particular reasons for emigration during that time period, perhaps the potato famine or other causes? One gentleman replied in German. Angela told me later he'd been explaining about the Indonesian volcano of 1815, which clogged the planetary atmosphere with so much ash that 1816 was the "year without a summer," a time when crops never ripened and many people starved.

"I hadn't heard of that," she told me. I hadn't come across it in my research, either.

I confessed to Angela on the drive back to Freinsheim that several people had spoken to me afterward at length in German. "I'm just so sorry I didn't understand a word they were saying."

Angela laughed. "That's funny. You gave your talk in German, so of course they thought you could speak it. You sounded so scholarly and professional."

I was pleased to hear it, and relieved we'd put the presentation behind us.

In yet another example of the generous Palatine hospitality that last week, Tante Gretel and Onkel Otto Kopf invited Angela and me over a second time for coffee and *Kuchen* (German-style cake), and to meet Sigrid Steil and her family. And also, to share a surprise.

"We have found another letter!" Onkel Otto announced.

Tante Gretel beamed at us from her place at the head of the dining room table, then stood somewhat stiffly and made her way to a dark wood desk along one wall of the living room. She and Onkel Otto were into their eighties by then. Wearing her tailored gray skirt and cardigan, with her white hair gently coiffed and her blue eyes sparkling, Tante Gretel reminded me so much of my grandmother. Grandmother had had a similar spry, diminutive frame, and often wore a similar gray suit, one of her favorites, for special occasions.

Tante Gretel rustled through some papers on the desk, picked one up and turned back to us, holding it in front of her like an offering.

"*Ein Brief von Achtzehnhundert sechs-und-funfzig,*" Tante Gretel said with emphasis, then paused to think. "Eighteen hundred fifty-six," she said for my benefit, then continued in German in a voice warm with excitement.

"What?!" Angela turned to me. "She says it's another letter written by Johann Rapparlie. They found it in their old papers. It tells how Rapparlie lost his leg."

"Johann did? No. It was Rapparlie's wife Katherina who lost her leg," I said.

Angela shook her head like she shared my disbelief. An expectant pause ensued as Tante Gretel came back to the table, moved aside the china cups and plates in front of Onkel Otto, and spread the letter out before him. As he leaned over the Old German Script, I realized I needed to catch every word, so dug hastily in my backpack for my audio recorder.

I managed to push the record button just as he started to read out the contents, translating to English as he went.

30 April 1856

Much beloved brother-in-law and sister-in-law,

Now that I have a good opportunity to write a few lines to you, so I want to send them to you with my neighbor or maybe you can directly speak with him about how it goes with us and has been going in the last 2 years.

I am still alive and have my health back like before but my foot has been taken away from me approximately 12 Zoll[1] below the knee where I had been lying on the sickbed for approximately 21 months before they have taken the foot away from me. I have taken the chance for such a long time until I saw that if I wouldn't let it be removed I wouldn't be able to live another 2 days in this world.

I have had to pay 12 hundred dollars for the doctor bill in 2 1/2 years that was because I have needed our professor from the university[2] who never makes a visit to a sick person or broken leg charging less than 5 dollars and at the beginning he came three times a day because I was so dangerously sick. Later I have thanked and ended with this professor's care and needed another one. But unfortunately it was no help. I have used all the doctors in the area where one believed they understood but dear

1   A zoll is an obsolete measure equaling approximately 1 inch.
2   Presumably, the Medical Department of Western Reserve College that once stood on E. 9th and St. Clair, founded in 1843.

God it was no help the leg had to be removed. My first
doctor or professor had told me that before that the leg
could not be healed it had to be removed. But at first
I didn't want to accept that. I kept saying, first remove
my head then my foot. But if one has three young boys[3]
and my wife, then my heart became heavy. Then I gave
in. Then the doctors removed my leg on the edge of life
and death. Dear brother-in-law and sister-in-law, I have
endured more than a beast of burden could ever endure.
Amidst all of that, in addition, my house burned down
where in my sickness I almost burned in it but I did not
despair. Always I waited firmly for improvement. Praise
and thanks to God I am now quite healthy again like
before but I have to walk on two crutches. Now I will have
an artificial foot made for me in Philadelphia which will
cost me again 150 dollars without travel cost.

Now I want to close this my time is short because Frey
from Rheingönnheim has promised to certainly deliver
these few lines to you and he is in such a hurry if not I
would have written more to you. If Frey should come to
you, he can tell you about all of my condition. Last year,
I have rebuilt my house which was burned down [it cost
me] 2700 dollars. My business is still going well. I now
have four [forge] fires going with eight blacksmiths, five
wheelwrights, three painters and two saddlers [4]and [I] do
all the organizing.

Our brother-in-law Jakob is still single and is still with us.
He earns a large wage and receives two dollars per day.
Our brother-in-law Scheuermann is still quite healthy and
[also his] wife and has two boys and works as a barrel-
maker craftsman. Jakob works in a manufactory where
the locomotives are made for the rail road. My family is
all quite healthy and so [are] all of us and we stay your
faithful ones brothers and sisters and brother-in-law and
we hope that these few lines will meet you in as good
health as they have left us,

---

3   Johann (8/25/1849), Jacob Rapparlie (9/7/1851), William Rapparlie
    (2/7/1854)

4   Also known as trimmers or upholsterers, who sewed seat cushions and dashes
    for fine coaches.

John Rapparlie

As Onkel Otto finished reading, I glanced over at Angela, at her stunned gray-blue eyes.

"If not for this letter, we would never have known it was Johann Rapparlie," she said in a tone of hushed awe.

It had been Johann Rapparlie, the Cleveland blacksmith shop owner himself, who'd had his foot amputated. When Angela and I had read the 1858 letter, which contained Katherina Rapparlie's signature just under the note in the margin about the leg, we'd assumed it was her note, her leg. All this time, we'd misunderstood.

While the others talked and exclaimed in German, I laid out the documents on the dining table and snapped photos. Such good fortune, I marveled, during a simple afternoon gathering with family for *Kuchen* and coffee. On the walk back, it occurred to me how the presentation Angela and I had given at Bärbel's must have spurred the discovery of this remarkable letter. Angela had been hoping all along for this outcome, that the family gathering would prompt further information. And so it had.

Chapter 32

I'd been in Germany almost a month, and the tug to return home, to my family, to Aunt Elizabeth, grew stronger with each passing day. With all that was happening, though, I hardly had time to dwell on it.

Every single day, we headed out on new adventures. To the vacation mansion of King Ludwig of Munich, called *Ludwigshöhe*, where tall yellow-leaved chestnut trees stood in majestic rows along the drive, littering the ground with their prickly-skinned shells. Matthias showed me how to peel the chestnuts, removing the bitter inner skin, for a delicious snack eaten raw. Chestnuts are a fall staple in Palatine cuisine, used in soups and sometimes in the *Saumagen* (stuffed sow's stomach), or served roasted on their own, accompanied by a cold glass of new wine.

Markus Kopf, the son of Tante Gretel and Onkel Otto, took me to Hambach Castle near Neustadt, where I learned about the 1832 "crib of democracy," as Matthias had promised I would. The *Hambachfest* event at this castle in 1832 is considered the start of organized rebellions against monarchical rule.

One evening that last week, Bärbel invited me to a *Schlachtfest*, the traditional German-style pig butchering, offered at the Herbel Restaurant. A *Schlachtfest* is a community occasion, a tradition gradually fading out in modern times. In the old days, when a family butchered their pig, they'd hold a feast for the whole village. The sign of a *Schlachtfest* was the pig's bladder, filled with air and hung outside the door of the home where the feast would be held, a sign not dissimilar to the party balloon of today.

In the Freinsheim 21st-century version, Herbel's restaurant advertised their *Schlachtfest* via a few rudimentary signs and word of mouth. Bärbel invited Ina and her teenage daughters to join us, although the two teenagers looked often at their cell phones and seemed unwilling to fully engage. When my "combination plate" arrived, featuring a pallid array of blood sausage, liverwurst, boiled pork belly, sauerkraut, and a slice of the pig's snout, Hannah and Helen scrunched up their noses and looked away. Shortly afterward, they left to meet up with friends.

While we were dining, the proprietor Frau Herbel stopped by our table to talk with Bärbel. I recognized her from the day Bärbel had taken me for a visit to the Herbel stables. At that moment, I realized with a shock that the grumbling pink sows I'd photographed in their sty were now cooked up and served on my plate. Later, on the walk back to the house, Bärbel told me with some merriment that Frau Herbel had been explaining how she didn't mind the work involved in a *Schlachtfest*, preparing the soups and different kinds of sausages, the huge mess it made of the kitchen. What Frau Herbel couldn't stand was the squeal of the pigs when the butcher cut their throats.

Philipp Harm, wife Margaretha,
and daughters Elizabetha and
Margaretha in Freinsheim in 1869.

For the Palatine Germans, the *Schlachtfest* was a familiar, if old-fashioned, ritual. For me, I felt like I'd struck the motherlode of sensory imagery. I practically dipped my nose into the soup trying to inhale the aromas, greasy and a bit off-putting from my 21st-century perspective. How differently Michael Harm must have viewed it. For a hungry young boy who worked in the fields, a meaty broth soup at a *Schlachtfest* would have been a rare and enormous treat, a precious opportunity to gorge on much-needed fat and protein.

In the Herbel Restaurant, I gazed around at the other diners and imagined I might even be sitting among descendants of Michael Harm's friends and neighbors. It struck me that, in this rural village, one generation passed to the next, and in some ways, cultural traditions remained surprisingly constant.

I ALSO RECEIVED ANOTHER INVITATION to the home of Tante Marliese Weber, Manfred's mother, who lived on *Wallstrasse*. The street is named Wall Street because it runs along one side of the fortified wall encircling the old town, a square half mile at Freinsheim's central core. I knew my way around well enough by then, so could walk from Bärbel's to Tante Marliese's in a few minutes. Michael Harm's family had lived on Wallstrasse, too, although these

Michael Harm, Amerika,
photo in Tante Marliese's
photo album.

days no one was entirely sure in which house. Several had been pointed out to me.

Since Tante Marliese's English was very limited, her teenage granddaughter Kristina, Manfred's youngest daughter, was there to help out as our translator. Tante Marliese shared with me the old family photo album, which contained photos of Michael's brother Philipp, his wife Susannah Margaretha and their daughters. Then we moved on to the subsequent generations. As the years flipped past, in many photographs the men wore military uniforms, a poignant reminder of the wars suffered in this region. At the talk at the *Heimatmuseum*, one history club member said there'd been some twenty wars in the Palatinate since the Thirty Years War of the 1600s. Hans Weber, Tante Marliese's husband, had served in WWII. He was taken prisoner of war in Russia and put to work in a Russian mine. He didn't return home until several years after the war ended, and his health never fully recovered.

Gazing at the photos, I felt relieved that my interest lay in the previous century. The 19th-century images were relatively scarce, but one in particular was a treasure. A photo of Michael Harm at his anvil, apparently taken sometime after he advanced from apprentice status to journeyman, certifying him to go into the blacksmith business for himself. The same photo Manfred had digitized for us years earlier. The handwritten caption, something I hadn't seen before, read: "Michael Harm, Amerika."

Michael stared out at me steadily, as if daring me to tell his story, to resurrect him from this tucked away still-life.

NEAR THE VERY END OF the week, Angela had another meeting in store for me, set up with Dr. Hans-Helmut Görtz. A resident of the village, Dr. Görtz had written books about many sites of historical interest in and around Freinsheim. He avidly researched area history as a hobby. In all my time in Freinsheim, there hadn't been an opportunity to meet with Dr. Görtz because he still worked full-time. But Angela persisted, in the end setting up a meeting with him at around ten o'clock at night.

"Are you sure this is okay?" I asked Angela as we set out at a quick pace along the dimly-lit stone-cobbled streets.

"Yes, it's the only time he could meet with us. He works days at BASF."

By then, I'd heard about BASF, a sprawling German chemical company in the nearby city of Ludwigshafen, the largest employer in the Rhine-Neckar region.

Sure enough, Dr. Görtz welcomed us at the door as if he saw nothing whatsoever unusual about guests arriving at his home after ten at night. A slight man with close-cropped, salt-and-pepper hair and silver, wire-rimmed glasses, Dr. Görtz invited us in, then sat down behind a large, dark wood table coated in papers. From the looks of it, his formal dining table.

"What part of the U.S. are you from?" he asked me as Angela and I took seats across from him. The only light in the room came from a low-hanging chandelier, which lit our faces in a yellow glow.

"Seattle, Washington."

"Oh, in the Northwest U.S.? I have not been there."

"It's a pretty long flight," I admitted. "But it's worth it. You should come."

Then Angela interjected, explaining in English about my thesis research, the novel I was trying to write for my MFA degree. "We were hoping to visit the Freinsheim archives. Claire's looking for an immigration record of her Cleveland ancestor, Michael Harm."

Dr. Görtz gazed at me, a bit cautiously, it seemed to me. "I don't think we can get in there at the moment. What year did he emigrate?"

"1857."

"I also wish I could find information about Pfarrer Bickes," I said. I'd been reminded by the retired pastor Herr Walter how Pfarrer Bickes was a key historic figure in Freinsheim during the 1848 rebellion.

Dr. Görtz's eyes lit with interest. "What kind of information?"

"How long he was a pastor, maybe something about what his sermons were like," I said.

"Otto Klamm, the former Freinsheim historian, was working on a book about Pfarrer Bickes. He had collected some of his writings, diary entries I think. Klamm is deceased now, but I have some of his old papers. I might be able to find something upstairs."

Angela and I waited in the semi-darkness while Dr. Görtz disappeared for a while. When he returned, he handed me just what he'd promised, typed-up pages transcribed from the journal of Pfarrer Bickes. The pastor's own thoughts, in his own words. Better, even, than what I'd hoped to find in the town archives.

OUR MEETING WITH DR. GÖRTZ at an end, Angela and I returned to the house, only to be met by her mother in the hallway. From the dark worry in Bärbel's eyes, I could see right away something was wrong.

"Dave called," she said. "You must call home right away. Your aunt had a fall."

I felt a raw tug of helplessness in my gut. With the time difference, it was early in the morning in Seattle, so when I called, I caught Dave before he left for work. He told me that, while walking with her walker in the courtyard at Bayview two days ago, Aunt Elizabeth had somehow fallen and smacked her forehead. Although she'd tried, at first, to refuse medical treatment, they'd sent her to the hospital anyhow. Since then, there had been swelling and fluid in the brain, and the doctors were recommending surgery.

It all came crashing down on me, the terrible distance, how I was powerless to be of any real help to my aunt. Dave said Aunt Elizabeth was lucid (although her speech had worsened and was starting to slur). She'd agreed to the surgery, which would happen the next day. I shouldn't try to come home early. I'd be home in just four days, anyway, which would allow time for her to be in recovery. He'd keep me and my brother Craig updated via email.

October 15, 2010

Claire and Craig: I went to see Eliz. She was o.k., but somewhat sleepy and groggy. She complained about 8 times in the hour and a half I was there that they hadn't given her any lunch yet, she really wants her lunch, etc. But she is under instructions not to receive anything by mouth (she just gets a moisture swab in the mouth) ... she is scheduled for surgery later today.

I told Eliz. that we love her and I said that Claire sends her love and that Eileen sends her love (I talked to her last nite) and I gave her a kiss (yuck!). Eliz. said, "Well that's o.k. then." I gave Eliz. a card from her neighbors on the 7th Floor (I went by Bayview this morning) and also a personal card from Nita (short for Annette, she's 89). Flora - the nurse at Bayview - told me that Eliz. was angry with the grounds crew after she fell and asked what took them so long [to come help her up].

Mary Swartz at Bayview reports that there is a nursing facility there in the basement with an open bed, so Eliz. can recuperate there if need be. Apparently medicare covers it if Eliz. has to spend at least 3 nights in the Hosp., which she will have done tonight (you go girl)

More later, hopefully, Dave

The surgery to remove fluid in Aunt Elizabeth's skull area, Dave reported the next day, seemed to be a success. I pinned my hopes on this and convinced myself she'd recover. Anyhow, I'd checked into the possibility of flight changes, and learned everything was booked. Even flying standby, I wouldn't get home any sooner than the flight I already had.

So that Saturday, two days before my flight home, I tried to compartmentalize my worries about Aunt Elizabeth and kept to the pre-arranged schedule. The family in Freinsheim had invited me to harvest grapes with the town council in the City of Freinsheim's vineyard rows, an annual tradition. Manfred Weber was on the town council at the time and had arranged with the Mayor for me to participate.

Grapes weren't harvested by hand anymore, it was all done by machine. Town council members harvested their grapes by hand more as a community-building exercise, and, I suspected, to avoid the cost of renting a harvester. Local wine-makers pitched in, providing the truck to haul away the grapes, and part of their facilities to make the wine. The following year when the wine was ready, the City of Freinsheim's town council gave bottles of it to the elderly in the village on milestone birthdays, and also poured it at council-hosted events.

On a wet, gray day, I went with Manfred and his brother Hans-Günter to the town vineyard. Most of the council had gathered, in yellow and green and black puddle boots and rain slickers, for the harvest. Two wine princesses were present, the princess of Freinsheim, and the princess of the broader district, both wearing their tiaras despite their work clothes and rain jacket apparel.

To my surprise, the first activity at ten in the morning was uncorking last year's vintage and passing glasses of it around. The mayor made a toast, and we tossed back the Riesling. For a few moments, people joked and talked in the constant drizzle. Then, bellies slightly warmed and moods slightly lifted, we grabbed our deep plastic buckets and knives and set off down the rows to begin the harvest. Manfred showed me how to snip the grapes and settle the bunches in the bucket, and left me on my own. I reveled in this opportunity, taking note of how some grapes had mildewed over this cold, wet summer, feeling the sticky sap on my fingers and the heft of the bunches as they released into my hand.

A short time later, the mayor came tromping over in his rubber boots with the two wine princesses. Manfred was also with them and leaned over to speak in my ear.

"The *Rheinpfalz* newspaper is here for a publicity story," he said in a low voice. "They heard an American author is here and want to take a picture of you harvesting grapes with the mayor and the princesses."

Although taken aback, I did as bidden. Would this really appear in the newspaper, I wondered? My family connections here were making so many things possible, so many chances I wouldn't otherwise have had.

We finished in a little over an hour, then trooped off to a local restaurant. Long rows of tables and benches had been set up in an underground, arch-ceilinged room. A chef in a white toque and apron served the wet, bedraggled harvesters a hot soup of potatoes and vegetables, plus bread, accompanied by more glasses of town council wine. The mayor stood and made speeches, and the chef received an enthusiastic toast for his cuisine.

At the table, I sat listening to my cousins Manfred and Hans-Günter talk and joke with their friends, a conversation centered on heavy metal rock music. I enjoyed myself, but felt on edge about Aunt Elizabeth, and had to keep reminding myself throughout the day there was little I could do.

THAT EVENING WHEN I CHECKED my email, the news was bad. Dave reported that Aunt Elizabeth had woken up after the surgery, but a short time later the fluid had returned, and she was now unresponsive.

Early the next morning, as I was loading into Manfred's car for the drive to the airport, Bärbel handed me a copy of the morning *Die Rheinpfalz* paper. Sure enough, the local news section featured a photo from the previous day. The heading, in German, read: "Search for roots leads to vineyard: In the city vineyard, a US author is making her debut as a harvester." There I was, crouched in the foreground reaching for grapes, the mayor and two wine princesses smiling behind me. In the background were the rooftops of Freinsheim, the spire of my ancestor's Evangelical Protestant Church rising above it all.

There were hugs all around as we said farewell. As amazed and grateful as I was for absolutely everything, at that moment I could think of little else but returning home.

WHEN I ARRIVED IN SEATTLE midday on Monday, October 18, Dave told me my aunt had fallen into a coma from which the doctors said she would not awaken. As soon as possible, Dave took me by Swedish Hospital to see her. Aunt Elizabeth, a healthy 89-year-old, quite strong for her age, now lay inert, a large purple bruise the size of a lopped-off tennis ball on the left side of her forehead. As for the rest of her coloring, she looked pale, and asleep. Despite what Dave had told me about her condition, I couldn't help but hope desperately she might still awaken.

That first day, still jet-lagged, I sat by her bedside in the silence, listening to my aunt's regular breathing. Off and on I talked to her, saying things I needed to say. I read a long email to Aunt Elizabeth from her friend, Eileen, and held and stroked her hands and arms. The next morning, I returned with a radio and tuned it to her favorite classical music station. I sat in the room for another day and a half before I realized Aunt Elizabeth didn't have her hearing aids on, so the radio idea was a bust. The nurses told me they appreciated it, though.

Whether she could hear me or not, I kept talking to her. At some point in the ensuing days, Dr. Steege, who'd performed the surgery, stopped by on his rounds. He assured me that Aunt Elizabeth's brain scan showed no activity, that it was really only her body, not her mind, hanging on to life. A hospice care specialist also came by. She had spoken with insurance, she murmured, and they determined it would be undue cruelty to move Aunt Elizabeth, so Medicare had agreed to allow her end-of-life to occur in that eighth floor room at Swedish Hospital. I was welcome to be with her as often and as long as I liked.

As the hours slid by, I read through my notes from the trip to Germany, and then through the pages I'd written so far to see if I could fix them somehow. Doing so brought fresh despair. The voice and details of that draft were all wrong. I had new voices, more vibrant scenes in my head. The third person version felt distant, pallid. It captured none of the immediacy of those highly turbulent times.

AUNT ELIZABETH LAY PRONE IN her hospital bed for an interminable five days. Each time I left the room, I told her I loved her, and thanked her, and kissed her cheek. She passed away around midnight on Saturday, October 23, 2010. I was not by her side—I got the call at home and immediately drove down one last time to Swedish Hospital to sign the papers. My son George came along, and I appreciated the support. I went in and stood by Aunt Elizabeth's side, to tell her one last time I loved her and kiss her cheek good-bye. But without her steady, even breathing, and in the stillness of her pale, inert body, I knew she'd departed this life.

The next morning, I woke from an exhausted sleep to a call from the funeral home managing Aunt Elizabeth's arrangements. It seemed, Nicole informed me, that Grace Elizabeth Lindsey's body had been taken to the morgue in error. Since her death had been the result of an accident rather than a prolonged illness, they were supposed to have taken her first to the coroner. As such, they'd taken her back to the coroner first thing, then would return her to the morgue. When might I be able to come down to work through the paperwork and details?

Even in the midst of my grief, I hung up feeling bemused. Aunt Elizabeth, I thought, would have made the most of that final mix up.

"It was really very funny," I could hear her saying. "One minute they had me all tagged and bagged, shelved and chilled at the morgue, the next minute I'm bouncing across town in the back of a van to the coroner's, where I should have gone in the first place."

As if that would somehow help, I thought, tears welling in my eyes. No matter what the coroner found, it wasn't like it could bring her back to life.

It just didn't seem right, that Aunt Elizabeth could be gone so fast, without notice like this, without saying good-bye. We should have had so many more conversations. Shared so many more jokes. I'd thought we'd have years ahead. If only she hadn't fallen like that. If only we'd had more time.

Chapter 33

Since I'd helped my brother Craig sort out and pack up Dad's assisted living apartment after his death, I knew the drill for clearing out Aunt Elizabeth's studio apartment at Bayview Retirement Community: Inform management the apartment would be emptied by October 31, pack up boxes, get a wheeled cart from maintenance, make numerous treks to and from the elevator between the seventh floor and my car, all the while wishing her death had never happened. I couldn't deal with thesis work just then, and put it entirely aside.

Aunt Elizabeth's belongings didn't amount to much—in addition to small furniture items, clothing, and a few kitchen utensils, she'd kept memento art objects from her years of traveling abroad—a clay turtle from Mexico, a few jade pieces from southeast Asia, a cloisonné pear from China. There were numerous tchotchkes along a rooster theme, something her friends got a kick out of giving her, I think due to her red hair and generally cocky personality.

Back when she left Michigan, my aunt had parted with her personal library of books, but on her bedside table stood a tall stack of newly published hardcover books, each with a piece of paper marking the place she'd left off reading, almost as if she'd been reading them all at once. When I returned the books to the community library downstairs, the volunteer informed me Aunt Elizabeth had been a voracious reader. Whenever new titles arrived, she was first in line to check them out. I think it was a matter of personal pride to my aunt, to keep up with the latest titles.

Aunt Elizabeth had died on a Saturday. I focused the entire week following on handling her final affairs. On one of my Bayview trips, as I wheeled a cart load down the hall toward the elevator, I encountered Sue Donovan, the intake specialist who'd helped make arrangements to move Aunt Elizabeth to Bayview just fifteen months before, and who'd been printing out my blogs for her while I'd been traveling. I didn't much want to interact with anyone at Bayview just then. My heart ached with fresh wounds over my loss, my grief still stuck in the denial and anger phase. When Sue recognized me, though, she reached out and pulled me into a strong embrace.

"Oh, I'm so sorry, Claire," she said, genuine sadness in her voice. She pulled back but kept holding me by the shoulders, searching my eyes with her intent brown gaze. Searching for what? I wondered. Accusation? Forgiveness? I didn't hold Bayview responsible, but I didn't feel all that great toward the place, either. Sue released me, her eyes brimming with tears. "I was hoping I'd see you. I wanted to tell you, Elizabeth was enjoying your blog posts so much. I was, too. She came by daily, and we often chatted about them." Sue put her hand to her nose, presumably to tamp down the tears. "It was so hard, that day she fell. On her way out for her walk, she came by my office and handed me a thank you note, a thank you note for printing out your blogs. I thought it was odd. You weren't due home for almost a week. It was like she knew she was going to go."

"That was Aunt Elizabeth," I said, marveling that her quirky personality manifested even in her last moments. "Always ahead of herself, early for every appointment."

Sue chuckled through her tears. "I really liked your aunt," she said. "It's such a loss for us all."

Another day I encountered Herb Keppler in the stairwell, a church friend I'd known for years. To stay in shape, Herb often used the stairwell rather than waiting for the elevator, something I did, too, when I didn't have a load. At Bayview, Elizabeth had the daily habit of joining Herb's table for breakfast.

"It was really strange," Herb said to me, his glasses glinting at me in the fluorescent stairwell light. "That morning she fell, Elizabeth stood up from the table and said, 'I won't be seeing you for a while.' I said: 'Why not? Where are you going?' But she'd already turned and was walking away, pushing that walker of hers. I don't think she had her hearing aids turned on."

I clung to these stories people shared, accounts of Aunt Elizabeth's final moments. With her death, I felt bereft not only because I loved her, but because I'd lost my last connection to the women of generations before me on my mom's side of the family.

"When is your aunt's memorial service?" Bayview residents would ask.

Again and again, I confessed that, at Aunt Elizabeth's request, there would not be one. My aunt had stressed that point to me over the years. Her ashes were to be taken back to Berea, Ohio, per her prepaid funeral arrangements. She would be laid to rest beside her parents, grandparents, and eldest sister Anna. She left a note behind with her important papers, too, in case I somehow forgot, "No memorial. Bagpiper to skirl a dirge." This latter instruction meant she wanted a bagpiper to play at her graveside service. A tribute, no doubt, to her Scots-Irish heritage.

Aunt Elizabeth's full name was Grace Elizabeth Lindsey. She loathed the name Grace, however, so gave strict instructions to leave that name off her headstone. Her urn, and her grave marker, too, should read only, "Elizabeth Lindsey."

I called my brother Craig about the arrangements, and we decided to delay the burial until that following summer, a time when our two families, including our college-age kids, could all be together. In the meantime, I'd keep Aunt Elizabeth's urn with me, a heavy, white-marbled, sealed block with the words ELIZABETH LINDSEY engraved in the top.

As OCTOBER DREW TO A close, I turned in the keys to Aunt Elizabeth's apartment, and returned home to my life, and my thesis. I found it hard to face all that had to be done. Clearly, with third person, I hadn't captured the sense of immediacy and uncertainty of 19th-century European peasant farmers, a life tied to the seasons, and subject to the whims of despotic rulers. Plus, the new information about Johann Rapparlie having lost his leg made for a better story. I imagined the pain he endured would have nagged him endlessly. I knew so much more now than I had when drafting these pages. But without having drafted them, when I went to Germany I wouldn't have known what I was trying to discover.

While my efforts had not been a total waste, I knew now I had to scrap the whole thing. I'd been leaning toward the first person point of view for months, especially since, in reading and rereading the letters, the voices of these immigrants had taken up residence in my head. Plus, it was a stylistic convention of 19th-century novelists to write in first person, so that felt right, too. At one point I'd mentioned switching over to first person to my thesis adviser, but Kathleen had advised against it. She said third person worked fine, and it would be too difficult to switch. But if I had to start over anyhow, I became convinced, now was the time to switch. It couldn't hurt to try, at least. Or, maybe I couldn't write this thing, after all. Maybe the reason everything was taking so long was that I simply couldn't do it.

Digging deep in search of courage, on Monday morning, November 1, I logged onto my thesis site. I'd been at it for three whole semesters with Kathleen, sending her report after report, and chapter after chapter, but it felt as if I'd gotten essentially nowhere. Since Kathleen would be heading off on sabbatical come December, I'd have to switch next semester to my new thesis adviser, Wayne Ude.

November 1, 2010

Kathleen—here I am—after a hospital vigil of about five

days, my aunt died Oct. 23 - since then I have been making necessary arrangements, moving her stuff out of her apartment, talking to her octogenarian friends in Michigan, etc.

Much knuckle-cracking and throat-clearing going on over here, as I incorporate my notes and writing. I have signed up for Thesis Continuation next semester, because obviously, I will not be finished at the end of Fall 2010.

[Reply from Kathleen November 1, 2010]

Hello Claire –

I'm sorry about your aunt. It seems to me you were able to take her on some fun outings until quite recently, so you both were lucky.

You have packed a lot into this semester, so don't feel bad about lapping into next semester. I think Wayne will be a good reader for you. If you can get a draft together by mid-December, that would be great! I'll give you as much feedback as I can.

Kathleen remained optimistic because I hadn't had the heart to confess my discouragement. I didn't bring up switching to first person, or starting over, because I figured it might not even work, so why worry her unnecessarily?

The month of November also marked the start of the annual event known as National Novel Writing Month (NaNoWriMo). Started in 1999, NaNoWriMo invites writers to sign up online from all over the world. The goal is to produce 50,000 words of a novel in one month. I didn't actually sign up, but the thought that many other writers were hunkering down just like me that November added incentive and made me feel less alone.

Each morning that next week, I rose out of bed at a pre-dawn hour and cranked out the words. I started writing with the first scene that came to mind, Michael Harm as a young boy in Freinsheim, with travelers on their way to America arriving at the door. Two chapters flowed from my pen, and I never thought once of turning back. At the end of the week, I submitted almost 3,000 words to Kathleen with sweating palms. Would she be upset, and advise that I cease and desist from the rewrite? I sure hoped not.

November 7, 2010

Thanks, Kathleen, for your encouraging words.

As I begin again, I am finding the first-person point of view is the one that resonates most strongly. I hope I am on the right track with this ....

[Reply from Kathleen, November 10, 2010]

I am standing and applauding. This is fantastic. Keep going.

Kathleen's support gave me a surge of elation, and huge sense of relief. By semester's end, I'd written about 45,000 words, which, by my estimate, put me about halfway on a first draft. Posting my thanks to Kathleen for her patience, I wished her well on her sabbatical.

Chapter 34

By the end of my third semester of thesis, and five weeks into writing it from scratch, I had much to share in my Monday writing update to Michele.

December 7, 2010

Dear Michele,

...Early last week, I got stuck in my writing, so I printed out the most recent five chapters (7-11) and realized my timeline was completely messed up .... My goal (again) was to get Michael out of Germany by last Friday, and I missed that deadline. But ... finally, as we speak, Michael is at the French border, so I'm awfully close.

I get goosebumps about the "magical" part of this experience. Saturday ... I was writing ... a scene where Michael is asked by the town mayor to sing at the Silvester dance (the New Year's Eve ball). So I referred to the book of traditional German carols my cousin [Angela] gave my children as a gift when they were little. The one that grabbed my attention was "*Es Ist Ein Ros Entsprungen*"— "Lo, How a Rose E'er Blooming." ... it was written in the 1600s, a traditional German carol. So I write this scene, with the song swirling in my head. Then Sunday morning I go to church and the scripture reading is Isaiah 11:1-10 (the text for "Lo, How a Rose"). The Offertory the organist played was "Lo, How a Rose E'er Blooming." Goosebumps.

My writing journey is hand in hand with research ...

During Thanksgiving weekend, Angela sent me some photocopies– pages and pages of published letters of other German immigrants. One letter describes in detail the trip from Germany through the border at Forbach, then on to Paris, then on to Le Havre. So when I feel I'm losing my footing, I head over to Google translate and start typing in some of these letters for a good dose of immersion.

[Since the emigration route went through Paris] I made a quick Google search of Paris in 1857, and learned the Salon of 1857 that year signaled the shift from Romanticism to Realism. At the exact moment when I need it in the book. 23,000 people a day went to the art exhibition at the Champs-Elysee—I believe it's quite possible my great-great grandfather attended. Goosebumps.

I have incredible angst that I won't be able to finish on schedule, since everything is taking longer than I expect. On the other hand, I feel guided by a greater hand, a community of saints, that won't quit.

Blessings,

Claire

[Reply from Michele]

December 7, 2010

Claire,

Thank you for sharing the "Lo how a Rose" story. It gave me goosebumps also as that is one of my favorite Christmas songs. If you are frustrated at how long it is taking, think about how frustrated Michael must have gotten regarding his long journey to the U.S.

Peace,

Michele

As I drafted scenes of Michael and his companions traveling through Paris at the same moment as the Salon of 1857, I found it compelling that Michael Harm had been born in 1841, just at the tail end of the era of Romanticism, a movement that championed the emotional over the logical, idealized the untamed wilderness, and idolized heroes. At age fifteen, Michael was no doubt still naïve and idealistic when he headed off for America. He would have had to grow up fast, and be thrust into harsh realities. As he toiled away as a blacksmith apprentice, he must have been forced to cope with a mundane and largely thankless everyday life. It stunned me that the shift to Realism seemed to be happening both within Michael Harm, and in the world around him. Perhaps, I reflected, our personal growth and understanding go hand in hand with events around us more often than we realize.

Two days after I sent my update to Michele, Dave and I drove south on I-5 to hear our daughter Vivian sing as part of the choir at the Christmas concert at Willamette University in Salem, Oregon. The Christmas carols sung in such beautiful harmonies raised my spirits and lent support to my growing conviction that music had a powerful influence on creative thought.

By then, I'd come across Peter Watson's *The German Genius*, a book that included 19th-century German philosophies about music, how it was believed to be integral to all aspects of human existence. If one entered into music fully, the thinking went, one could forget the self and enter a higher realm. I felt inspired by my daughter's concert, in no small part due to the things I'd been learning. Hence, my research was informing my life, which was informing my research, in ways I could not have predicted.

My family and I shared a relatively quiet Christmas at home. Without Aunt Elizabeth, it felt all too quiet, but we tried not to dwell on our loss. Between Christmas and January 3, I rose at five a.m. almost every morning and cranked out more pages. A strong impetus to rise out of bed was the thought of the Freinsheim family. Whether or not I could actually do this, I had an obligation to try. If I kept at it, I told myself, just maybe I could make it happen. Incredibly, the discipline and persistence seemed to be working. By early January, I was able to email 174 pages of the manuscript to my new thesis adviser, Wayne Ude, in advance of our face-to-face consulation at residency. If I could keep up this pace, maybe I still had a chance to graduate come August.

THE JANUARY 2011 RESIDENCY WAS held on Whidbey Island at Captain Whidbey Inn, a madrona-log lodge on Penn Cove near Coupeville. An inspiring setting, with views of the beach and with shifting waters of the cove visible through almost every window.

As I prepared to attend the nine-day intensive, I did worry about what Wayne would think of my manuscript draft so far. Would he have different ideas than Kathleen, and would those stall my progress or force me in a new direction? I hoped not. Actually, I hoped the switch would work to my advantage. Now that I was writing from a first person male perspective, I saw it as a good thing to be working under Wayne, especially if I somehow missed the mark in gender characterization.

Sometime during that residency, Wayne and I sat down together to discuss what I'd accomplished so far. He was a published author in his own right, now nearing 70 years of age. He dressed a bit like a Northwest lumberjack, in plain earth-tone clothes, suspenders, and heavy vibram-soled shoes, and carried a black briefcase with him everywhere. His hair still maintained a cast of brown amid streaks of gray, but his beard was entirely, shockingly white.

"You've accomplished a great deal," he told me in his soft-spoken voice. He didn't have my manuscript with him, and kept his hands in his pockets, his legs crossed in a relaxed manner as he sat in the chair across from me. "I'm especially enjoying the German component, since I have Lutheran Germans in my ancestry. I'll not comment too much, since you know the story much better than I do. But I do hope for some clarity on Harm's reasons for telling his story."

I understood. When I'd been in Wayne's Craft of Fiction class, he'd emphasized the functions of various points of view, how first person narration is often confessional in nature, the narrator sharing his or her story to set the record straight or make things right.

I hesitated, wondering how to answer. And trying not to panic. With my frantic, driven production of pages these past few months, had I overlooked this key element?

"I think," I said slowly, my brain searching for the right words, "it's because, at the end of his life, Michael Harm isn't sure if he made the right decision in coming to Cleveland, after all."

"He regretted immigrating? What makes you think that?"

"Well, I found a phrase about him in a book, *Cleveland and Its Germans*. It has write-ups about Clevelanders who were German immigrants. Michael Harm doesn't have a bio, though. His name only appears in a write-up about his son-in-law, W. F. Hoppensack. Something about how he's a German through and through. When I saw that, it made me think about how Michael Harm had been in Cleveland for a long time by then, almost 40 years. Yet he still clung to his Germanness. Did that mean he regretted leaving Freinsheim?"

Wayne tilted his head to the other side. "I like that," he said. "He's reviewing his life, trying to figure out his German American identity."

At the close of our discussion, Wayne pointed out to me that I had a good deal of work ahead if I expected to graduate in August. We targeted April 1, just two and a half months away, as the deadline for a completed first draft. We'd meet in person then, at the Whidbey Island Writers Conference, to take stock of where things stood.

I was not enrolled in a class that residency, but I did attend many of the afternoon Profession of Writing sessions, being sure to choose topics that addressed writing about history. One such class was taught by Kirby Larson, author of the middle grade nonfiction book *Hattie Big Sky*. During her session, Kirby explained about the importance of historical accuracy when writing historical nonfiction.

This discussion came at a very tough moment. I continued to struggle with writing scenes of my own invention, especially when it felt as if they departed from the historical record. For instance, when writing about the ocean voyage, I had no idea if Captain Lewis Higgins was mean or wise or witty. And what, exactly, were the hierarchies on board the ship between steerage and second class passengers, and with the ship's crew? How did that work? By that time, I'd read some first person accounts of ocean journeys, but none were specific to Michael Harm's voyage on the *Helvetia*. After the class, I went up to talk to Kirby about it.

"I'm having trouble with scenes in my historical fiction novel," I told her. "I have no information about a particular ocean voyage except that it lasted 43 days—although even that is in question, because by some family accounts, the voyage lasted 46 days. Anyhow, I'm getting stuck trying to write about it."

Kirby had close-cropped, dark brown hair, a lean face and deep brown eyes, which she fixed on me kindly. "This is fiction, you said?"

I nodded.

"Aren't there first person accounts of other voyages to draw from?"

"Right, I've found some great stories, like one about a second class passenger who climbed up in the crow's nest. It was against the rules. The first mate made the man pay a fine before he'd let him back down. I'd love to write that scene, but it feels wrong, because I doubt the same thing happened on my ancestor's boat."

Kirby looked thoughtful. "But you're writing fiction? Let me ask you this: could it have happened? I mean, if it happened on one ship, might it have happened, or a version of it, on other ships, too?"

"Yeah, I guess it probably could." I saw what Kirby was saying. With historical fiction, as long as something was within the realm of possibility, it qualified if it worked for the scene.

The idea was liberating.

At home after residency, I felt tense and bottled up from all the work that lay ahead, and from the terrible prospect that I wasn't going to make it. I was supposed to finish the whole first draft by April 1? In one-and-a-half years, I'd barely gotten Michael on the boat to America. Pulling this off would mean countless hours at the computer.

But by this point, the last thing I felt like doing was sitting all day at the computer. I needed a way to counteract the spread in my hips. My body had begun to take on the shape of a ripe pear. Back in my teen years, I'd done some yoga and, during my first years in college, I'd been a daily practitioner. The discipline and stretching of it, especially of my spine, had relaxed me and also stimulated my energy and creativity.

So one day in February, feeling stiff and irritable, I gathered an old black mat, loose shorts, and a t-shirt and went down to a local yoga studio, Yogabliss, to try out a class. In the lobby, I filled out the first-timers paperwork and scoped out the other students, all dressed in tight-fitting yoga outfits with trendy lavender- and sage-colored mats and towels. I felt out of place, and not sure I was up for it. *You need an energy boost*, I reminded myself. *You really need this.*

In the class, I tried not to dwell on how athletic all the other students were. As the teacher led us in the poses, I found I knew many of them, but alas, my body did not respond as it used to. I was badly out of shape. I felt like quitting, but I stuck with it, enduring the full hour.

Afterwards, feeling a little looser, I sat in the front lobby to put on my socks and shoes, then picked up a flyer to examine the schedule and the price breakdowns.

"So, does it make sense to get a 10-class card?" I asked the young woman behind the counter.

"Well, it depends," she replied, swiveling slowly from her computer screen. She had clear, tanned skin, and long brown hair highlighted blond. About half my age, if not younger. "If you're going to come three or more times a week, it's a better deal to pay month to month."

"Oh." I continued to sit. A few people exited, the door whooshing open to the wet February day, then closing again. "So, if I pay for a month, I can take any class?"

"Yup, any class."

"But I'd probably only be able to manage the lower level ones."

She tilted her head, considering this. "You probably wouldn't want to take a class that has 'advanced' in the title, but otherwise you'd be okay. Everyone is at different levels. We just do what we can and don't stress too much about it."

I nodded, and kept sitting there, internally debating.

"My name's Lena," she said. "What are you thinking? What can I help you with?"

"Well, I want to sign up for a month, but I have this huge project I need to work on full time. So I'm wondering—do I want to sign up to help myself get through it, or do I want to sign up to procrastinate?"

"I see." Lena studied me. "It's up to you, of course, but I can't see how taking a few yoga classes a week would be a mistake."

Her argument worked. After another moment's hesitation, I stood, walked over and signed up for the month.

The yoga did help energize me as I slogged ahead over the next two months. But it didn't help me figure out a decent plotline for Michael Harm during the Civil War. Nothing I'd heard about Michael Harm's life indicated he'd fought in the war. How I wished I had more letters to fill in the gaps. Such a strange thing, how the Rapparlie letters dropped off in 1858 after Michael Harm arrived, and the Michael Harm letters to Freinsheim were so few. One in 1869, and none in the 1870s, when his carriage works on Champlain Street must have been doing well, according to what Martin Hauserman had dug up for me at Cleveland City Records.

In the 1880s, I had just one, painfully short letter:

> Cleveland, O., 1st August 1883[1]
>
> Dear brother sister-in-law and children,
>
> Those who bring these few lines Mr. H. Lederer and wife,[2] doubly neighbors and friends, will make you the favor of a visit. And because they are entirely informed about our circumstances so you can learn from them everything you wish to know. Therefore I don't want to add anything concerning my family and me, as these few lines are only meant to introduce you to Mr. Lederer and his wife. With this I want to close and greet all of you many times and further wish that these few lines as well as those who bring them meet you as healthily as they have left us. And I stay like always yours
>
> M. Harm

As I read through this unenlightening letter, I felt let down. How nice it would be, I thought sarcastically, if Mr. H. Lederer and his wife were still living, so they might also inform me of everything I wish to know. During

---

1   Here Michael wrote Aug 1te, which is a curious mix between German and English: instead of 1st from the English "first," it is the ending of "erste" (der erste August).

2   Possibly, Henry and Kate Lederer, appearing in the 1900 Census in Cleveland's Precinct B, Ward 3. Henry (Heinrich) Lederer (1839) possibly emigrated from Wachenheim, a town just 10 km from Freinsheim. Also see December 16, 1889 letter following, regarding Michael Harm's later lawsuit against this man.

my five a.m. writing jags, I did my best to conjure what life had been like in those years, the phase of necessity in his life when Michael Harm worked as a journeyman blacksmith, fell in love with my great-great grandmother, Elizabeth Crolly and started to raise a family. And just how and when did he start his own carriage-making business?

When it came to that, I still could find little information about carriage-making. I'd made many visits to the on-line *Encyclopedia of Cleveland History* and the *Cleveland Memory Project*, but nothing that clued me in to everyday life at a carriage works. As a blacksmith, what kind of things was Michael doing, exactly?

Following the 1883 letter came a postcard from October of 1893, when Michael Harm was 53 years old, written in a rather drunken script. Apparently he'd written it after a visit to Freinsheim, as he was boarding the steamship Columbia to journey back to the U.S. I remembered Angela giggling about it back in 2008.

"Oh," she'd said, putting her hand to her mouth and rolling her eyes in a comical gesture, "it says here they drank the rest of the Freinsheimer wine. That's why he writes in this crazy handwriting."

We'd never gotten around to translating the postcard, but I didn't imagine such a brief, dashed off note would help me much anyhow, other than to confirm he was on his way back to the U.S. Presumably this was the visit mentioned long ago in that first 1922 letter Angela sent us at Christmas. "For all that it has been such a long time, since our dear uncle had stayed with us (1893)!"

Regardless of what I knew and didn't know, during February and March of 2011, to get through the whole manuscript, I had no choice but to barrel ahead, writing about 6,000 words a week, only pausing every so often to go down to the yoga studio to stretch and sweat. My body was not used to the exercise. Often after a session, I'd come home and fill the bathtub near the top, then ease my aching muscles into the hot water.

In all the stress and busy-ness of working on my thesis, I'd compartmentalized my grief about losing Aunt Elizabeth. Once in a while, though, a feeling would emerge unbidden. A guilt that I'd somehow let her down. I had this nagging feeling that she'd trusted me to take care of her, but she'd died while under my care. A guilt I found it hard to cope with.

One afternoon after an hour-long yoga session of stretching and bending and balancing, the compartment broke open. I was lying on the mat with my eyes closed in the usual resting savasana pose at the end. The instructor was speaking to us quietly, intoning how the English name for the pose is the "corpse pose," and the image of Aunt Elizabeth appeared, once loving and stubborn, witty and smart and brash, then pale and still on the hospital bed. I missed her, pure and simple, and the tears began streaming from my eyes down my hot temples onto the mat. Maybe that was the real reason I'd turned to yoga. To work out the struggle of emotions so tangled up right then inside my heart.

Chapter 35

In a race to the finish of the first draft of my thesis, I wrote several "firsts" in the life of Michael Harm, scenes I'd delayed writing until now: a first fist fight, a first sex scene, a first marriage proposal (in that order). As for the scenes of Michael Harm's return voyage to Germany in 1893, I had a pretty strong picture of Cleveland in those years, changed dramatically in the four decades since Michael Harm's arrival in 1857.

How? John D. Rockefeller's oil refineries, for one thing. Chernow's biography *Titan* described how Rockefeller built his first oil refineries along the Cuyahoga River in downtown Cleveland shortly after oil was discovered in Titusville, Pennsylvania in 1859. The black gold of oil refineries was kerosene, a key source of illuminant for lamps. Oil refining was a brand new technology, and a boon for business, but the process had serious environmental side effects.

> "Before the automobile, nobody knew what to do with the light fraction of crude oil known as gasoline, and many refiners, under cover of dark, let this waste product run into the river. 'We used to burn it for fuel in distilling the oil,' said Rockefeller, 'and thousands and hundreds of thousands of barrels of it floated down the creeks and rivers, and the ground was saturated with it, in the constant effort to get rid of it.' The noxious runoff made the Cuyahoga River so flammable that if steamboat captains shoveled glowing coals overboard, the water erupted in flames." *Titan*, Chernow, p. 101.

The Cuyahoga River erupted into flames? This account from the early days of oil refining meant the much-publicized 1969 Cuyahoga River fire, an event that lives in perpetuity in Randy Newman's song "Burn On," had not been the first time flames erupted on that river. It had happened starting 100 years earlier. I imagined a snaking fire through the center of downtown must have horrified the citizens of Cleveland, Michael Harm included.

Oil refineries permeated the air in Cleveland with an acrid, burning-rubber odor. Even worse, refineries had a tendency to explode, causing violent fire storms that blackened skies with oil-gritted clouds and licked up entire city blocks. Besides the pollution due to oil refining, Cleveland's skies became smudged from coal-burning industries, home furnaces and cook stoves. As the Machine Age progressed, for entire days, even in summer, Cleveland lived without the sun, which only broke through the thick smog at sunset as a glowing red ball on the horizon. For a breath of fresh air, Clevelanders took to purchasing cottages along Lake Erie's shores, where women and children spent the summer months for the healthier air.

Meanwhile, by 1893 in Freinsheim, the landscape had changed very little. In my thesis chapters, I imagined my great-great grandfather returning to his homeland, to the ancient pastoral village of Freinsheim, encountering clear, blue skies just as I'd witnessed them on my visit that previous fall. I imagined Michael Harm breathing in the crop-sweetened air and gazing across the green rolling countryside. No doubt the clean air and sunlight stood in stark contrast to the industrial smokestacks and blackened brick and steel landscape of Cleveland.

What would Michael Harm have been thinking, to stand there in Freinsheim after going through so much in America? My great-great grandfather had emigrated as a true romantic, I surmised in the early chapters of the thesis, dreaming of the American Indian and pristine wilderness. But by 1893, instead of a free, romantic Ohio wilderness, Cleveland had become a fast-paced, noisy, recklessly polluted metropolis. And, in 1893, the U.S. was experiencing another staggering financial crisis. When Michael Harm arrived in Freinsheim that fall, surely part of him questioned his decision to ever have left in the first place.

His attachment to his German culture no doubt compounded his regrets. My grandmother had told me both her Grandpa and Grandma Harm only spoke German to her when she was a child. Her parents, though, counteracted this by mainly speaking English, an indication that they wished to be seen as Americans and raise their children as Americans. In the final chapters of the draft, therefore, I wrestled with how Michael Harm felt about this. He'd worked tirelessly to keep a strong German influence in the family, yet his own children were turning their backs on their German heritage. Out of Necessity (that fourth life phase of Goethe's "Primal Words, Orphic" poem), he'd worked hard to establish a family, but it wasn't turning out as he'd planned. In what way, in his last years, did Michael Harm find Hope?

For insights, I turned to the last letter in our possession, written in 1900.

Cleveland, April 1rst, 1900[1]

Dear brother, sister-in-law and children[2],

These few lines are intended to introduce to you Mr. F. B. Schweizer, [3] an old acquaintance and business friend of mine. Additionally, a small gift, a real American-made pipe along with the tobacco that goes with it, a sign that I've not altogether forgotten about you, so go ahead and stuff and light it! Furthermore, one photo of our Kretchen,[4] who is now four years old, mentally very advanced, especially with a remarkable strength to grasp things.

As Mr. Schweizer was so kind to do me this favor and his visit will be short, and he saw me every week at least once or twice, so he can testify to you over a glass of wine whether I belong to the young or old men. As Mr. Schweizer has lived in America for a very long time, and he is a good narrator, so go ahead and ask him many questions.

We have received your letter on the 6th of January and have seen that you are all well, which is ever of the most importance. Also, we are all without exception healthy and well except Ph. Heinrich[5] [who] suffered eight months with stomach problems. However, now he is improving.

Last spring, I had been tied to the bed with pneumonia for four weeks, but I improved since then and am healthier now than in my younger years. Our family is again increased by one girl in the youngest daughter's family of Mrs. Becker. [6] She is 14 months old now,

1   Written on Harm & Schuster Fine Carriages stationery.
2   Elizabetha, Margaretha, and Katherina were the three daughters of Philipp Harm and Susannah Margaretha Hisgen (Harm).
3   Possibly, Frederick B. Schweitzer, listed in the 1920 census as having immigrated from Germany in 1871.
4   Marguerite "Gretchen" Becker (3/7/1896), fifth granddaughter of Michael and Elizabeth Harm. Photo apparently lost.
5   Ph. Heinrich—Philipp Heinrich "Henry" Harm (1864), oldest son of Michael.
6   Emma Becker nee Harm (5/18/1866), youngest daughter of Michael and Elizabeth Harm, married 6/21/1893 to Paul Becker (1869).

healthy and above all the strongest and heaviest of all six grandchildren, her name is Leonie.[7] By subscribing to the "Pfälzer in Amer[ika]"[8] I am learning again what is happening in Freinsheim. Deaths and other incidents, the bad luck of Ph. Aul was also reported about, as well as the the obituary notice of the neighbor Mrs. R. Pirrman.[9] I ask you to send both my cordial greetings and tell them that I share in the hardness of their loss.

Business has been good recently and in the former years. If my wife should hold on to her decision, we will visit you in 1901. According to the newspaper last year alone 5,000 people traveled to Europe from Cleveland. From my whole family to yours, we all wish you many warm greetings through the sending of these lines.

I now endorse and wholeheartedly wish that these lines, together with the bearer, meet you all as healthy as they leave us. I remain together with you as one of yours,

Michael Harm

In 1900, Michael Harm seemed quite proud of his American-made pipe and tobacco. Despite his struggles, he identified strongly, for better or worse, with his new homeland. Regarding the 1901 visit, I could never find evidence that it occurred, with or without his wife Elizabeth. Michael Harm had visited Freinsheim once in 1864 and once in 1893, but for whatever reason, he'd never been able to convince his wife to travel to Freinsheim. My great-great grandfather would die ten years after this letter was written, in 1910.

ON MARCH 29, 2011, FIVE months after I'd begun the rewrite of my thesis, I uploaded the final chapters for review to my thesis adviser Wayne, this time under a new title: *Harm's Way*. The *Harm's Way* inspiration flashed into being sometime around three o'clock in the morning during yet another sleepless night, a common occurrence in those last months. I wrestled with all kinds of thoughts in the sleepless wee hours of the morning—scenes I might include,

---

7   Leona Elizabeth Becker (2/7/1899), sixth granddaughter of Michael and Elizabeth Harm.
8   A newspaper founded by Conrad Voelcker of Edenkoben in New York City in 1884. Hartkopf, Herbert. Die Voelcker Brothers, Edenkoben-New York, Und *"Der Pfälzer in Amerika"*. Ludwigshafen Am Rhein: Pro Message, 2007.
9   Aul and Pirrman are names frequently mentioned in Michael's letters.

images I might add, and the pervasive anxiety that I'd never finish the book.

When the title *Harm's Way* first popped into my head, it seemed so obvious I wondered why I hadn't thought of it before. By emigrating, Michael Harm had put himself in harm's way, first on a perilous ocean journey, then under a cruel blacksmith master in Cleveland. And, taking the book as a whole, this was Michael Harm's way, his life, his journey to a new homeland. It may have been a journey taken, in one form or another, by millions of others, but in the end this book told the story of the unique, singular experience of my great-great grandfather.

The next time I logged into my thesis advising site, I was delighted to learn that Wayne wasn't the only one privy to the fact that I'd completed my first draft. Even on sabbatical, Kathleen Alcalá still had access to our site and had been eavesdropping behind the scenes. "Yay Claire!" she'd posted on the same day I turned in the pages. It felt great to know she was cheering me on from the sidelines.

Wayne was congratulatory, too. To my relief, he accepted the new title, and didn't fuss much about the hasty manner in which I'd dashed off the final chapters: "These pages feel a bit more like summary than have your earlier pages, perhaps because you're focusing on finishing this draft," he posted.

Wayne was spot-on with his critique. I could hardly argue the point.

Two days later, on April 1, Wayne Ude and I met at the Coupeville High School on Whidbey Island to talk about my thesis progress. We were both there to attend the 2011 Whidbey Island Writers Conference and had agreed on a time between sessions to meet.

My thesis advisor appeared before me wearing his usual suspenders, khaki pants and hiking boots. Sitting in chairs in a high school hallway, we began with small talk and pleasantries. Wayne's thick glasses were a little loose, I noticed, so that every so often he had to lift them back up on the bridge of his nose. As we chatted, my insides longed to cry out: "What did you think? What did you think?" Wayne was the only other human being on Earth who'd read this story, who could provide informed feedback and insights. Deep down, I hoped for nothing less than: "It's brilliant. Magnificent! The best book I've read in my entire life." Ah, the vanity.

"Well now," Wayne said as if calling the meeting officially to order, "about the thesis. You have a first draft, which you've accomplished in an impressively short amount of time." He paused to push his glasses back up on his nose. "There's a beginning there, and a middle, and an end." My heart sank. Faint praise, that. "Really overall, it's a pretty good story," he continued. Wayne's legs were crossed, his hands in his pockets. He wasn't looking at me, but at his foot, which he raised and lowered as he stared at it thoughtfully. "You've got the love interests, and the growth and change of the protagonist. That's a good start. The secondary characters need strengthening, and I think you need a subplot or two. But what you're really lacking ..." he paused and looked up at me with a slight crease of worry between his eyebrows "... is a villain."

A villain? The hallway felt suddenly over-bright. "A villain?" I said aloud. This was bad. Very bad.

"Yeah," Wayne nodded with conviction. "A villain. Now, you had a villain, that was Rapparlie, the blacksmith master. He was working as a villain for a while. But then later, he turned out to be a mentor. Yeah, what you really need here is a villain."

It struck me like a sledgehammer. All along, I'd been wrestling with the issue of Rapparlie's role in the book. I'd started out making Rapparlie a brutal taskmaster based on the 1858 letter where he'd reported on Michael's progress to Michael's parents: "In the beginning it came hard to [Michael] to swing the heavy blacksmith hammer ..." But as Michael began to succeed in his craft, I'd softened Rapparlie into a mentor. Wayne was right.

I swallowed, my throat dry. "But Rapparlie was a real person in history. How can I make him bad when I have no real proof?" I tried not to whine, especially since people were loitering around us in the hallway, but this news felt devastating.

Wayne looked off to his left, then back at me. "Well, now, I don't think you have to." He pushed his glasses back up on his nose. "Rapparlie works just fine as he is, as a mentor, a shapeshifter character who seems evil at first, but turns out to be okay. No, the kind of villain you need is someone in the carriage-making business, a rival to Michael on a professional level."

Lord have mercy. A second punch to the gut. Wayne had zeroed in on another of my struggles. I hadn't been able to dig up much of anything about the carriage-making trade. I'd found a newspaper advertisement or two, plus a chapter here and there about carriage-making in books on 19th-century life. But nothing about how they operated, what the various workers did. All along, it had felt like a big black hole in my knowledge. Of course it showed up in my draft.

"Okay, I'll try to come up with something," I told him, although I had not the slightest idea how. At that moment, I felt devoid of all hope.

As we wrapped up our meeting, Wayne and I settled on a schedule of deadlines going forward. In order to graduate, he said, I needed to get him the revised draft by the first week of May, five weeks from the day of our meeting.

As Wayne and I went our separate ways, I thought my head might explode. Five weeks? Five weeks to find a villain? Five weeks to bone up on everything I could find out about carriage-making? Five weeks to revise the novel with a whole new character and plot element, start to finish, that I hadn't even thought of yet?

Reeling in my private agony, I went through the motions of the remainder of the writers' conference, even going so far as to meet with an editor and a literary agent to pitch *Harm's Way* to them. They both expressed an interest in seeing the book "once it was finished." I did not feel Hope. I felt Defeat, with a capital D.

The saving grace of that weekend was the talk by the keynote speaker, Garth Stein. The author spoke about the state of the novel at a time when it felt as if movies, Internet and digital entertainment were all but eclipsing good old-fashioned books. Stein said he'd read a study about the difference between viewing a story on the screen and reading it in a book. For the most part, viewing is a passive activity, the images fed to the viewer without requiring them to use much imagination. The illusions are created for them, so all they have to do is absorb the story. Reading, on the other hand, demands active participation. Readers lift words off the page and transform them into scenes and images in their minds. Reading another person's story, therefore, causes the reader to walk in someone else's shoes. Hence, studies have shown, reading builds compassion. It may seem like a tangential point, but hearing Garth Stein's talk kept me from giving up entirely.

Chapter 36

In other news, Wayne informed me, I'd reached the point in the thesis process where I needed to secure a second reader. Here's how it worked. To graduate from the Northwest Institute of Literary Arts (NILA) with an MFA degree, in addition to meeting course requirements, the student had to write a book-length, publishable thesis of approximately 60,000 words. Approval of the thesis came from two published authors, each of whom had read and signed off on it.

My thesis adviser Wayne counted as the first reader. As for the second reader, although the Northwest Institute of Literary Arts funded the cost, he or she didn't have to be a faculty member in the MFA program. It could be any published author (who met the approval of faculty), preferably someone who wrote books in a genre similar to the student's thesis. I could have gone with Kathleen Alcalá, but the general practice was to find an author not associated with the program. Since my connections, especially in historical fiction, were few, another MFA professor, Larry Cheek, suggested I contact his friend William Dietrich, the Pulitzer Prize-winning journalist. Dietrich had received the Pulitzer for his articles in the *Seattle Post-Intelligencer* about the Exxon Valdez oil spill of 1989. But he'd also written best-selling historical novels, notably *Hadrian's Wall* and the Ethan Gage series.

The recommendation both excited and terrified me. Here I'd been floundering like mad to pull off a first draft, but my adviser and other faculty seemed to think my writing could meet the standards of someone of Dietrich's caliber. I understood that with this recommendation, Wayne and Larry were doing me a great honor. The upside to having a big name author sign off on the thesis included receiving expertise and tips from him that might enhance the manuscript going forward. Furthermore, if William Dietrich liked my thesis, he might agree to "blurb" it, an endorsement that would help me find an agent and add marketing appeal should his endorsement one day appear on the published book jacket.

The downside was the possibility that Dietrich wouldn't like it; that he'd send in a report to the program saying my thesis needed major revisions before he'd sign off on it. It could happen. It had happened to a close friend of mine in the MFA program the previous year. What if Dietrich said I needed another year or so to get it in shape? A frightening prospect, not helped in the slightest by my ongoing quicksand of self-doubt.

Scared or not, I had to go forward if I wanted to graduate. Using the email address Larry gave me, I sent William Dietrich the details and my request. Right away, he graciously agreed.

"Dietrich is my second reader," I posted in the student forum that week. "I'm doomed."

Fortunately, my classmates understood. One pointed out the auspicious nature of his last name. With a German name like Dietrich, he'd have to love the book, right?

All joking aside, I needed to find a villain. First, I revisited the historical newspapers online, but turned up little of use. Then, during another sleepless night of tossing and turning, it occurred to me I might be able to dig up an old lawsuit of some kind. Would law libraries have something like that, maybe even old cases between warring carriage businesses?

This brainstorm led me back to the University of Washington campus, this time to the Gallagher Law Library. I didn't even try to figure it out on my own. I went straight to the reference desk and, to my amazement, the reference librarian turned up old court cases from Ohio in the mid-1800s. Soon, she and I were winding through the stacks of centuries-old, leather-bound tomes. After some searching, the librarian handed me *Western Law Journal: Decisions of the Courts of Ohio Volumes 1-10, 1843-1852*—a canvas-covered book with a crumbling leather spine.

The journal opened with a case about a 24-year-old barkeep named Noble who accidentally killed a man during a fight over a turkey for sale at a market stall. Accidentally, by all accounts, but still, should the killer hang? Reading through the case, I especially loved how it included direct quotes, great source material for the vernacular of the day. "My God I have killed a man," Noble said when he learned his foe McCann was dead. And, in another case I perused, Lawrence v. Jones, the text quoted a man as saying: "There goes a coward and a scoundrel." Each summary of a court decision, I discovered, was a fascinating entrée into a former time.

Unfortunately, as I paged through the volumes, no lawsuits between rival carriage makers emerged. Returning home, I browsed online again, for the umpteenth time, at the *Encyclopedia of Cleveland History* website. In 2011, this site was still under development, indexed with a list of topics from A to Z in one long vertical column. Topics like breweries, churches, and Germans in

Cleveland had all been helpful. I believed I'd harvested just about everything I could, but that day, scrolling aimlessly down the index, I made it to W.

And there it was, all the way at the bottom of the column. Not under "C" for Carriage-making, but under "W" for Wagons and Carriage-making. My grandmother had always described Michael Harm's business as a carriage works. She'd never once mentioned wagons. It had never occurred to me to look under W.

Clicking on the link, I found a substantive article, not only about the wagon and carriage industry of Cleveland in the 1800s, but specifically about the German wagon and carriage industry.

> As it happened elsewhere, Cleveland's trade came to be dominated by skilled foreign-born craftsmen, particularly GERMANS. Large numbers of these immigrants—many skilled in various trades—began flooding into the region in the 1830s and 1840s establishing a marked presence in crafts such as horse-drawn vehicle manufacture.

The article listed names—Lowman, Hoffman, Drumm—and noted they'd been a vital component of Cleveland's carriage-making industry. It explored how the carriage trade expanded in the 1870s and 1880s. Rauch & Lang, the article noted, transitioned from the carriage business into electric automobiles at the turn of the century.

Why no Harm & Schuster? I wanted to scream. To hear my grandmother tell it, Harm & Schuster Carriage Works was a premier carriage-maker of high repute in Cleveland. I read the article several times, desperate to concoct some kind of plot rivalry. Then it occurred to me to check the byline. The article had been written by: Kinney, Thomas A. "From Shop to Factory in the Industrial Heartland: The Industrialization of Horse-Drawn Vehicle Manufacture in the City of Cleveland."

Browser-searching the author's name to locate the thesis, I could hardly believe my good fortune. Thomas A. Kinney had written a book, published in 2004 by Johns Hopkins University, called *The Carriage Trade*. Looking it up on worldcat.org, I learned the book was on the shelf at the University of Washington's Suzzallo Library.

How had I missed this? I'd been working on my thesis for a year and a half, virtually in the dark about carriage-making, and all along, this book had been under my nose. I contacted my son and arranged for him to meet me at the library, to use his university ID card to check it out, to which he readily agreed.

The minute I cracked the cover of *The Carriage Trade*, I could see the details of the operation of this 19th-century industry were all there. The carriage works departments—blacksmithing, wood-working, painting, and trimming, and how each one functioned. When it came to trimming, here was another revelation for me, answering a question Angela and I had long ago about the women employed by Rapparlie in his wagon shop. Trimming departments, also known as saddlery or upholstery departments, produced seats and dashes, cushions and fringe for finished carriages and coaches, essentially a sewing department that often employed women.

The development of carriage-making technologies and business operations, often with illustrations, were all there in *The Carriage Trade*. I found a whole section devoted to the artisan craft hierarchy of apprentices, journeymen, and masters. In the author's note, Dr. Kinney explained it had taken him ten years to research and write the book. Ten years.

As I dove into this refreshing pool of information, Michael Harm's world opened up for me. Every so often, as I read along and took notes, I returned to the website of the *Encyclopedia of Cleveland History*, doing my best to figure out how, based on this new understanding of hierarchies and the various approaches to the business—small family-run shops or large factory enterprises—I might incorporate scenes having to do with rivalries among Cleveland German carriage-makers.

Every time my eyes lit on the name Rauch & Lang, I felt a strange, nagging sensation. The name Rauch seemed oddly familiar. Then, at a random moment—was I loading the dishwasher? Feeding the cat?—it hit me. Rauch was one of the names on the *Helvetia* ship passenger list, right near that of my great-great grandfather. At least I thought it was.

Hardly daring to believe it, I dropped whatever I'd been doing to rifle through my files searching for the *Helvetia* passenger list printout, the one I'd brought home from NARA over a year ago. Locating it, I scanned down the list to Michel Harne (Michael Harm), and sure enough, there it was, right beneath Philipp Haenderich (24-year-old U.S. Citizen): passenger 258, Rausch, Charles, age 15, Bavaria.

Or maybe Roesch. The handwriting was terrible. Michael Harm's name wasn't spelled right (Michel Harne), and neither was Haenderich's (Handrich). Regardless, in my mind that passenger became Rauch. The plot began to hum like a well-oiled clock.

What if, I speculated, it had actually been Charles Rauch, of the future Rauch & Lang carriage company, who'd sailed across the Atlantic on the *Helvetia* with Michael Harm? In one way, it seemed like too much of a coincidence, in another, weirdly plausible. Two young men had arrived together in Cleveland, at the same age and in the same carriage trade, but in vastly different circumstances, one as an apprentice entirely beholden to his master, the other as the entitled son of a carriage shop owner.

By now, having read Kinney's *The Carriage Trade*, I had a much clearer idea of the changes taking place in the carriage industry in those days. Even with the rise of the industrial revolution, some carriage-makers adhered to the time-honored practice of small family businesses crafting custom vehicles. Others, like the Studebakers who claimed to produce "a wagon every six minutes," shifted their focus to quantity production. In the latter model, skilled work was not as essential, a development that drove down wages, lessened the need for skilled artisans and hence, in part led to the demise of the apprenticeship system.

Based on how Michael had been trained under Rapparlie, I felt certain he leaned toward the family business model, whereas Rauch & Lang, I speculated, leaned toward larger factory production. Via the 1880 census, I'd learned that Michael Harm had even gone so far as to make his son Henry an apprentice at Harm & Schuster, at a time when apprenticeships were all but obsolete. In the end, I felt sure, the smaller Harm & Schuster business model couldn't compete. It had closed in the early 1900s, while Rauch & Lang built an enduring reputation with electric automobile manufacture. I'd found my rivalry, and maybe, just maybe, I was also hitting on a broader story of what really happened in the carriage trade in that era. Or one version of it, anyway.

THIS BREAKTHROUGH SET ME ON a path that was ambitious, yet felt achievable. I had to change the relationship between Michael and his shipmate Charles, then add in a whole series of scenes and altercations. In addition, I decided to email Professor Kinney, hoping his expertise might help ensure my manuscript's historical accuracy.

May 18, 2011

Hello Professor Kinney,

My name is Claire Gebben. I am a student in the Northwest Institute of Literary Arts and am working on my thesis for an MFA in Creative Writing.

I was so delighted to come across your book *The Carriage Trade*, because the subject of my thesis is my German immigrant great-great-grandfather, who was an owner of a small carriage works in Cleveland in the 19th Century …. What a relief to find you have done so much, and put it together so beautifully. It's impressive and has become my new bible.

That said, I have a few questions I am hoping you can help me with ...

My biggest and most pressing hope: in your research ... did you find any documents/information regarding the Harm & Schuster Carriage Works? I am attaching a couple of photos—of Michael Harm & Fred Schuster's carriage shop at the Champlain Street location and of the letterhead .... I will not take up any more of your time, but THANK YOU again, for writing *The Carriage Trade*. If you are interested, I have been keeping a blog about my discoveries as I work on this thesis at clairegebben.com.

Claire Gebben

Dr. Kinney replied:

May 24, 2011

Dear Ms. Gebben,

Thanks for the goosebumps!

One of the pleasures of writing for publication is the often surprising responses it elicits from people one would never otherwise know .... My goal [in writing *The Carriage Trade*] was a manufacturing-based history of the trade, something which had never really been done before. Since the demise of the industry the literature on horse-drawn vehicles has focused almost exclusively on the objects themselves (pictorial works, typology, restoration); the manufacturing side, including the lives of those so engaged, remained almost totally unexplored .... I do indeed have information about Harm & Schuster; when I pulled up your e-mail I walked over to a file cabinet and pulled my "Harm & Schuster" file from a collection I've maintained since the 1990s .... The photograph you attached (hence the goosebumps) is ... the first I've seen of a Cleveland wagon shop ..... Thanks again for writing, and know that I look forward to speaking with you soon.

Sincerely,

Tom Kinney

Thomas A. Kinney, Ph.D.

Associate Professor of History

Bluefield College, Virginia

In subsequent emails, Dr. Kinney promised to send me his notes on the Harm & Schuster business, and the Rauch & Lang business, but since he was wrapping up his teaching semester at Bluefield, those would not arrive before my thesis was due.

No matter, my cup was full. As I slogged away incorporating the "villainous" character of Charles Rauch, a wealthy peer of Michael Harm, into my thesis, I had all I could manage. I'd run out of time. Even if Professor Kinney had been able to send me his notes right away, I could not have worked in a single extra detail.

Harm & Schuster's Carriage Works circa 1878 on Champlain Street, in Cleveland, Ohio, present-day site of Tower City.

Chapter 37

That final month, I also leaned on Angela for additional help, sending her the chapters set in Germany to double-check for accuracy. I also pressed her with more questions, about traditional Freinsheim clothing, German dialect cuss words, and the German names of my characters. Despite all Angela had going on at home in Marburg, with school holidays for her daughters and helping Christoph renovate his parents' house and a talk to prepare on Renaissance art discourse, once again she found time for me. One afternoon, she reached me by phone to discuss suggestions.

"Some places are courageous guessing," Angela said. I could picture her leafing through the 146 pages I'd emailed, the part set in Germany, her eyes scanning the text. "It's an interesting twist, that Michael doesn't go on his own to America, unlike the story we always heard. It makes sense. His parents would not have sent him without knowing what he would do. And the knowledge that he would have a formal apprenticeship once he arrived, that was so important in Germany."

I chuckled my agreement. "It took me a long time to come around, but I think you were right. Like you said, he couldn't have run away, not even with a music band. I didn't realize when I started how little freedom he would have had. It was my American understanding getting in the way."

Angela laughed, too. "You know, Claire, I am telling Tante Gretel and Tante Inge about what you have written in the Freinsheim part, and they are really enjoying your portrayal of their town and its people. The only thing is, Tante Gretel thinks the names you've chosen don't sound like they come from the Palatinate."

"What do you mean?" In my MFA program, we'd been taught about the importance of names in a novel, how they can convey character traits and symbolic meanings. I'd looked up meanings for the names I'd chosen. "They're German, aren't they?"

"Tante Gretel says people with these names would not come from the

Freinsheim area. Herr Schulin, the schoolteacher, sounds Swiss, and anyhow, it is not a good name for a teacher. In an old Bad Dürkheim phone directory, we found a teacher named Herr Glock. 'Glock,' Tante Gretel said, 'That sounds like a teacher.'"

I made a note of it, marveling at this difference between our cultures. In the U.S., we also identify people by their last names, making assumptions about who they are, but those assumptions are often off base. In the melting-pot U.S., a person with a German name could appear to be of Asian descent. A fair-skinned blond might have a Hispanic last name. A person with a Scottish name can turn out to be African American. In general, we can't establish where a person is from based on their last name.

"Also, Tante Gretel and Tante Inge think your spelling of Ana Maria is too Italian."

"But that's how Michael Harm spelled it in his letters."

"His spelling in general wasn't so great, was it? But then again, he only went to school until age 15. Tante Gretel says we must spell it Anna Marie. Also, they did not get the idea of the name Haendi at all. They said people would be unsure about a person with a name like that."

Based on the name Haenderich on the *Helvetia* passenger list, I'd given that character the nickname Haendi. Apparently, the concept didn't translate across cultures.

I ran into name issues later, too, when working with Freinsheim historian Dr. Hans-Helmut Görtz. In reviewing my manuscript, he pointed out I'd picked a last name for Michael Harm's sweetheart that would require further plot development.

"Harm is Evangelical Protestant, while Gumbinger is a Catholic name in Freinsheim," Dr. Görtz said. "If you use that last name, you'll need to include something about the general disapproval of the villagers. Back then, for Protestants and Catholics to marry went against accepted conventions."

Once again, I was humbled. The novel would not have been nearly as authentic without the help of my German relatives and friends.

MEMORIAL DAY WEEKEND CAME AND went. June arrived, and I'd missed the deadline for completing thesis revisions. I kept plugging away, doing my best to revise the novel, villain and all.

I use the term "villain" loosely. Charles Rauch was a real person, after all, with a genuine carriage business in Cleveland just like my ancestor. I was loathe to vilify him. What evidence did I have that he and Michael Harm were "enemies"? My thesis adviser kept urging me to increase the tension, to write more knock-down-drag-out scenes, but I continued to struggle. Wayne and I had several back and forth posts in the thesis advising site before I came to a decision about how to proceed.

June 3, 2011

Wayne - Thanks SO much for your comments, once again. I have now looked through them, and I think I see the gist of your point.

As you can tell, I am not keen on this whole villain thing. I think part of what is holding me back is that Rauch is a real person ... [In addition] there are a couple of other justifications for why I resist the idea:

- For one, the Palatinates are known for their good humor. Twain and Cooper and others note it in their writings about travel in the region. Plus, there's the story I found in my research of when Carl Schurz went to arrest a Catholic priest for telling his peasants not to join the provisional army. Schurz and the priest drank wine together and it was all pleasant and civilized, almost like a college prank. So I want to keep up that "admirable foe" concept.

- For another, I don't think anybody is right here—the times were changing, and everyone was adapting— no one could foresee how the internal combustion engine would be the winner in the automobile market, or that horse-drawn vehicles would so dramatically, so quickly become a thing of the past.

- Third, I think the real "villain" is man vs. himself, because citizens of the nineteenth century seemed to have an insatiable desire to conquer nature and amass wealth and rise to the top of the heap in society. Harm and Rauch both got forced onto the hamster wheel, as the entire human race has in this progressive age, and we seem compelled to keep spinning that wheel.

- Lastly, [with all the scenes I've already written], I've reached the climax and we're in denouement mode—I have trouble believing the reader wants more. (Altho, based on your comments, perhaps it's only the writer who has had enough, I'll grant you that.)

I have been working away polishing the manuscript diligently all week … I'll do what I can to address your concerns.

Three days later, on June 6, I mailed a hard copy of the thesis to Wayne and posted in our advising site to let him know it was on its way. Kathleen chimed in then, with smiles and congratulations. While she hadn't had time to read what I'd been uploading, she was rooting for me, which felt great.

Wayne promised he'd get to it right away, and he did.

June 10, 2011

Claire - I just finished the manuscript. It's well written, definitely focused throughout on [Michael Harm's] questions of identity, with just enough of the conflict with Rauch over the years for its present structure … I'm ready to sign off on the novel in its current form, and you should send it on to Bill Dietrich.

The key thing is that even after several readings of most chapters, I continued to find the novel interesting—after all, I read the entire 425 pages in two days and enjoyed it. Harm is likeable; he's an interesting person moving through an interesting time. And the other characters are nicely drawn, convincing.

Well done!

Reply on June 10, 2011

Wayne, you've made my night, my week, my month, my year. I'll send it off to Dietrich right away, fingers crossed. I realize more will need to be done, but bless you for letting it be what it is. And truly, I appreciate how you hung in there with me—your comments and input have been invaluable.

(And I haven't forgotten the three semesters you hung in there with me, Kathleen. Bless you, too.)

I was so late, I worried about how little time I was giving my second reader. We were required to get the thesis to the bindery no later than July 15, but my deadline came even sooner. I had plane reservations to leave for Ohio

July 6. If William Dietrich had major changes for me, I'd have little or no time to make them. As I stood in line at the post office waiting to mail off the draft to my second reader, I still couldn't say, even after all the work I'd done, that I'd be graduating that August.

Fortunately, William Dietrich didn't make me wait long. Just a few days after receipt of my thesis, on June 16, he sent me a follow-up email:

> Claire, I've finished "Harm's Way" and was quite impressed; your writing is superb. I've written a report to the Northwest Institute of Literary Arts that says just that. But I also urge you in my response to take the next step as a fiction writer toward more inventive and gripping plotting, being unafraid to break free from the historical record. You'll see both comments in more detail in my report. Meanwhile, I encourage you to keep developing your writing; you have real talent. Good luck! —Bill

Of course Dietrich was right about my needing to break free of the historical record, but I hoped with all my heart I wouldn't have to "break free" in the next three weeks. What would the MFA faculty think of this assessment? Could I call it done, or not?

When I checked with Wayne and Kathleen, they assured me it was the green light. The thesis could stand without further revision. What a relief! Come August, I'd be receiving my MFA degree in Creative Writing.

As fantastic as I felt about this news, I had little time to rejoice. With three weeks remaining before my departure for Ohio, my next job was to format the book per bindery specifications, and to fix as many typos along the way as possible. Plus, I hadn't finished tracking down the endnotes and bibliography. Once bound, the thesis would be shipped to the MFA office to be displayed at graduation and become part of the library that held the work of all graduates of the NILA program. Published, in a sense. I had to make it as perfect as I could.

I set to work with a sense of frantic, focused haste. Proofreading the later chapters, I again regretted how little information I had about Michael Harm's life during the Civil War, and about his years building his business and raising a family. Wayne referred to it as a "leap" in the text. One day, I hoped, I'd find a way to fill in those gaps. But it wouldn't be before I galloped to the finish line of July 6. Enough was enough. By the time I formatted it all, the thesis numbered 439 pages.

In the midst of it all, on the upcoming trip to Ohio, I also faced the prospect carrying Aunt Elizabeth's ashes with me to her memorial service and burial. Her urn had been at home with us in Seattle all these months, ever since last October when she'd passed away. My brother Craig and I had arranged July 12 as the date for her burial next to her parents and her eldest sister Anna Lindsey at Sunset Memorial Park in Berea.

As usual, I'd overdone the travel arrangements and planned to visit Columbus, and my brother in Cincinnati, flying out a week ahead of the rest of my family. *You're being ridiculous*, I told myself more than once. *Just forget about Michael Harm for a while.* But I'd caught the genealogy bug. As long as I was making the expensive flight to Ohio, I couldn't resist checking out the renowned Ohio History Center in Columbus, Ohio, a place I'd not yet been that held a vast archival collection.

Also, while in Columbus, I wanted to visit Eileen Teall, the very dear friend of both my mother and my Aunt Elizabeth. From a distance via phone and email, Eileen had been such a help to me during my aunt's knee injury, and later during the move to Seattle, and we still corresponded often. Craig and I had invited Eileen to Elizabeth's burial in Cleveland, but she'd emailed us that she couldn't make it. She didn't drive long distances any more, and her daughter wasn't able to take the time off work mid-week. If I came to Columbus, though, she assured me I'd be welcome to stay at her house and she'd love to see me. I could even use her car to get around town.

So, I planned my itinerary accordingly. First, I'd spend two short days in Columbus, then take a bus to Cincinnati to meet up with my brother Craig and ride with him and his family up to Cleveland.

A few days before the start of my trip, I gave Craig a call.

"When I'm in Cincinnati, I'd like to spend some time going through Dad's things," I told him. Boxes and boxes of Dad's belongings still lined several walls at Craig's home, from back in 2009 when we'd cleaned out his place after his death.

"What are you looking for?" he asked.

"It's a long shot, but I'd love to find records from the Harm & Schuster business. I know we haven't come across anything yet, but it doesn't hurt to look again."

Two days later, Craig called back.

"I found more letters," he said.

My pulse quickened. "What do you mean? What kind of letters?"

"They were folded up and stuck in this little leather pocket thing. I can't read them, but it looks like they go back to the 1800s."

"Originals, not copies?"

"Looks like it. It was a fluke I even noticed them stuck in there like that."

"Who wrote them?" Were these letters, I wondered, written long ago from the German side of the family to Cleveland, the other side of the correspondence?

"That's the weird part. They're all written by Michael Harm to Germany. It makes no sense why Dad would have them."

My brain raced, trying to imagine what Craig held in his hands. "How many are there?"

"A lot. I'd say over a dozen. I'll show them to you when you get here."

Close on the heels of the 4th of July holiday, I uploaded my final thesis manuscript to the bindery, packed my suitcase, and nestled Aunt Elizabeth's heavy, boxed urn into my wheeled carry-on. At the airport check-in, I learned it's no small matter to carry a deceased person's remains onto a plane. The Bleitz Funeral Home had supplied me with the paperwork, but still I had to go through a separate line and interrogation.

I filed up to two guards in military black and, as gingerly as I could, extracted the box with the urn out of my carry-on and set it on the stainless steel table. The guards, a man and woman all in black and wearing assorted weaponry, glared at the box, then at me, with suspicion.

I handed over the letter, which the woman received and began to read. The man opened the box lid and stared at the bold words ELIZABETH LINDSEY engraved on the urn. He dusted it with his gloved hands and looked up at me, his eyes a piercing brown.

"You say this contains a deceased person's—"

"Can't you see it's a burial urn?" The woman guard interrupted. "The paperwork's all here. For God's sake, just let her through."

Gratefully, I accepted the pass.

I kept Aunt Elizabeth with me during my Columbus visit, her urn tucked neatly in Eileen's car trunk as I bustled around town, to the Ohio History Center, and with Eileen to the supermarket and out for dinner at Bob Evans Restaurant. Eileen was full of stories about the days when she and the Lindsey sisters, as she referred to my mother and my aunts, barreled around Ohio. They'd traveled in my mom's Ford, a car they'd nicknamed the "Red Demon." My mom was the only one of her sisters who knew how to drive back in the late 1940s.

"Since I was newly arrived from England," Eileen said, "the Lindsey sisters took me on as a sort of project. They were determined to educate me about America. They took me down to Zoar Historic Village and to Dover, Ohio to see that wood carver. Warther, I think his name was. Another time your mother drove us in her Red Demon all the way to Washington, D.C. That was quite a trip, before they put the highways in." I had not heard these stories, from my mom or from Aunt Elizabeth, and pressed Eileen for as many memories as she was willing to share.

Our visit, and easy camaraderie, meant so much to me. During our time together, I realized I'd been worried Eileen might blame me somehow for having lost her dear friend Elizabeth, for having not taken good enough care of her. The sense of forgiveness I felt from Eileen did much to salve my grief wounds.

And my stop in Columbus brought other benefits, as well. The library of the Ohio History Center offered old issues of carriage-making trade magazines, and the museum featured an exhibit of a 19th-century carriage works. I also spent much time in a special exhibition on taboo subjects, about methods of torture and early forms of birth control. Interpretive displays covered little known statistics on birth control, such as: "in 1800, the average American woman gave birth to 7.04 children. In 1900, the figure was 3.56." In part, this was due to the arrival of the India rubber industry, which made the manufacture of condoms and feminine caps more accessible. Moralists, however, rose up against birth control as "unnatural," and 24 states had outlawed contraceptives by 1885. Back in the day in Ohio, it was illegal to even possess instructions for their use.

In the Ohio History Center archives, I found records on the Hoppensack side of the family, my grandmother's father and grandfather. It turned out that my great-great grandfather Hoppensack had a brick-making business in downtown Cleveland on Broadway Hill, where Rockefeller's Excelsior oil refinery later stood. I also learned Michael Harm lived on property that had once been Hoppensack's truck farm. Later, Michael's eldest daughter Lucy would marry Hoppensack's son.

Now I had additional historical characters and details to add to the novel. Once I graduated, of course. First things first.

ALL TOO SOON IT WAS time to hug Eileen good-bye and catch a midday bus to Cincinnati. My early arrival in Cincinnati, though, meant I had several hours to fill until Craig got off work. Wandering aimlessly through the downtown area, I passed a nail salon and decided to treat myself. With everything else that had been going on, nail care had been something I'd neglected. I entered with my heavy wheeled suitcase and carry-on dragging behind me and discovered the manicurist alone in the shop, ready for a walk-in. Parking my belongings, I settled in across from her at her counter.

"So, you're not from Ohio?" She asked, glancing at my luggage propped against the wall.

"No, Seattle, Washington."

"What brings you to our fine state?"

I thought about skirting the subject, but changed my mind. "I'm here to bury my Aunt Elizabeth," I said. "Her urn with her ashes in it is over there in my carry-on. She's such a quiet travel companion."

Holding back a giggle, I waited for a reaction. The manicurist looked up at me, then again at my luggage.

"I'm serious," I said. "It's the quietest she's ever been." I nodded and chuckled, but the manicurist seemed unsure whether she should laugh. "My aunt was quite a character," I said, trying to ease the awkwardness, my grief. "I miss her, but in a lot of ways, she's with me in spirit, even her sense of humor."

She didn't reply, just focused on removing my cuticles. Perhaps she didn't know what to say. Perhaps, I reflected, gallows humor wasn't for everyone.

A few hours later, fingernails now a gleaming gold, I met up with Craig and we drove back to his house on the Kentucky side of the Ohio River. I was happy to see my sister-in-law Cheri and nieces Erica and Lisa, but truth be told, I also couldn't wait to have a look at those letters. When Craig pulled them out, I sifted through them in awe. Every single one was written by Michael Harm, starting in July of 1857, apparently immediately after his arrival in Cleveland. Eighteen letters in all, six from the 1850s and 1860s, and at least two for each of the decades following, the last written in 1908, two years before his death.

Craig and I puzzled over how Dad had obtained the letters, deciding he must have received them from Gunter Faber, Tante Inge's husband, during one of his visits to Freinsheim. He must have brought them back to Cleveland, only to tuck them away in the little leather pocket and not think of them again.

Although I could barely read a word, for my book, I knew this meant I had a serious revision ahead.

ON JULY 12, 2011, THE entire immediate family—Craig and Cheri and their two daughters Erica and Lisa, and Dave and me and our children George and Vivian—all gathered at Sunset Memorial Park in Berea, Ohio for Aunt Elizabeth's memorial and burial. The previous day, Craig and I had already dropped by the cemetery to sign papers and leave her urn, so the details were all taken care of. We arrived in two cars, winding through the peaceful expanse of lawn and trees and headstones until we arrived at the location of the service, marked by the green tent staked over the Lindsey grave plot.

The day was blazing hot. We walked across the sun-drenched lawn to the shade, to two short rows of folding chairs set up underneath the tent. Aunt Elizabeth's urn rested on a pedestal. Amid the dim green light under the tent, the white marble let off an ethereal glow.

The funeral director stood with hands folded in proper respect. To complete the scene, a bagpiper in full regalia paced outside under the hot sun, prepared to skirl a dirge in fulfillment of Aunt Elizabeth's last request. Having just made this long journey with my aunt's urn, I felt a bit raw again, wondering at the mystery of life, and death, and the pell mell, yet awe-inspiring ways we survive during our time here on Earth.

As we stood there quietly, the rest of the family seemed to be looking to me to get things started. At which point I suddenly realized, I'd made all these preparations to get here, but hadn't given thought to what words I would say in parting.

"If Aunt Elizabeth was still here," I began, casting about in my mind for a way to capture her high standards and no-nonsense demeanor, "she probably would have made some comment about how I was dressed, how I'd put on a little weight ..." I didn't get much farther before tears robbed me of my voice. I wanted my aunt back again, keeping an eye on me, prodding me to be the best I could be.

After a moment, Craig stepped forward, pulled a piece of paper from his pocket, and began to read.

Grace Elizabeth Lindsey

8/3/1921-10/23/2010

In her 89 years of life, Elizabeth accomplished a great deal, especially when it came to travel, libraries, and liberal activism. She looked forward to travel to exotic locations, such as Brazil, India and China. She took on assignments that many Americans would never consider, including United States Information Service jobs in Indonesia and East Pakistan. This trust in the unknown broadened her perspective. Elizabeth never failed to improve libraries in Cleveland and Michigan including libraries in jails. She always gave us thick hardcover books for Christmas. Elizabeth could read a book in an evening. She was active in the Democratic Party and supported many female candidates ....

I could almost see Aunt Elizabeth nodding her approval, as if to say: "That's how it's done." As Craig read on, I was grateful to him for his well-written tribute, and also for how our children were hearing things about Elizabeth Lindsey they'd probably never heard before.

When my brother finished, others said a few words, and then the funeral director stepped forward. To the mournful tones of the bagpipe, the director lowered her urn into the ground. The bagpiper had only played a few bars before we recognized the tune: "Amazing Grace." My aunt may or may not have appreciated the irony, but my brother and I sure did. We grinned at each other, both for how much Aunt Elizabeth hated her given name Grace, and for how truly amazing she was.

Soon the service was at an end and we left the tent for the sun-dazzled lawn, my brother and I and our spouses talking together while the younger generation cousins joked around, glad to be together again after such a long time. On this, my family journey, so much had already happened. My gratitude for the lives of those who went before, on whose shoulders we all stood, ran deep.

Chapter 38

The saying goes that funerals are for the living, not the dead. Present at the burial of Aunt Elizabeth in Ohio were her sole survivors. Craig and I were her only niece and nephew. Since my father was an only child and my mother was the only one of her sisters to marry, we'd grown up with no first cousins. We'd lost our older brother Sandy, too, over two decades ago. After the burial that afternoon, it hit me with a jolt of clarity and dismay that Craig and I, although still in our fifties, were the last survivors of our generation. Each of us had two children—one son and three daughters in all—but Craig and I were the patriarch and matriarch of the Patterson/Lindsey family line.

So this is how we survive here, I thought, remembering again Rapparlie's phrase in his 1847 letter. *We dwindle down to a mere handful of souls.*

How we survive here. That phrase kept echoing in my head, so I made an inventory of the news in Rapparlie's missive. His account of the family's survival in the New World included: details of wages and occupations; further family dispersal as siblings went their separate ways; dogged determination to launch a business; the marvel of newfound political liberty; looking after elderly parents, one of whom had been sick; life events of births, marriages and deaths; news of safe arrivals of common acquaintances; instructions for how to travel; and greetings and hospitality to family and friends.

In quite similar ways, his account echoed how we have been surviving here in our present day lives. We work, and love, and grieve, and gather during times of travel and celebration and loss. We survive here moment by moment, and generation to generation, across time.

Johann Rapparlie's descriptive letters were some of my favorites, his voice direct and no-nonsense, capturing the rapidly changing conditions of their pioneer immigrant existence. I couldn't claim to have inherited his writing talent, however. My great-great grandfather's uncle was not a blood relative. Rapparlie was related to me by marriage only, the husband of Katherina Handrich, a younger sister of Michael Harm's mother.

Nowadays, we are able to expand our family associations via DNA, but blood relations have always played a role in the search for identity. Regarding the two different sets of letters from Cleveland—fifteen of them found in 2008 in Tante Inge's attic written mostly by Handrich and Rapparlie, another sixteen found that July of 2011 in Dad's belongings written by Michael Harm—I believe blood relations factored into how they became separated in the first place.

Once upon a time, these letters were all in the possession of Gunter and Inge Faber in Freinsheim. During one of Dad's several visits to Freinsheim, Gunter Faber, a cousin of Dad's generation, brought out the letters so they could look through them together. Gunter and Dad must have determined that Dad should have all of the letters written by Michael Harm, since he was Michael's blood relative. For his part, Gunter would keep the letters written by Rapparlie and the Handrichs, since Gunter was a direct descendant by blood of those people, a descendant of the Freinsheim family of Johann Philipp Harm and Elisabetha Handrich Harm.

Regardless of how it occurred, the restoration of the letters into one collection was, for me, a godsend. That July of 2011 when Craig first handed them over, I could only speculate about the priceless find. With great excitement, I took them back to Seattle and shared news of the discovery via email with Angela. Immediately, I made scans and within days sent Angela email after email of high resolution .jpg images. I hardly dared hope she'd have time to look them over, but inwardly longed for her to do it soon.

As it turned out, Angela was as thrilled by the discovery as I was. Soon she was sending me news of the contents of the first letter Michael wrote to his parents, a letter he sent to Freinsheim within weeks of his 1857 arrival in Cleveland.

July 25, 2011

Re: July 1857 letter p 1

Claire, this letter alone is a treasure! It is so amazing, how different and eloquent it is from the first note we had, the one Michael added to Rapparlie's 1858 letter. I was moved by the last page, [Michael] writes he would not miss Germany at all if his parents were also with him. The greetings go to the dear parents and his beloved brother.

In her email, Angela was emphasizing Michael's affection for his Freinsheim family because we'd wondered about it all along. We'd never been sure if there'd been ill will between Michael and his parents. These additional letters revealed to us how Michael Harm maintained a strong affection for his family in Freinsheim, and as more letters were translated, it became clear it was an affection that endured to the end of his days.

An affection that, as it turned out, was handed down through five generations to where we are today. While writing my thesis, I'd come to appreciate this abiding love most of all. The constant support and help of the German family saw me through the tough times, and helped me persevere, sometimes against daunting odds.

Thanks to Angela's quick translations, that August of 2011 as I rode the ferry from north Seattle across the Puget Sound to Whidbey Island for my MFA graduation, I already knew many more details about Michael Harm's life.

As I walked forward in the procession to receive my MFA degree, my head swirled with plot twists. The new batch of letters astonished me in their richness. In many cases, what actually happened was better than the fictional storyline I'd invented. On arrival in New York City, my great-great grandfather had fallen prey to a common scam of the day and been robbed of his last $20. He and Rapparlie had truly had a major falling out.

Angela had not yet translated all the letters, so there was much more to learn. I dearly wanted to know what my great-great grandfather had written in 1908, just two years before he died. Had he found hope, as I'd surmised for the conclusion in my thesis? My burgundy and gold, hardbound *Harm's Way* thesis gleamed on display at the graduation reception, but my mind couldn't let it rest.

Post-graduation, it would take me over a year to complete major revisions based on the new information in the letters. The revision process was an ongoing journey, inviting me ever deeper into an exploration of the novel's themes of the forging and shaping of a life, of the transcendent quality of music, and of what hope my ancestors may have found amid the dramatic cultural shifts and fast-paced technological changes occurring during their lives.

By the fall of 2012, I had the novel in good enough shape to think about next steps. I needed to get it published, especially for the sake of the family in Germany who had been so wonderful in helping me research and earn my MFA degree. As a member of a local Seattle writing group, I'd once attended a presentation by Catherine Treadgold, editor of Coffeetown Press, a small independent press in Seattle. Formerly, she'd been an opera singer and majored in German in college, so she seemed like a perfect fit as an editor for the book.

Double-checking Coffeetown Press's website, I saw they accepted historical fiction. I knew finding a press could take years, so I decided to leap in then and there. Nervously, I followed the query guidelines and submitted an excerpt of *Harm's Way*. I heard back in a few days with a request for the whole manuscript. That November, just before my 55th birthday, Coffeetown Press informed me they wanted to publish the book.

"Good job," the acquisitions editor Jennifer McCord said when we met in person. "We want to offer you a contract." As joy rose inside me, she added, "You'll have to change the name, though. *Harm's Way* doesn't do it. Start thinking of title ideas and keep a list. When you have some good suggestions, send them our way."

"What's wrong with *Harm's Way*?" I bristled at the very idea of a new title. Angela too had liked *Harm's Way*, similar to the title of a German tale with an immigrant theme: "*Der lange Weg des Lukas B.*" [The Long Way of Lukas B.] What's more, I felt emotionally attached. For three years I'd been walking in the footsteps of my great-great grandfather, doing whatever I could to accompany him along Harm's way.

But Jennifer had a more objective view. She pointed out how a book called *Harm's Way* could be about anything: a war novel, a science fiction book, an adventure story. It didn't immediately point to a historical novel, let alone the 19th-century era.

When I thought about it, I knew she was right. Whenever I talked about my book to friends and acquaintances, I had to elaborate on the title.

"I've been working on a historical novel about a German immigrant blacksmith to Cleveland," I'd tell people.

"Oh really? That's great. What's it called?"

"*Harm's Way*." At their blank stare, I'd feel compelled to add: "It's based on the true story of my German great-great grandfather. His last name was Harm."

Then, realization, and interest, generally dawned on their faces.

So, I scribbled down title ideas, and selected several favorites, all of which did not pass muster with Coffeetown. At last, we hit on one we both liked: *The Last of the Blacksmiths*, a title reminiscent of James Fenimore Cooper's *The Last of the Mohicans*. The deciding factor for me was test marketing. When I told people "I'm thinking of calling my novel *The Last of the Blacksmiths*," I was generally greeted not with blank stares, but with sparks of recognition and open curiosity.

Angela, on the other hand, was not thrilled. She explained Germans would find the title confusing. There are still working blacksmiths in Germany, after all. There are still working blacksmiths in the U.S. when it comes to that, but certainly not the blacksmiths of my great-great grandfather's era. Their role, so essential to the pre-machine, pre-petroleum age, has not existed for over a hundred years. In choosing that title, I hoped the novel might provoke some controversy, opening up discussions about what's been lost with the waning of the artisan craft era. To some extent, that conversation has managed to come to pass at venues where I've spoken.

With the publication of *The Last of the Blacksmiths* in February of 2014, the ultimate celebration of family and friends ensued. My book launch, somehow, turned into a really huge party. Just about everyone I knew and loved came from all over the globe to celebrate the book's release. My father-in-law came from Michigan, my brother Craig and his wife Cheri from Cincinnati. That's just for starters. Dear friends of a lifetime flew in from South Korea and New York City, and drove up from Portland and Eugene. Friends and colleagues came from Seattle and Bellevue, from British Columbia and Whidbey Island, from Los Angeles and Olympia and Bellingham. Perhaps best of all, Angela's brother Matthias Weber and his partner Ina Dörr-Mechenbier flew all the way from Freinsheim to celebrate with me. I couldn't get over how the book launch brought together descendants of both Michael and Philipp Harm. If only Angela could have been there, I wouldn't have wanted for anything else. Our house overflowed with guests all weekend, and I loved every moment.

How do I account for this outpouring? On the face of it, I planned big. It felt almost like a destination wedding. I booked a party venue in Seattle's 19th-century Georgetown neighborhood and hired a horse and carriage to give rides around the block. A blacksmith friend brought his anvil and gave demonstrations on the back patio. I scoured local wine stores for vintages from the local Palatinate (Pfalz) region, even the signature *Sekt* (German sparkling wine) from Bad Dürkheim. A big fan of theater, I roped local Seattle actors into presenting a 10-minute scene from the book. I also noted in the invitation that a percent of the proceeds of book sales would go to the Northwest Carriage Museum in Raymond, Washington, where I'd learned much about urban carriages and how cars with their bright, colorful finishes were a natural next step. Cars today still bear the names of carriage styles: Brougham, Cabriolet, Victoria.

When the books stood stacked on the venue table, I felt so incredibly fortunate. For four years, I'd been living with this undertaking, so tentative and afraid, uncertain about my ability to actually write the novel. This massive project grew and grew, so many things coming together, both past and present. Even as I pursued the realization of this dream, everything around me seemed to be slipping away, losing my father, then Aunt Elizabeth. Yet time kept propelling me inexorably forward, everything taking longer, and being more difficult, than I ever could have foreseen. All this time, I hadn't been pretending to be a writer, I'd been practicing and learning how to write, while growing into a new understanding of myself, and of those around me. We all have to survive within a constant duality, the push and pull of hope and despair, of looking back and looking forward, and somehow cope.

How wonderful it felt, when the book was finished, to celebrate and appreciate everyone around me. I'd gone on a surprising, tumultuous, challenging journey, and had something to tell about.

Chapter 39

Since publication of the historical novel *The Last of the Blacksmiths*, I've had the privilege of giving over 70 talks to audiences at universities, libraries, genealogy and historical societies, German and other interest groups, retirement communities, clubs, and book stores. It is the encouragement and interest of these audiences that led to the writing of this memoir, which I hope serves as an inspiration for others to explore and write their own family stories.

Through the process of writing that novel, I began to look at my own life trajectory through a new lens, as a continuation of, and at times a repetition of what has gone before. Writing it changed me. I no longer think of my life as beginning at birth, but as reaching back through layers of generations and personalities. I no longer think that everything happening in my life signifies progress, whereas what happened in the past was always outmoded and backward. I've come to realize that in many ways in our modern era, we've lost more than we've gained, especially in terms of diminishing knowledge of agriculture, hand-crafted materials, and sustaining the environment around us for posterity. And I've also gained the perspective that how I live my life has an impact on those who come after me.

Writing *How We Survive Here* has taken me to a whole new level, deepening my perspective on how I survive here, for better or for worse. Originally, Angela and I had talked about publishing the actual letters. Already in September of 2013 she visited me in Seattle for an intensive couple of weeks of letter translations. All twnety letters found in Dad's belongings follow in the second part of this book. Angela and I view the publication of these 19th-century letters as adding to the lexicon for scholars of history and material culture.

The historical novel *The Last of the Blacksmiths* is a fictional account, in which I invented characters, and dialogue, and feelings, and scenes to allow the imagination of the reader to picture and better understand a little-known era. But while it's based on a true story and on real events and people in history, it's not what actually happened.

As such, I'm also eager to provide the letters here in order to set the record straight. Thanks to Angela's careful and diligent work, the letters have been translated as accurately as possible. Furthermore, I have written this memoir as close to the truth as I remember it. While the dialogue is not word-for-word, I've scoured my memory, and also reviewed the manuscript with those I've quoted in an effort to come as close as possible to what actually happened.

As I got down to the business of writing this book, something unexpected emerged. As I kept returning to old emails to reinforce my memory of what had taken place, I noticed how Angela and I were going through similar experiences to those of our ancestors: economic uncertainty, political elections, the death of loved ones. It wasn't until I began working with the 19th-century and 21st-century letters in juxtaposition that I better understood the phrase: "history repeats itself." This project has brought me to view time differently, as having patterns that repeat in sometimes surprising ways from generation to generation.

The appearance of Aunt Elizabeth in this narrative was a genuine surprise. I'd planned to bring her in as a subplot, but she kept emerging and demanding (or should I say commanding?) her time on stage. Until that last fifteen months of Aunt Elizabeth's life, we had barely seen each other twice a year, yet in writing about her in these pages I came to realize what a strong influence she had on my life, and on who I am today. I realize now how much she did to foster in me a passion for literature and writing. Her high standards demonstrated to me a way to live that I admire very much: as an independent thinker, without apology, living from the heart with creativity and flair. Within a year after she passed away, I changed my hair color from brown to red, a subconscious act that I later came to think was more than a coincidence. I've kept it that way ever since.

While the estate of Elizabeth Lindsey was not large, after her death, a surprising windfall came in the form of three paintings. During the 1950s while working for the United States Information Service, Aunt Elizabeth became friends with two important Southeast Asian artists, Zainul Abedeen and Quamrul Hasan, and returned home with paintings by both. While abroad, she also traveled to Calcutta, India on one occasion to the studio of Jamini Roy, where she purchased several paintings. After her death, when my brother and I queried Christie's in New York about these works, they agreed to add them to their Southeast Asian Art auction. I attribute my liberal spending on the book launch in part to the serendipitous money raised from the sales. It's my hope that the works went to museums or collectors who could truly appreciate them and make the artwork more accessible to the public. And I'd like to believe Aunt Elizabeth would have been pleased to know she supported my writing dreams posthumously.

After Matthias and Ina returned from the 2014 book launch to Freinsheim, they started planning an event for me there that coming fall. This event, to be held in a recently renovated old hospital, would be open to the public. I admit to having another case of nerves. Worried about what Freinsheimers would think of me, and wanting to communicate with them to the best of my ability, I felt compelled to again read from a German script to go along with my PowerPoint images.

When I arrived in Freinsheim, Angela had not yet arrived from Marburg. Despite a busy schedule, Matthias sat down with me to translate my English script into German. We also walked over to the *Alte Spital*, a restored community building that used to be a hospital, to set up the presentation. The event would take place in a spacious, wood-floored room on the second level, which had large windows and a huge, sandstone-manteled fireplace. Matthias and I set out 60 chairs and, in a separate room, glasses for wine to be served at the reception afterward.

That evening, all but two chairs were full. During Matthias's introductory remarks, I did my best to breathe deeply and stay calm. As things got underway, my nervousness subsided. The event wasn't really about me at all. In the audience were many of Philipp Harm's descendants, relatives who rarely gathered together anymore. This was a celebration, I realized, of the family, and of the town, and of our shared history.

After the introduction, I read an excerpt of my book in English, then Matthias read the same passage in German from a translation by an English schoolteacher in the town, Astrid Stapf. Next, Angela read excerpts from the old letters. When it came time for my PowerPoint presentation, Angela received enthusiastic applause for teaching herself to read the Old German Script, and I received the same for attempting to learn blacksmithing.

Afterward, as people lingered to talk and drink Riesling, a man I had not met came over and introduced himself.

"Hello," he said in halting English. "I am Michael Harm. I am called after an ancestor first time in Freinsheim. He was blacksmith—Johann Michael Harm? Perhaps related to you also?"

Goosebumps. We are indeed related. My father's family tree lists our common ancestor, Johann Michael Harm, a blacksmith, at the start of our tree—the first Harm to come to Freinsheim. Delighted, I shook Michael Harm's hand and gave him a copy of my book.

I have my writing professors at the Northwest Institute of Literary Arts to thank for their patience in helping me learn how to write. Perhaps this memoir might inspire others to want to attend that program, but unfortunately, in

2016 the Master of Fine Arts program on Whidbey Island closed its doors. It had been in existence for a brief eleven years. The program made a significant difference in the lives and careers of many writers, but could not be sustained.

All along as I was writing the novel, I dreamed *The Last of the Blacksmiths* would be translated into German, especially for the sake of my elder relatives. "I cannot read your book," Tante Gretel said to me on a 2015 visit to Freinsheim. "It is in English." This reality made me sad and inspired me to have a translation made for my German family, young and old, whose English, like my German, is not so fluent. As of December of 2016, such a translation exists, accomplished by a young professional translator of the Freinsheim community, Corinna Schlachter. I am currently seeking a publisher for the German edition.

In 2011, Angela was accepted into a Ph.D. program at the University of Bonn, and in 2017 earned her doctoral degree in cultural studies via her thesis, Indigenous Positions within the Canadian Art Discourse Since the 1960s.

In 2016, Matthias Weber was elected Mayor of Freinsheim, an honor that makes me—and the whole family, I hazard to say—very glad. Wouldn't the two brothers, Michael and Philipp Harm, be proud? I like to think so.

And the reverberations of this journey continue to expand. The photo of Michael Harm at his anvil, which appears on the cover of my novel, is now included in a permanent exhibition on blacksmithing at the Metal Museum in Memphis, Tennessee. In a new publication by Dr. Hans-Helmut Görtz, Michael Harm's bio appears as one of 120 Freinsheim personalities. The German title of the book is *Freinsheimer Gestalten. Miniaturen aus anderthalb Jahrtausenden Freinsheimer Geschichte* (2016). [*Freinsheim Personalities: Brief Biographies from One-and-A-Half-Thousand years of Freinsheim History.*]

Again and again, I'm reminded to be open and grateful as the mystery of our lives unfolds. Due to the publication of my novel, I've become reacquainted with Cleveland Hoppensack relatives, descendants from my grandmother's paternal side of the family. And, in the spring of 2016, a full two years after the U.S. publication of *The Last of the Blacksmiths*, I received an unexpected phone call from another relative.

"Claire, it's Mark Gressle. I finally got around to reading your book. What a story. I had absolutely no idea."

I knew Mark by name only. His father, Lloyd Gressle, and my father, Clyde Patterson, were close first cousins, but by the time I was born, Lloyd and his family had moved to Pennsylvania. Apparently, Lloyd's youngest son Mark had picked up my book based on postcards I sent out to distant relatives.

"I had no idea, either," I agreed with Mark. "It's been such an amazing journey, finding all that stuff out."

"Here's a thought," Mark said. "We have a Gressle family reunion every summer. Why don't you come this year?"

I told him I'd think about it. A month or so later, I called him back and confirmed I would attend. "It's so great of you to invite me," I added. "I mean, I'm coming to this reunion, and you and I have never even met."

"That's right!" Mark said, laughing. "I guess it's about time."

Which is how, in July of 2016, I wound up sitting in the Gressle family home amid a passel of Michael Harm's descendants, meeting most of them for the first time. In addition to relatives of my generation, the house swarmed with young adults and grandchildren, including five children under five years of age and a baby on the way. We shared stories and laughs and, at some point during that afternoon, Mark produced a pile of my books for me to sign, to be dedicated to fifth, sixth and seventh generation descendants of our great-great grandfather.

In the course of the three years recounted in this memoir, my immediate family may have dwindled to a mere handful of souls. But as the matriarch of the oldest generation, instead of feeling very much alone, I feel as if the opposite has occurred. My family and friends have grown and continued to expand. After returning from the Gressle family reunion, I received an email that September with the subject line "She's here!," announcing the birth of a beautiful, healthy baby girl. Not to mention the ever-expanding clan of Philipp Harm's descendants in Germany. Of course, they've been there all along. But since this project began, my affection and appreciation and friendships with them have deepened immeasurably. I count them now not only as the "relatives in Freinsheim," but as family.

In reading over this manuscript, Angela expressed to me how she did not see my novel as a fait accompli, a foregone conclusion that would be the end of it all. "I have to admit," she wrote in her comments in the margin, "I never thought about your book as the main and sole outcome of this project. Really, I saw this project in a very broad sense and didn't want us to forget about aspects we were finding on the way." She added that, even though we did not know about these ancestors until the discovery of the letters: "Omissions and oppressed histories sometimes leave tiny reminders, which will become motivations for a search …. So, you see, I cannot but think beyond this family story, and it is certainly just the beginning."

Indeed, that's how we survive here, moment to moment, in the midst of all the "aspects we're finding on the way." As I've written this account, I've come to understand that, often without realizing it, we live along a continuum of generations, our days filled with joy, and with sorrow, and with everyday living, not in isolation, but amid the broader tides of human history. Our family history influences us more than we recognize. We don't always have as much power over our lives as we'd like to believe, but we can influence how we survive here. It does matter what we do, what kind of lives we create with the opportunities and materials at hand.

Since writing and giving presentations on *The Last of the Blacksmiths*, many people have come forward to tell me my story has inspired them to write their own family histories. May *How We Survive Here* continue to spark such endeavors. Becoming aware of our family history deepens our understandings of who we are, enriches our present-day lives, and contributes to our ongoing legacy for the generations who follow.

Part Two

A collection of twenty additional 19th-
and early 20th-century letters written
from Cleveland to Germany, spanning
the years 1857-1908

Letters Written by Michael Harm,
Discovered in Clyde Patterson's Belongings in 2011

———◆———

In Part One, letters written by Philipp Handrich, Jakob Handrich, Johann Rapparlie, Michael Höhn, and several additional letters by Michael Harm are scattered throughout the narrative.

Page locations and years of those letters are noted in the Index starting on page 317.

This first letter by Michael Harm was written at age 16 shortly after his arrival in Cleveland.

Cleveland 9 July 1857[1]

Much loved parents and brother.

With joy I pick up the quill (feather) to send you the news that I have arrived healthy in Cleveland. I want to describe the voyage a little bit for you as follows: we were taken aboard on May 18th[2] in the evening at 8 o'clock and in the morning at 4 o'clock our ship left the harbor with good wind, which stopped at noon though and the ship rested quietly/motionless. Our ocean journey was not very good, because when one hovers around on the water for 43 days, that's not very fast, and still time does not get boring because once one is on the water for 8 days, one gets accustomed. When the 43rd day came along, we still didn't see land in the morning at 6 o'clock and at 10 o'clock our ship cast anchor and we were riding at anchor in front of New York, such a good wind did we get.

In the afternoon at 4 o'clock we were brought to land by steamboat, because in the summer no ship is allowed to cast anchor inside the harbor. We put up at Hartnung's[3] from Dürkheim[4], who owns the "Freischütz", at whose place we were treated very well, and I advise everybody who comes to New York, if he wants to be treated well, to put up at this same place.

We stayed in New York for three days. I met a lot of Freinsheimers there, the Borner's Franz, Joseph and Ana. I also met the Hawer's Fritz, and Philipp Kirchner,

---

1   According to the *Helvetia* passenger list, Michael's ship arrived in New York Harbor on June 30, 1857. Michel Harne. Year: 1857; Arrival: NY, NY; Microfilm Serial: M237, 1820-1897; Microfilm Roll: Roll 175; Line 3; List Number 737. Nearby on the same passenger list, the name Philipp Haenderich, age 24, U.S. citizen, appears.

2   Corroborative evidence that Michel Harne and Michael Harm are one and the same. June 30 is exactly 43 days after May 18.

3   Trow's New York City directory of 1857 lists a William Hartung, hotel owner, at 161 Washington.

4   Bad Dürkheim, 6 km from Freinsheim

whose house I visited and he is very well. I also met the old (man) Borner and (the) Fischer's Ana, who were very happy about the encounter. We traveled then from New York away to Philadelphia, there we stayed three days, too, then we continued our travel again to Cleveland. We arrived late in the evening, but still went to their house[5] and they were very glad. They are all still quite healthy and have a happy family. Cousin Jakob is still unmarried and still works at his old place and has everyday 2 ½ dol. The next day I also visited cousin Scheuermann and his family,[6] they are also quite healthy and have two boys. When I was barely two days in Cleveland, it was known to the Freinsheimers all over and whenever there was market day I saw many. Adam Höhn[7] comes weekly to Cleveland to the market with his two white horses. He has visited me immediately and was very happy when he saw me. He asked me also right away if I didn't have a letter by his brother. When I told him No and why I don't have one, he was very sad, he said he had written once before and had wanted to send another one along with Schantz from Dackenheim and also a present for his sister, but when he arrived at the place where they were supposed to meet Schantz, he had already left. [Adam Höhn] has shown me the letter he wanted to send. I later went out with him to his farm and stayed two days with him.

He is doing very well. He has an inn and a store or retail shop. He houses almost every 14 days music or a dance, all the farmers and Freinsheimers from the surroundings come together and there's dance to notes.[8]

Also, Mathias[9] and I were hunting in their forest, then we

---

5 Presumably, Johann and Katherina Rapparlie's home at Michigan and Seneca Sts. in Cleveland

6 Georg Scheuermann was born approximately 1815. His marriage with Katherina Margaretha nee Handrich (12/12/1813) occurred in Cleveland on 2/14/1844. Sons Georg (5/24/1846) and John (11/20/1851)

7 Adam Hoehn is listed in Ohio County Death Records as living in Parma, Ohio, born 1815 in "Frunsheim," died 1872 at 57 years of age.

8 Presumably, musical notes

9 Records indicate a Mathias Hoehn, son of Adam, was born in Freinsheim in the same year as Michael Harm, 1841. "Deutschland Geburten und Taufen,

visited with the Försters, who are all very well, and we visited Riethaler and his family, he is still so healthy that he outruns a young man of 18 years. He was so happy to see me, he said, if only your father came in this door, then I would want to be jolly once more!

I also told Höhn what he would say about how Jakob and Margarethe also want to come to America[10] later this autumn, and he said if they want to come they should not hesitate to do it, as I will want to care for them as if they are my own children, but the very best would be if they would come all together.

I could not deliver the presents from Beringer, because Georg and Jakob are both away in Minesore [Minnesota]. I have kept the things until one of them returns.

Dear parents, up to now I like it very much in Cleveland and wouldn't feel any longing anymore for Germany, if only you, dear parents, would be here with me. I learn the blacksmith business, which I like very much, as I am all healthy now and am thanking our dear God for that.

I don't know any more news for now, except that in this moment there are very bad times in America and the money is very scarce and it is being believed that many banks will fail again.[11]

Now I want to close my writing and I remain your true son and your brother who loves you

Michael Harm

Many greetings to all good friends and acquaintances and neighbors. Please greet my godfather and his family, Richard Pirmann and his family and our female cousin Bas, also greet for me Phil Hilberth, his wife and Auguste, a greeting to cousin Daniel[12] and his family and all the Meckenheimers, who ask for me. Also a greeting to the

1558-1898," database, Mathias Hoehn, 18 Jul 1841; citing ; FHL microfilm 193,848.
10 The letters always refer to immigrating to the U.S. as "coming in" to the country.
11 Financial panic of 1857.
12 Possibly Daniel Ohler

neighbor Michel and his wife and then at last to my friends and their parents and brothers and sisters. If once one of them should come to see me, then it will still be like the old times.

[Transverse]

Write an answer to this letter immediately and the address is:To Michael Harm at Joh. Rapp. Clev Oh.

[Vertical in margins]

Dear parents, you do not have to worry about me, I am well taken care of, as well as or even better than in Germany. I believe that Jakob will come over (travel out of the country) and the Handrich's Jakob also wants to come along once more.

In case someone from Michael Höhn's family should come here, Jakob or Gretel, they should just come to me into the city and I will guide them to Adam Höhn, and the BK [blacksmith shop?] Rapparly they will find easily, everybody knows him.

22 December 1857

Much beloved parents and brother!

Your letter I have duly received and I have seen from it that God be thanked you are still quite well, for which I'm glad of heart. Also, I am still quite healthy and I am doing very well.

As I have heard from your letter that Lebhard's wife has died, which is surely hard for him. But he must find comfort and think that what God did is well done.

Much beloved parents, I would have written to you earlier but I always wanted to wait for the arrival of Jakob and of Johannes later this year as you wrote [they are coming], and I also wouldn't have written by now but I see that they are not coming and winter is already close to the door so I do not think anymore, that I will see them this winter.

(The) Höhn[1] had already been looking forward to seeing them, and has been coming to see me as often as he came to town in order to see whether they are still not there? Another thing, (the) Stein[2] wanted to know where his brother is and how he is doing and what he is doing, on that I can give him a little news, he lives approximately 30 to 40 steps from Höhn on a rented farm and farms half of it, but he is doing very well.[3] I have visited him myself.

Much beloved Parents, you need not think that I am regretting that I went to America. No that is not the case, instead I am rather glad that I am here,[4] here I can learn a craft from cousin Rapparlie that is needed around the world, and if, in 5-6 years, it no longer pleases me so I can go back to Germany again and then I will have traveled and seen the world, and think to also be able to stand my ground as a businessman.

---

1   Presumably, Adam Höhn of the other 1857 letter.
2   The Stein name is a common one in Freinsheim and neighboring villages.
3   Possibly, farms in Parma, Ohio.
4   It is now almost six months since Michael arrived in America.

A couple of days after I wrote my letter Jacob Siringer returned again, he has bought a house here and has an inn and [illegible]. He is doing very well. I know no other news than that this year is very bad in all the businesses in America, because almost all of the banks have failed.

Now I will close my writing, and I remain your faithful son and your brother who loves you

Michael Harm.

Many greetings from cousin Rapparlie and Jakob and cousin Katherina they are all still quite healthy.[5]

I greet all of my schoolmates and all good friends and acquaintances and neighbors and all who ask about me. Also pass on a nice greeting to the wagon-maker Bart from Jacob Hoffmann, who works here at cousin Rapparlie's.

---

5   Michael sometimes refers to his aunts and uncles as cousins.

1858 letter written by Johann Rapparlie is found in Part One, Chapter 7.

27 January 1861[1], from Cleveland[2] to Freinsheim

Much beloved parents and brother

Your last letter we have rightly received and in there I have seen with regret that the few lines I added to the back of uncle's letter have caused you to be very sad, although I only attribute this to the times at the moment in Germany and to the gossip of our countrymen.

What they said I cannot write again because I don't know whether it was lies or truth. That's why we want to leave it to the future, and if God the Lord wants to, perhaps we may be able at one time to speak about it directly.

As for the allegations uncle made towards you, I want to write something orally about it to you that is the following: First, he has written to you that you sent your child into the wide world, [but] my own will was part of it, and you did not send me, instead I have asked you for it, and therefore have gone for myself.

Then secondly, there was no money? That is true because when I came to Cleveland, indeed I admittedly had no money anymore, but when I came to New York at that moment I still had 20 dollars, and if I had settled on the next piece rate[3] [of the journey] immediately and would have gone to Cleveland, I would have had at least 10 dollars free money, but then I had such a good opportunity to be led around on a fool's rope by a certain Mr. Cousin, the same as it happens to many green Germans who rely on their American cousin.

Therefore I advise all who wish to go to America, and want to rely on such people, better to go alone, because

1   At the start of 1861, Lincoln had been elected to the presidency and would be inaugurated that coming April.
2   By 1860, the population of Cleveland had reached 43,000 persons.
3   Michael apparently did not contract for the whole journey, but bought fares for the next leg of the journey at each stop along the way, a method of travel advised by Rapparlie in an earlier letter.

otherwise they are abandoned.

Now we'll stride into the third and final writing, there were also no clothes. Although I had no clothes, the uncle did not buy any for me although he had also written that he had provided so much for me, what kind of clothes I had you know and also I was satisfied and would I have made the journey again, then I would have taken even less because they [the clothes] have no importance here.

About the next of the accusations there, you have not sent me any money with our compatriots, but I think he did not want money for [accepting] me, but he just wanted a small cask of wine for himself to pay for what he had done for me, then he had also written again that I was angry because of the socks that you sent to me, but that is a lie and that is as big as the others, I have worked for everything he had done for me, and I could go on telling you many stories, if paper would not be so expensive to me for such things. The answer to his letter has made me very happy but it had made such an impression on him that he told me I should not write to you anymore, therefore I also wish that you don't write a letter to him anymore, because I do not believe he is worth one. Amen.

Now I also want to write something about Uncle Jakob, he is as you know in California, he is doing very well and he earns 5 dollars a day. As he wrote to us, he will stay there for approximately 2 more years and then come from California to Germany, then you will maybe see [him] again, he is still single and I believe he makes a wedding.

As for me I am still pretty healthy so far and am doing very well. I am still working on my craft and also with Lord Rapparlie. My apprenticeship was over in August and my current salary comes to about 20 Dollars per month.

Uncle Scheuermann and family are also still quite healthy and they are very well.

I know no further news than that it looks very warlike in America, and the times are so bad as they have never been before because many businesses are closed and thousands and thousands of workers walk around without jobs.

Now I will close my letter and wish that these few lines will meet you in such good health as they have left me and I remain your faithful son, and your loving brother

M Harm

Greet from me all good friends and acquaintances and neighbors and all who ask about me

Greet from me Richard Pirmann and family, Peter Michel and family, Jacob Rälber and family, also cousin Philip Hilberth and family also many greetings to my cousin Michael Harm[4]

Also a greeting to cousin Daniel Ohler and family to Bernhard and Jacob Ohler and family

Also a greeting to the Ana Maria Gumbinger and her husband.

I wish that you write soon, because I want to know whether Philipp[5] is a soldier or not, or how his luck went because I dream almost every night about you.

If you write so write the address M. Adam Crolly,[6] Cleveland. Ohio so Rapparlie won't get the letter.

---

4   There was a second Michael Harm, just a few years older, in Freinsheim in that era.

5   Once he turned 21, Philipp was eligible for the draft lottery, where numbers were drawn and worn on the hat.

6   Adam Crolly (1815–1886) of Friedelsheim, a Palatine village neighboring Freinsheim, emigrated circa 1839, and is the father of Michael Harm's future wife, Elizabeth Crolly.

1st of May 1862

Much beloved parents and brother,

Today on the first of May Michael Höhn[1] who was in town for the market brought me the news that he got a letter from you. About the contents of the letter he did not tell me any further, just that you are complaining very much about me because of lack of attention in writing to you my dear parents and he told me that you wouldn't even know whether I am still alive or not. At the same time he said you carry the belief that he and his family had told me a lot of [silly] things therewith you shall receive no more letters from me.

Dear parents, you should not believe anything like that, even less write about it if one is not entirely certain about it because then you hurt people a lot, and especially if they are wrongly judged. The Höhn family has not chattered anything about you and even if they would have said anything I would still do what my duty is and never believe that my parents would do anything else than what is right.

Much beloved parents, I had written a letter to you last year and it was immediately after the family of the Hoffmans from Obersülzen arrived here and I can see now that you have not received it. And I am very sorry too, because I can imagine that you have waited in agony for a letter but I still couldn't help it, because as you have hoped for a letter, so did I hope, and almost no day passed when I didn't go to the post office. Then one day, Jacob Handrich who was just then visiting us brought me one and when I unsealed it, it was my own writing which I had written shortly before leaving Germany to Rapparlie, so you can see how long the letters are being left somewhere.

Much beloved parents now I also want to write you how I am what I do and where I am at home. As far as my health is concerned I am God be thanked quite healthy

1   The Freinsheim Emigration Archive lists a Michael Höhn and family emigrated in 1858.

but last year late in the year I was very sick for about eight weeks. My sickness was the old nuisance. At the beginning I sought help with doctors but it didn't help. Then I took Russian steam baths, that helped me on my legs again but it cost me heavy money because the people let themselves be paid well in America.

I have left our Uncle Rapparlie and work now with an American by the name of Leycker and receive 9 dollars per week. The work is purely carriage work. I won't enter Uncle Rapparlie's threshold anymore, because he is a human being you have to avoid and you have to flee his closeness. I don't want to describe to you his personality, neither do I want to damn him, because it is said "don't damn anybody so you won't be damned," but I only say what he has sown, that he will reap. Now I want to write you too where our cousin Jakob is living. He is until now in California amongst the gold people because he still has not enough even though he has already $10 - $12,000 dollars lying around in the banks and he owns a nice house in addition.

In his last writing we received he was still quite healthy and fine, but he wrote he wants to come back by August of next year. And then his first visit will be dedicated to you in Germany and I shall also greet you many times from him. If I knew his address now exactly I would send it to you, so you could write from Germany to him once, because that would make him very happy, but so far he is not at a stable place

Concerning our cousin Scheuermann and his family, they are all still quite healthy and doing fine as I go to see them almost every week even though it is far because there I really feel at home because there is no falseness and hypocrisy present like at the rich and still so poor Rapparlie, who owes almost all of his factory project to our cousin Jakob and still betrays him where he can because Jakob is too good and this is a mistake in America, and a big one.

Dear brother, the harmonica that you sent me I have rightly received, and that it made me happy you can imagine, as it makes me happy almost all days. I could have been able to sell it often for double the price that it cost you, but I would rather sell myself than the magnificent present from you which is so dear to me. Dear brother don't be mad at me that I haven't sent you a return gift yet. Since then I didn't ever have a good opportunity but soon a good friend of mine will travel outside our country and then in addition to sending my portrait I will make you and father and mother a gift.

In your last letter you wanted to know what kind of a man Adam Crolly is, and how I stand to him. Adam Crolly comes from Friedelsheim and his wife is a sister to the teacher Gerhard Crolly of Gonnheim. They have both emigrated about 20 years ago from there, and have founded themselves here in Cleveland a new refuge, through rightful behavior and a name without any stains and through diligence and thrift they have accumulated a considerable fortune and at the same time they are blessed with three lovely children in my age and these are girls.

Cleveland, 9th of November 1862

Dear parents and brother,

I have rightly received your letter from the 10th of July and have seen from it that you are God be thanked all still living quite healthily which makes my heart happy and I will also ask God every day that he should let you my dear parents and brother still live together healthily and contentedly for many long years. The next is to write a little bit because of my conscription, as far as this is concerned, I think that you will know best and you will find out what to do. I can't go to Germany in this moment because I am a citizen of the U.S. and it is not allowed for any citizen under the age of 48 to leave the country as long as this disastrous civil war is not finished.[1] We live here now in a bad time, and have to be ready always to be called to arms, because already in many states as also in the state of Ohio, about 300,000 men have been drafted by lottery. The second evil of the war is inflation which is being felt in all corners of America, because all the products like food are doubly expensive than they have been before.

As I have understood from your writing you [Philipp] were lucky enough to draw yourself free in the lottery about which I am very glad. Also, I have often wished I would just have been one day with you or only that evening when you came home with your number on your hat from Neustadt.[2] I would have been more happy than a king, but now I am in America, it is far but still not outside of the world, and God's dear sun shines here the same as outside [of the country] and whoever trusts in God has built well, wherever he might be. And whoever works has bread and whoever does not do it has nothing here and

---

1   On May 26, 1862, Michael Harm became 21 years of age, in that era the age at which a white male citizen was eligible to vote.

2   This section appears to indicate that, in the military draft lottery in Neustadt on the year Philipp became liable for military service, he drew a very good number, so chances were slim to none that he would be conscripted.

nothing there. As far as me and my little betrothed[3] are concerned we are both quite healthy and in a good mood and she, like I, think of you all days even though she does not know you by sight, so she still wishes to see you, even though it is perhaps not by speaking to each other, but through a portrait or image, if you have an opportunity to send it.

Our day of marriage we have moved to next spring because of the war and if you have the opportunity until then to send us a little barrel of 1861 so we want to drink to your health on our marriage day God willing, I would surely like to pay the importing cost.

As far as our relatives are concerned, namely our cousin Rapparlie, he wants to give up his carriage factory and wants to enter a special trading company because he can't, as he says, conduct his business anymore. He and his family are healthy as I heard, but I don't visit him.

Cousin Scheuermann and his family are all quite healthy and they are very well. Dear brother in your last letter you have written to me that you would marry yet next spring, but I think, that you will not keep secrets from me. You will certainly let me know who it is whom I shall welcome as my sister-in-law. I don't know any further news but that Katherina Ohler is entered among the [words missing—a square piece of letter clipped out here].[4] Now I want to close my writing and stay your faithful son and your loving brother —Michael Harm.

Many greetings from Adam Crolly and wife and a very heartfelt greeting from me Elizabeth Crolly

[Vertical in margin]

You can expect my portrait and that of my betrothed by mail shortly after my letter because almost no people go

3   Elizabeth Crolly (1845–1926), middle daughter of Adam and Katherine Crolly. In 1862, she would have been about 17 years old.
4   Katherina Elisabetha Ohler, wife of Philipp Henrich Handrich, the letter writer of 1841. Born in 1804, she would have been 57 years old. She was preceded in death by her husband Philipp, who died in 1855 at age 71.

to Germany anymore.

Here I send you a sample of American small [paper] money.[5] Silver money is not to be had anymore.

Here I send you a list of the drafted ones from Cleveland for soldier duty.[6]

[Vertical in margin]

Address to Mr. R. Adam Crolly

Just write soon.

Beloved parents and brother.

I don't want to omit writing a few lines to you namely how I am doing, and what else I want to write to you as follows. As M. Höhn told me, you would have been willing to go to America if Philipp would have come. What I think about this is, namely: I think if you would come in [to this country], it would be much better for you. You could buy for yourself here a beautiful farm and live much happier and more content on it than in Germany, as here the house is not invaded the whole year by tax people and other bailiffs, here the farmer or townsperson pays his tax and then he has his peace for the entire year, also the tools to work the land are much better and more successfully furnished than in Germany and some of the grains grow here as in Germany. Specifically, the wine does not grow as good as outside [of the country = in the Palatinate] and is not planted as much but still there is more of it each year.

Dear parents you ought not to think that I want you in here, so that I can later rely on you, oh no, I think if I stay as healthy as I am now, I am living better in America than in Germany with your help.

I write my opinion because, if one accepts that Philipp will

---

5   Additional notation: These are three cent, 1 cent [Small money sample not kept with letter]

6   List not kept with letter.

be a soldier [conscripted] next year, a substitute man [to serve] for him that costs a lot of money which in such war-like times can hardly be paid.

If Philipp becomes a soldier, then you stand there abandoned, because I hardly believe to see Germany once more [to help while he is gone]. Should one of you die or both of you die in this time, dear parents, then the government draws half of the fortune which you have so dearly earned[7], and Philipp will have to do back-breaking work as long as he lives and have nothing. The journey is not as dangerous as you believe and could maybe become quite healthy across the water, because so many have received their health across the water which have left sick from Germany.

That is all what I can write about this. Think about it if you want to come but I do not want to have the fault if anything should happen on the journey. If you really feel like coming so first write us once more then we will write down what you should take along. I don't know further news except for that Ludwig Winter has supposedly been hanged in Baltimore because of a murder but you mustn't say anything further.

Now I want to close my writing and greet you all many thousand times and stay your obedient and thankful son until death and your loving you brother M Harm

---

7   Presumably, because Michael Harm emigrated from the Palatinate illegally, without permission of the authorities.

Letter from Michael Harm on letterhead from Bremen written to the family in Freinsheim.

Bremen, 23rd of September 1864[1]

Much beloved Brother, Father and Sister-in-law[2].

As I have just a little bit of time left, so I don't want to omit writing a few lines to you. So far my comrades and I, God be thanked, have arrived quite healthy and well kept in Bremen today at noon as well as Ana Beringer whom we did not meet earlier than in Bremen, because of an all too strong fog on the Rhine during which the steamships usually lie still to avoid collision. What comes next, tomorrow we will be taken aboard[3] and therefore the hand of the Lord may guard and protect us as he has done up until now so we will happily reach our new home again. With this I will close my writing and stay yours until the death

Mich. Harm.

Greet from me all good friends and acquaintances who ask about me and all those to whom I could not say good-bye especially Pirrmann Rich. and family and my godmother Juliane Harm and children.

Another greeting to Ana Maria Gumbinger and Heinrich Harm, Sophie and mother, also Richard Michel and wife

---

1   Presumably, the reason Michael Harm returned to Freinsheim in 1864 was due to the death of his mother Catherina Elisabeth Handrich (Harm), who passed away May 14, 1864. There may have been matters to settle regarding her estate.

2   Philipp Harm married Susannah Margaretha Hisgen on August 20, 1863.

3   Aboard the ship *Hansa*, Bremen, Germany and Southampton, England to New York, arriving on 10 Oct 1864. Year: 1864; Arrival: New York, United States; Microfilm serial M237; Microfilm roll: M237_246; Line: 43; List number 1022.

[Note from travel companion Konrad Bender[4]]

Dear sister just be without worry for me I have happily and
healthily arrived today at noon in Bremen as well as my
comrades and will tomorrow be transported on. Greetings
from your dear brother Konrad Bender. A heartfelt greeting
to my brother-in-law Richard as well as to Heinrich and
Sophia, Mr. and Mrs. Harm to Philipp Harm and his entire
family. More later. Greet from me father and brothers and
sisters. Konrad Bender

[Note from travel companion Heinrich Mäurer[5]]

Dear all of the well-meaning friends, Now it is my wish to
let you know that we have all arrived healthily and happily
in Bremen. I hope that our few lines will reach you as
merrily and happily as they have left us. I am greeting all
of you from my heart. Philipp Harm and his wife, [and]
his father, Heinrich Harm and Sophiche and your mother.
Now good-bye all my greetings

Heinrich Mäurer

Greet from me also Reichert Michel and his wife

---

4   On the passenger list, Konrad/Canrad Bender is listed as age 29, a smith from
     Kallstadt.
5   On the passenger list, Heinrich Maurer (Friedrich Heinrich Maurer), age 27,
     is listed as a farmer from Hornbach.

Addressed to M. Harm, care of Daniel Selzer

Box 2091, Cleveland, Ohio

Cleveland, 21 October 1864

Much loved Father, Brother and Sister-in-law,

Before everything else my most heartfelt greeting bound together with the news that I have re-entered the circle of my family healthy and intact. But what was waiting for me, of that I have not even dreamed in Europe, namely I was drafted (drawn) and that on the 24th of September. Many of my friends had pleaded for me but all of that didn't help. On entering American soil I had to become a soldier or pay $600. My wife had borrowed the money in her anxiety over me and bought me free. So now I am free for two years and the war will thus hopefully be ended by then. If God wishes, we humans can't do anything about it.

What this war has inflamed already no quill can describe. Draft follows draft (drawing follows drawing), the fathers are taken away from their families, the [substitute] men are now so expensive that you can't get one under $1,000 and the savings of years for which poor people have labored many years, have to be given away for the men.[1] In this distress I turn to you dear brother. Let me have $500 Gulden more.[2] I know that you don't have the money but you can get it and please note down $550 for me, because I can now cover the debt because the paper money is so low. I am very sorry that I have to bother you. How much I would have liked to do without but where

1   The Enrollment Act of 1863 made all male citizens ages 20 to 45 eligible for the draft. It also allowed draftees to pay for substitute soldiers willing to serve in their stead. The amount for a substitute soldier in 1863 was around $300. By 1864 the sum was closer to $1,000.
2   Since Elisabetha Harm had already bought Michael Harm free of the draft, was this to pay the debt? It is unclear, but according to Cleveland City Records, in 1864 the Beach & Co. Carriage Works at 102 Champlain Street was formed, of which Michael Harm and Ernst Butler were also partners. They bought the firm from Beach in 1866, and it was renamed to Harm & Butler.

to get this sum in this time? The paper money rises [in value] as soon as the war is ended again and then I will be able to give away my entire fortune for soldiers. If you want to do it, so let it be sent through a secure bank and let us note it in [plain] sight.

As far as my family is concerned they were all not quite healthy and merry and my small son has grown astonishingly tall. My travel partners[3] are both healthy and merry and taken care of but they were seasick during the entire travel. I work again in my shop as before but if the war goes on like this I will look for a new home. Cousin Jakob Handrich is still in Cincinaty [Cincinnati], but he prepares himself again for Callifornia [California]. Of John Rapparlie one doesn't hear anything anymore. Now I want to close my writing and stay like always yours,

Michael Harm

Many greetings to all good friends and relatives. Greet for me Juliana Harm, his Gethel one to Richard Pirrmann, to your father-in-law and to your brother-in-law, to the Fuhrmann family. Michael Harm

Here I am sending you also a list of those who have been drafted with me.[4]

---

3   Konrad Bender and Heinrich Mäurer (see letter of 23 Sep 1864)
4   No list found.

Cleveland, 4 February 1865

Much beloved Brother, Father and Sister-in-law,

After having received your letter dear brother and seen from it that all of you enjoy the best health and your little daughter grows up well, the same that I can report from my family, so there is nothing left to us, than to wish that the Lord of the heavenly host, would gift this mercy on us for a long time to come and especially to us here on this side in our new fatherland a peace soon to come.

As far as the bill of exchange is concerned, I have received the payment for it in a Cleveland business house and therefore this is settled.

As I have further seen from your letter, this sum of $500 Gulden was too heavy for you, and then it is not equivalent according to our contract. That it was a little heavy dear brother I know, because first of all I know your circumstances too well not to know how strongly it touches you, and second, I know well that lending does not come naturally to you. But I simply thought I might try it even though the matter troubled me very much. First of all, I called on your good heart and secondly, I thought possibly he has sold some wine, and if he wants to lend so the additional 50 Gulden will already pay two years of interest, if he doesn't want to then I will have to help myself, but I have not been wrong, even though what was requested was not entirely filled, I thank you with a full heart and if I can further do something for you, so I will always be aiming at living fraternally in relation to you because we want to stay brothers in the right sense of the word even when the oceans flow between us. Further I know little to write to you than that we have limitless inflation, at this moment we pay for pork, that earlier was sold for 6 to 7 cents 20 — Beef 12 earlier 3 to 4 cents — Sugar 35 per lb earlier 12 — Coffee per lb 55 cents earlier 18 to 19 — One pair of boots earlier sold for 5 dollars now costs $10 to $12 — a cord of wood costs 10 to 12 dollars earlier 3 to 3-1/2. 300 pieces of matches 10 cents. Rattan and cotton articles are the most expensive.

Also we have another draft until the 14th of February for 300,000 men, of those 85 men will have to be drafted out of 500 men in the city quarter of the 6th Ward, but in general according to the war news one speaks about that the war will come to an end and one hopes that until summer most will be done.[1]

How things stand here with our relatives, I know little. Jakob[2] was in Cincinaty but at this moment I can't learn more about him, Cousin Scheuermann[3] has married again with a Swiss woman. I don't hear anything about John Rapparlie anymore. And I also don't care about it. Then I want to additionally report to you that Philipp Schäfer, who travels around in the states on behalf of the draft board has visited me and instructed me to greet you many times from him.

Now I want to close this. My wife and I greet all of you many thousand times and stay yours

Michael Harm

Elisabetha Harm

Greet from me Fuhrmann's family and all those who ask about me

Many greetings from my parents-in-law to all of you

Also greet your father-in-law from me

Further greet from me Lui Aul, Richard Piermann and family

also to Ana Maria Gumbinger

1   The War Between the States ended 5/9/1865
2   Presumably Jakob Handrich, Michael's uncle.
3   Katherina Margaretha Scheuermann nee Handrich passed away about 1863 in Cleveland.

Partial letter from Michael Harm in Cleveland, presumably to his father and brother and sister-in-law in Freinsheim. The date is an estimate, based on contents of the letter.

1868 November

[page 5—middle of sentence]

to fulfill my duty as a child better like my dear sister-in-law is expressing herself but because it is hitting the nail on the head but I will better myself. More news I don't know but the results of the presidential election namely that General Grant[1] is the winner in the big fight for freedom and human rights and in his hands as president is laid the destiny of the Union. So far, no president has been elected with such a majority as he has been. Business is in general average at this moment. Groceries, clothes are partly high and partly low so the barrel of flour 1 jar $9.50 … potatoes 75-80-90 … Apple Bushel 50-60-75 … meat pork leg 100. 10 … in small sale 15 … beef 7+8 in bulk, wholesale 12-13. Petroleum gallon or 8 Schopfen 40 cents.[2]

You will probably know about Jakob Huck's sad end. You will probably know what has brought him to his doing is probably in the dark because until now I have not heard other than speculation. The last time that I saw him was at the Cleveland Turnfest. We only exchanged a few words because since the time when the thing with the wine became known he has avoided me even though I have once called him to account, it is very much to be regretted for bringing such sorrow to his old parents.

Now I want to close my writing and greet you father brother sister-in-law many thousand times and stay yours. M. Harm Greet from me Richard Pirrmann, my classmate J.

---

1   In the first post-Civil War election, Ulysses S. Grant beat the Democrat candidate Horatio Seymour on the Republican platform of "Radical Reconstruction."

2   In this passage, abbreviations are sometimes illegible, and quantities (Schopfen) unclear.

Fuhrmann and tell him he should write once where he is.

Greet for me Anmaria Gumbinger and relatives, as well as your father-in-law Hischen (sic) and your brother-in-law Johannes and wife. Then my Gethel Harm and family as well as the Meckenheimers if you are still in contact with them. Until I will come again

The next address is Mr. M. Harm care of 102 Champlain Street[3]

Cleveland Ohio North America

No more with Selzer Address.

Many more greetings from my parents-in-law to all of you. Don't forget to answer.

Dear sister-in-law,

I have heard your request to remind my husband about his duty as a son. I have always done that. But then he said always tomorrow. And so it went from one day to the other. But I will from today on, when he is not writing, take over to do it myself too and we want to see if we won't keep up a regular exchange of letters. Your presents have made me very happy. We will most certainly not forget about you at the first opportunity.

What are the little children doing? Are they all quite healthy? How I pity you, you have in your short marriage gone through so much hardship[4] but be consoled sunshine will also be coming again. I would have so much on my heart but the space becomes narrow. It would make me very happy could I only be together with you for a few hours. With these few lines I will close now and stay your sister-in-law Elisabetha Harm.

3　Address of the Harm & Butler Carriage Works. Originally founded as Beach & Co. in 1864. Ernst Butler, Michael's business partner, would sell his interest the following year to Frederick Schuster, an immigrant from the same region as Michael, and a Civil War veteran.

4　Philipp and Margaretha Hisgen lost two infant sons born in 1866 and 1867 and one infant daughter born 1868.

1869 letter by Michael Harm is found in Part One, Chapter 24. The following partial letter was written around the same year.

II. [page number]

I hope and wish he has done it, then they will also be together in peace and happiness. My salutations along with best wishes to the young couple.

That John Fuhrmann is a groom is naturally nothing new to me because I have always expected such a thing but that he picks himself a girl from Kallstadt[1] I can't understand, as there are so many of beautiful girls in Freinsheim. I have received his letter, but I will only answer it when I know when his wedding will be. My greetings in the meantime.[2]

In addition, I should like to meet the German American who calls to me Lincoln's [Linkolns] words, Let us hafe Pice of ouer Country,[3] better he would have called over the sea. Let us have Pice bedween ouer Countrys Amerika and Germania.[4] Such a thing I would have understood and would have given my thanks for.

---

1 Kallstadt is a village three kilometers from Freinsheim.
2 Johannes Fuhrmann married Katherina Fleischmann in Kallstadt on May 12, 1870. "Deutschland Heiraten, 1558-1929," Johannes Fuhrmann and Katharina Fleischmann, 12 May 1870; citing Kallstadt, Bayern, Germany; FHL microfilm 193,950.
3 Michael Harm appears to misquote Lincoln here. A well-known quote by Lincoln in that era went as follows: "With malice toward none, with charity for all, with firmness in the right as God gives us to see the right, let us strive on to finish the work we are in, to bind up the nation's wounds, to care for him who shall have borne the battle and for his widow and his orphan, to do all which may achieve and cherish a just and lasting peace among ourselves and with all nations." It was Ulysses S. Grant who used "Let us have peace" as his 1868 presidential campaign slogan.
4 Presumably, Michael is referring here to unfolding military discord. In 1866, a seven week Austro-Prussian War forced alliances of German states with either Prussia or Austria, pitting Germans against Germans in a civil war. By late 1869, the Prussian Bismarck and Napoleon III of France were heading for a showdown over unification of the German states, which led to the Franco-Prussian War starting in July, 1870, concluded with a German victory in April of 1871, a conflict German Americans followed intensively in the newspapers.

Uncle Jacob is still living in town, and we are together very often he also lets greet many times. Uncle (?) Scheuermann is still healthy and also sends his greetings.

I still want to add that the photograph pictures an American Blacksmith who it is I can't say.[5] This summer I will have a family picture taken of my children and send it, too.

Now I want to and must close because it is already late, and I remain like always your brother and son M. Harm

Greetings also from my parents-in-law to all (of you)

My wife is already to bed she sends her greetings through me.

Please greet the Annemarie and family I believe she will probably be grandmother by now.

---

5   Presumably, Michael is referencing the photograph of himself at the anvil, mailed to his brother around this time, currently kept in a Freinsheim family photo album. (See photo on page 204.) This same photo of Michael Harm at his anvil appeared on the cover of my historical novel *The Last of the Blacksmiths*.

Cleveland, August 17th 1872 [1]

Dear Brother and Sister-in-Law,

I have received your letter with a check of $500.[2] In fact, in a time when it was not possible for me to answer it. And I did not believe either that I would ever pick up the quill in my hand again. Actually, already since the first of April, I am still until today not entirely restored. And I am very much in doubt if I will ever be fully restored—My sickness is still the rheumatic evil, which has, so to speak, emerged in this summer in its highest degree and has paralyzed my limbs heavily. Still I can't work but at least I can by now pretty well look after my business.[3]

As far as the ones of mine are concerned, they are all well and merry[4] and specifically now the three children diligently go to school and because apart from that they are quite well-behaved they make up for us many a friendly hour. Also, they all know just how many children you have, what their names are, and if I ask our little Emma how many children her uncle has, what are their names, so the answer follows exactly as if she would have been in personal contact with them. It has touched us quite hurtfully that your wife cannot come back to her health, something I hope when these few lines reach your hand would be the case. My wife thinks that she does maybe work too hard. And she should conserve herself more. But the German men out there, she says, don't have regard, it is all about labor and toil, not only looking after the housekeeping also the field work, I would say

---

1   Johann Philipp Harm, Michael and Philipp's father, died in 1872.
2   Perhaps this money is sent as part of Michael's inheritance from the estate of Johann Philipp Harm?
3   In 1870, Michael Harm became a partner with Frederick Schuster (1838-1914) to form Harm & Schuster Carriage Works. Fred Schuster was also Michael's brother-in-law, as Schuster married Elizabeth Crolly's younger sister Mary. The two couples both lived together on Henry Street in this era in the home of Adam and Katherine Crolly.
4   He uses the German expression: *wohl und munter*

"no thank you."

As far as my business is concerned, it goes very well. The demand for our work is so strong that we will probably have to enlarge our business again in order to meet our customers' [needs]. We have now a contract for the building of trucks [Truckes] which will be used on the railway for the largest railway company of the United States, which is the Lack. Schore. Michigan Southern Eisenbahn Co[5]. for many years and also for the United States Express Company. I don't know further news but that we have very good times here, if only hopefully no change occurs, which is usually the case if there is a presidential election, this time it will show what the German can do because the weapon dealer U.S. Grant stands against H. Greeley. The first one is supported by the Americans, the last by the German element. The young Krehter who was in Germany has visited me yesterday so I heard quite a bit of news I am now closing, next time more. Me and my wife greet all of you many thousand times and stay yours in honest love

M. Harm

Harm & Schuster's Carriage Works circa 1878.
Michael Harm is pictured third from left.

---

5   Lakeshore Michigan Southern Railroad Co.

Cleveland 20th December 1875

Dear Brother and Sister-In-Law,

We have received your letter written by the hand of my small niece, but we have seen from it with sadness that death has ripped a gap into your family. How painful such a loss is one can only know who has felt it.[1] We have been met by a similar hit that was on August 13 1874 our youngest child a boy in the age of 13 months was buried to his eternal rest.[2] It hit us like a bolt from the blue. We almost didn't want to believe it because he was always so healthy and merry and so well behaved, we rarely felt that we had a child, he woke up with a laughing mouth and that's also how he went to sleep, until he laid down to eternal rest in fact after three days of being sick. He died of the childhood sickness "summer complain[t]."[3] He was baptized in the name of Hermann. While we and you dear brother and sister-in-law are crying for a dear child also our uncle Jakob,[4] who lives at this moment in Columbus, has buried a little girl of two years old to her eternal rest. That's why, dear brother and sister-in-law, let's find comfort in the awareness that they have gotten through everything as they have left in the time when they have not yet known the sorrows and torments of this world which yet remain for each one to endure.

About the bad storms which have hit you I have read in the newspaper, according to the reports it must have been terrible. Now as far as my family and I are concerned so we are here up to this date all quite healthy and we

---

1 Philipp and Susannah Margaretha Harm lost three children. Infant boys born in 1866 and 1867, and a young daughter Katherina, born 8/16/1868, who apparently died near the time of this letter. The following year, in 1876, Philipp and Susannah would have another girl, also named Katherina, Angela Weber's great grandmother.
2 Herman Harm born 7/8/1873.
3 Similar symptoms to infant cholera.
4 Jakob Handrich married Mary Platt. Children (who lived to adulthood) were Anna Handrich (Steinbrick) (1869-1912) and William (1876-1914).

are also quite well, the children grow up, go to school diligently. I have bought them two years ago a new piano, which cost me 500 dollars, Heinrich[5] already plays very well, Lisabeth[6] starts now also to take lessons and all of them can sing like larks. But at the same time the main duties must not be left unattended. They have to knit, sew and also cooperate with the housework. We also have a horse. In the summer we drive out to the country on Sundays sometimes to visit Heinrich Mayrer [Mäurer] and sometimes Jacob Höhn, both greet you many times and they are very well. Many times my children ask me then: Father, why can't our German uncle[7] come in to us? Then if uncle and aunt would go to the countryside, we would have much more joy if we could visit him. I would agree, it is so to speak still my only remaining wish, but to talk him into it, that I won't take on myself. But if you would come over to us out of your own motivation we would welcome all of you with open arms.

About business life at this moment in America there is not much praiseworthy to be mentioned, because it is very flat, and it is especially the craftsman who suffers most from this, at this moment it is not advisable for craftsmen to come over because they might have to walk around entire years until they get work, but those who like to work in the countryside can find work everywhere.[8]

As far as my business is concerned so I am content because so far we haven't had to let workers go but the demand for finished work is not strong yet there are signs that next year there will come an improvement.

Please dear Philipp also write once some lines to Uncle Jakob in Columbus because he wishes to hear something personally from you, and be assured that you can't bring him a larger joy, I will add the address.

5 Philipp Heinrich "Henry" Harm (1864-1937)
6 My great grandmother Elizabeth "Lucy" Harm Hoppensack (8/8/1865-7/11/1961)
7 Michael's brother Philipp, to whom he is writing in this letter.
8 The U.S. underwent another financial panic and depression beginning in 1873.

The photograph of your passed away child will be within this letter, and also the same with ours.

Cousin Rapparlie and his daughter have visited us this summer. Aunt Rapparlie has died.[9] I don't know if I have written it to you, the children ask you for the photograph of their mother, if you have no opportunity [to send it along with someone] send it by mail they will be glad to pay the cost.

The old history from earlier times is buried. The children are all very well behaved, exactly opposite from the old man.

Uncle Scheuermann is also still healthy, as well as his two sons, who are capable machine builders. The oldest Georg is foreman or master builder in one of the biggest factories here. I have been after them for a long time that they should once take a short trip to Germany. Maybe they will surprise you one day. I will send you on occasion the photograph of our business and of the workers. Christmas day is on the threshold, may it gift richly to the small ones, but also shall they be quite well behaved and rightly obey father and mother and until that is the case, so I want to wait and see if maybe I can bring the American Christchild to also go to Germany, because it also has beautiful things to gift. Should these few lines reach you still before New Year's Eve so we wish you all a happy and merry new year and may the eternal guider heal all the wounds which he has inflicted on you in the past year. With this wish, my wife and I close and stay yours,

M. Harm, Elisabetha Harm

[Added note from the children]

Dear uncle and aunt and cousins

We wish all of you a merry Christday and also a Happy

9   In 1863, John and Katherina (Handrich) Rapparlie moved with their family to Fremont, Ohio, and six years later in 1869 to Toledo, Ohio. Katherina Rapparlie died 8/29/1873 in Toledo.

New Year. We have already so often wished if only we wouldn't live so far apart from each other that we could only once visit you because we are so fond of you even though we have not yet seen you,

Ph. Henry Harm Lizzie Harm and Emma Harm[10]

[Vertical writing in the margins]

[Page 1]

Many greetings from our parents-in-law[11] to you they are both still merry

[Page 2]

Greet from me many times Richard Pierman and wife and children, as well as John Fuhrmann, Philipp Brettinger and Ana Maria Gumbinger and my cousin's boys. If you write occasionally so send a small biography what the fellows are all doing.

[Page 3]

Dear brother please be so good as to not take revenge and write quite soon and don't forget to send the photograph of Aunt Rapparlie because if not I will receive each week a postcard if it has not yet arrived.

[Page 4]

Jacob Handrich, 23. Lassell Av. North of Russel Columbus Ohio

---

10 The three children of Michael and Elizabeth Harm. Henry (11), Lucy (10) and Emma (9).

11 Adam and Katherine Crolly, parents of Elizabeth Crolly Harm, emigrated from Friedelsheim.

Cleveland 5 April 1880

Dear brother, sister-in-law and children

Since a good friend of mine, Mister Friedrich Dietz has kindly offered to also visit in Freinsheim on a short trip to the Palatinate while visiting in his homeland of Baden, so I will not let this occasion pass by without using it and let you know about us once again after a long time of waiting. An excuse for this omission I unfortunately don't have any but simple laziness.

Dear brother, sister-in-law and children, my family and I are until this date all healthy and well, and an enlargement of selfsame has not taken place since my last letter. However, I had in this winter, which was very mild with little cold and little snow, again to deal with my old suffering, even though it didn't re-emerge as hard as the last time 8 years ago, but now I am on my legs again and look after my business, which goes well, and we are to this date overloaded with as many orders, as we can barely manage.[1]

Business in the entire country is exceptional right now, obviously after seven meager years we have to expect seven fat ones.

My children are now all confirmed. Elisabeth and Ema [Emma] were both of them confirmed together on Palm Sunday of this year. Phil Heinrich is with me in the business and will be a blacksmith. My parents-in-law are both still alive, and stay with me. They send you many greetings.

At the same time we have [added] to these few lines the two photographs of our girls and that of John Scheuermann who is a machine builder by trade—and a good one, too—his brother Georg is at this moment Superintendent in one of the oldest and largest machine manufactories

---

1   In 1880, Harm & Schuster Carriage Works moved east to 811 & 813 Woodland Avenue, near present-day E. 40th St.

of this town. Their father, our cousin Scheuerman, is still alive and is still well off.

I also wanted to send along to you a photograph of our business and the workers, but as Mr. Dietz does not take along any luggage but for handbag, so it had to be omitted, but I will send it later at a new opportunity.

Dear brother and sister-in-law it is now almost 23 years that I am in this land of America, but during all this time I have never proposed to you to come in here, but today, I believe I can call to you with all optimism to come. Because America is the land of the future for all people who have the desire to work. But, dear brother and sister-in-law, you don't have to attribute to this call any other motives than only the inner wish of my heart to see you here, and as content as I am at this day, I know that it is a hard step to tear oneself away from circumstances, from friends and from the familiar stove, because one loves one's fatherland. I myself love it even more today than those days when I left it, but if one reads day after day the reports from other countries, as well as from the immigrants and hears about the opinions of Europe's greatest statesmen. About the militarism. And about the future of Europe and especially of our common fatherland, this incredible tax burden which is resting on you, the eternal clouds of war, the entirely disabled industries, so one is beset by the wish to know that what one still has in this fatherland will be assured.

With these few lines I want to close this time and my friend Dietz is authorized to report everything to you whatever you wish to know.

With a thousand greetings to you, I stay your brother brother-in-law and uncle

M.Harm

Greet from me Jean Fuhrmann and also from Jacob Höhn, he will probably be dropping by your houses unexpectedly in two years.

As well greetings from me to Richard Piermann and his

family the brothers and the sisters and Kath. Gumbinger, the cousin of my godfather. Philip Brettinger say to him he should also once write to me

Asking for your answer soon.

To the many thousand greetings of our mother to all of you we add ours and we stay yours until death.

Elisabeth Harm[2]

Emma Harm

Phillip H. Harm

2   The eldest daughter Elisabeth Harm was later known in her family by the nickname "Lucy."

Cleveland 30th May 1882

Dear Brother, Sister-In-Law and children

Through the agency of Karl Schuster[1] my family and I have rightly received your dear letter together with valuable presents and have seen from the oral reports that you are with the exception of our dear brother your father[2] all quite healthy. This is in a family a hurtful event, may it pass by according to God's will and return full and fresh health for him

My dear brother, sister-in-law and children, the presents which we received from you now have all been right after their heart's desires, so that they cried out "we couldn't have wished for anything better."[3] The wine is now stored in the basement and it is better than the one of Karl Schuster because he claims that his wine has been diluted on the journey. This is a rare feeling when one comes home in the evening and is able to go to the basement and fetch and drink a glass of Rhine wine, and also many of my Palatinate friends take the opportunity and visit me. Indeed for all of this my full and heartfelt thanks.

Now as far as my family is concerned so we are all quite healthy and have the pleasure of our best well-being. Elisabetha[4] the oldest of the girls has learned dress-making, Ema [Emma][5] or our baby is not parting from her mother. She will, so to speak, be a housekeeper. Heinrich will be a blacksmith[6] and will later take over the business. The parents-in-law are still with us and have

---

1   A Charles/Karl Schuster (presumably Fred Schuster's brother) also worked in the carriage works.
2   The particular illness of Philipp Harm referenced here is unknown.
3   Quotations added for narrative flow.
4   Elisabeth "Lucy" Harm, 1865-1961), my great-great grandmother.
5   Emma Harm (1866-1950), third child of Michael and Elizabeth Harm.
6   Heinrich "Henry" Harm, eldest son of Michael and Elizabeth Harm, is listed in the Cleveland 1880 census at age 16 as working in his father's carriage shop.

the pleasure of the best of health[7], but Karl Schuster is working with us again, we have already tried more than once to marry him off but I believe we won't achieve it as he is afraid of the female gender.

Further the photograph of your two beautiful strong girls has[8] also given us much joy and as Karl Schuster says they can work like a man, a trait they don't have in common with me which they have inherited from their father and mother. When we will stay healthy for two more years and fate does not forbid our plan one beautiful morning I will stand with my wife and Ema [Emma] in front of our old father's door and start the song "Sei mir Gegrueszt mein Herz"[9] which song the Harmonie singing society to which I belong is convinced that nobody else sings better than me.

Our Uncle Jakob will now move back to Cleveland again after he has lived for eight years in Columbus, his wife and two children[10] are both here. We have in this year strange weather. It does not want to become spring mostly cold and wet. The fruit [trees] have all blossomed but I do not think there will be much fruit, all food items are very expensive. Potatoes 1.85/100 per Bushel. and everywhere debts amongst the craftspeople. Here in Cleveland alone a factory was closed in which more than 4000 workers had been employed.

What the transactions in general are, there is little to be wished for and especially our shop is this winter and still now overflowing with orders that one sometimes does not know where one's head is. So in this winter alone we had orders for 22 pieces fine wagons and buggys at 200 to 500 dollars a piece. And since the 1st of February

7   Katherine Crolly would die on 7/4/1885 and Adam Crolly half a year later, on 2/15/1886.
8   Probably, Philipp and Margarethe Harm's eldest daughters, Elisabetha (born 3/25/1864), and Margarethe (born 3/19/1865). Third daughter Katherina (1876) only 6 years old at time of this letter
9   "Be Greeted My Heart" (composer unknown)
10 Possibly, Anna Handrich (Steinbrick) (1870-1912) and William P. Hendrick, (1876-1914). These two are listed as children of Jacob Hendrick and (Anna) Mary Platt in Ohio birth/death records .

until today we have 107 pieces of wagons and coaches restored and painted.

As I don't know any further news that would be of interest to you so I want to close these few lines and I and my wife and children greet all of you many thousand times and stay yours. and hope that when these few lines reach you they find you in the best of health, Michael Harm

Greet from me also Jean Fuhrmann as well as Ph. Brettinger R. Biermann and his family and especially to Amerie Gumbinger.

[Vertical note in margins:]

Also Karl Schuster has asked me to greet all of you from him, also he was so pleased that you had asked after him in Dürkheim if he had arrived well.

I have given 2 dollars to G. Huck in order to subscribe to the Freinsheimer Anzeiger[11], as I would further like to receive it so please be as good dear brother to see that you will subscribe it for another year and put that to the bill of the costs for the barrel and the shipping from Freinsheim to Rotterdam because I am happily accepting the gift of the wine but I don't wish that you also carry the cost of the freight of the barrel. Send me that [bill] and I will remit it to you.

---

11 Newspaper of Freinsheim.

1883 letter written by Michael Harm is found in
Part One, Chapter 34

Cleveland, O., Dec. 16th 1889

Dear brother sister-in-law and children

Now that the year 1889 is getting to its end so I want to use this short time and surprise you in the old year with a few lines and the photographs of our daughter Elisabeth and her young husband William Hoppensack.[1] Their wedding took place in the month of May and as usual here inside of our house, as well as the marriage ceremony by Mr. Pastor Steppler[2] the pastor of the community to which we belong. Invited were only the nearest relatives of his side and of ours only brother-in-law Schuster and wife.[3] The young man whom [Lucy] chose is born here yet his parents come from Westfalia.[4] He is in his rank a lawyer and a notary public currently employed by the state as deputy recorder in the administration of mortgages.[5] He is an excellent young man very wealthy and esteemed and loved by everybody. He has built himself prior to his marriage a fine new house[6] and lives on the same street as us approximately six houses away. This is not to be considered further as a big separation if one considers how young people here often all too frequently move after marrying 1000 to 2000 miles to the west and parents and children don't see each other for years.

---

1   Elizabeth "Lucy" Harm and William Hoppensack were married 5/15/1889. William Hoppensack is the son of H.F. Hoppensack (1821-1890) and Maria Ilsabein Kämper (Hoppensack) (1826-1888), Cleveland Geman pioneers who emigrated from Nordrhein Westphalia in 1846.
2   Pastor Joh. Heinrich Stepler was elected as minister of the Second Evangelical Reformed Church in 1888.
3   Frederick Schuster (1838-1914), business partner in Harm & Schuster, and Mary Crolly (Schuster) (1847-1920), younger sister of Michael Harm's wife Elizabeth.
4   The groom, William F. Hoppensack, was the fourth child of nine.
5   See biography of W. F. Hoppensack in Rowan, Steven W (transl.): *Cleveland and Its Germans*, Cleveland, Ohio: Western Reserve Historical Society, Jan 1, 1998.
6   Present-day 6209 Francis Ave SE, Cleveland, Ohio.

But now to get back to your last letter in which we learned that you are all healthy and merry which is amongst all goods of the world the most precious. Also we anticipate with pain to your daughter Elisabeth's long-lasting sickbed first of all and then second the unlucky gunshot which happened through the mishap of the overeager hunter Friedrich. [We learned of it] not alone from your letter but read it here in the German newspaper. But as everything finally turned out fine and without disadvantage so we want to thank God for that.

The detailed letters of little Käthe[7] about the schoolhouse of Freinsheim and the big merits of Mr. Mayor Pirmann for it have brought me much joy. As well as the clean and firm handwriting, as well as that she is thick and tall in that we are only equal in one thing namely in being thick because I am small and thick and so now have a lot of similarity [in appearance] with a globe. Now that you are confirmed and don't have to go to school anymore dear Kätchen so we will certainly occupy you as our guide to our outings once we come out.[8]

Now as far as we are concerned so we are God be thanked very well and are not suffering and have no sorrow. If other people make us cry sometimes and especially those with whom one is well meaning like H. Lederer from Wachenheim who visited you that time[9] he is entirely on the docks. We have over the years loaned him very much money to hold him above water and have been very much mistaken with this man. We were forced to sue him for over 2000 dollars. It is still stuck in the court, but we have him closely. That man has made me more trouble than he is worth. In our 25 years of business this is the first time we had to sue but in spite of that he tried everything to trick us out of it, he didn't succeed. Our business is working exceptionally fine. Our carriages have a reputation and count among the best which are being built in this country.

7   Katherina Harm, born 1876.
8   The letters refer consistently to coming "inside" the U.S. to mean coming into the country, and coming "outside" or "out" as leaving the U.S.
9   See letter of 1883, Chapter 34.

Konrad Bender[10] has passed away this summer after a life full of hard work without children. He has left his wife a beautiful fortune she lives off her pension. H. Mairer [Mäurer[11]] is sitting lonely on his rented farm, left by wife and children. She wants nothing else to do with him. The guy could have it better but he was a fool. Jealousy without reason has brought him there.

On the occasion of a trip to Akron this summer my wife and I have visited Michael Selzer for the first time in 22 years. We have been very happy on both sides. He is doing quite well. His children are all adults and most of them married. They live all together on a farm very close to the city. Michael is a big light in the church and also a preacher. I am still communicating with Jacob Höhn. He is always a dear friend to me and that will last as long as we live. He is fine, two of his children are married. His mother is still alive and is very spry for her age. She has sent me this summer a little container full of her homemade handcheeses. They were thoroughly well done. I have eaten them with delight. Jacob is cultivating a good wine, a kind of sorrow breaker, always when we sit with it together and talk about you and your youth time, then the heart becomes weak. That Mr. R. Pirmann has offered his upstairs at our disposal on the occasion of a visit made me especially pleased and for that dear brother send him my heartfelt thanks and 1000 greetings to him and his dear wife. But there is room in the smallest hut for a modest human couple.

Now I want to close here because the hand of the watch is pointing to the ten and it is bedtime. Greet from me above all John Fuhrmann Annmaria Gumbinger and tell her she should only hold on until I come out. Because I have to see her once more. Greet from me your brother-in-law J. Hisgen and wife. As well as Ph. Prettinger, J. Reibold, then Ph. and Mich. Harm, Philip Aul and wife. Above all many greetings to you from my son-in-law and wife from

---

10 The blacksmith who traveled with Michael Harm from Freinsheim in 1864.
11 The farmer who traveled across with Michael Harm from Freinsheim in 1864 (see 1864 letter).

our children from my wife from Uncle Jacob who is again in Columbus [he] instructed me when he was here not to forget his greeting when I write. Uncle Scheuermann is still alive now 85 years old but spry like a 40 year old

I further wish that these lines will arrive well and healthily and I greet all of you sincerely from my heart and stay forever

M. Harm

Harm & Schuster Carriage Works craftsmen circa 1879.
Back row: 4th from left Anton Strom. 5th from left Charles Schuster (others not identified)
Front row: Adam Crolly, Wm Walker, Fred Schuster, Michael Harm, W Paplotzki, Herman Butter

Michael Harm traveled to Freinsheim with a friend then living in Berea, Ohio—Michael Höhn (see Höhn's letter, 7 November 1893 to Freinsheim in Chapter 21)—in the fall of 1893. The following note was written after the Freinsheim visit, as the two prepared to embark on the return journey to the U.S. across the Atlantic. Michael's three-masted sailing ship journey in 1857 lasted 43 days. In comparison, this steamship journey in 1893 on the Columbia lasted only eight days.

Letterhead: BrunsHotel, Osterstrasse 24, Hanover [Northern Germany]

Hanover, 18 October 1893

Dear brother, sister-in-law, and children,

I herewith send you my last greeting on German soil. We have arrived here yesterday afternoon healthy and fine. We'll be brought to Wilhelmshaven tomorrow morning at 9:50 a.m. At 4 p.m. the steamship will start its journey.[1]

The afterpayment of 17 marks was waived because winter prices are in place.

At Adolph Piermann's we stayed for half a day and received a friendly welcome. We also still drank new wine. Adolph has shown all of the town to us even though he's buried in work.

Further, I don't know what else to write, so farewell all of you once again and think of me in love.

With cordial greetings,

M. Harm

---

1 M Harms, New York, Passenger Lists, 1820-1957, departure: Wilhelmshaven Hannover, arrival: 27 Oct 1893 - New York, New York. Residence: Cleveland. Ancestry.com NYM237_620-0295.jpg.

[POSTCARD addressed to]

Herr Philipp Harm

Wallgasse. Freinsheim

Rheinbayern

Germany

Still 300 miles from New York I am writing to you still surrounded by sky and water.

Tomorrow, on Friday October 24 we will arrive in New York. The journey was magnificent, favored by the most beautiful weather, although 3/4 of the 700 passengers were seasick.

The two of us are both healthy, we have just now emptied the last bottle of Freinsheimer wine.

Thousand greetings

your brother and uncle M. Harm

Cleveland November 26th 1893[1]

My dear brother sister-in-law and children

Already at home for four weeks I am reaching out for the quill. You have certainly received my postcard from New York, the journey has been as beautiful as my ocean crossing to Europe.[2] I have encountered all of my family healthy and well yet they were full of longing and especially my wife and then the circumstance was added that on the ship Gellert fire broke out and they assumed I was on that ship. I came home on Sunday morning at 4. I had sent a telegraph to them from New York but not when I would arrive but I am home [now] and everything is in good order. Little Emma at first was estranged when she saw me but soon afterwards she recognized me and wouldn't leave my lap almost all of that Sunday. They were all very happy about the presents even though the rings are a little bit too big and will for now be laid aside until they fit.

I had also promised to write about Francke[3] the same was here regarded as lost for a while he didn't write neither to his wife nor to any other person. He arrived on 14th of November and visited me immediately the next day. He said he had written from Berlin again I should come to Frankfurt he waited there four days for me. Finally he said he had lost my address and had put as address on the letter Freising, Bavaria. Mind be mind not. Also Heinrich insisted on having written a letter and lets me ask whether it has ever arrived. As we have been in New York more than a day so we have visited with Schmidt Hannes, with Kröther, with J. Aul, with Joh. Ehrhard. Schmidt Hannes is doing fine [he] has a good position but his debts in Freinsheim he never pays. Ehrhard has the

1   Written shortly after Michael Harm and Michael Höhn's return to Cleveland from their visit to Freinsheim.
2   See Hanover letter of October 1893 above for passenger record regarding that Columbia steamship crossing.
3   Illegible handwriting, spelling may not be correct.

best luck he owns a nice inn and it is all his own property, the same with Kröther. Jacob Aul works as a sander in a furniture factory. It is good that he still has work in such bad times[4]. Godfather Michel's Jacob is so far run down that even the tramps don't tolerate him anymore among themselves. The Freinsheimers had at least collected the money together in order to send him back again, he took [the] money and drank it away.[5] A sad piece of human life but please do not tell anything about that to the old Mr. Michel. Dear brother, R. Pirmann is already instructed to buy wine for Paul Schmidt[6] from here. When it is ready in spring so you buy yours […][7] and send [it] along. Times are below the worst, we only have four workers left in the shop but we hope by springtime to fetch them all back again. We stand yet better than some other businesses in the profession. Because we don't have to pay rent, we can endure.[8] I will send you a newspaper each Sunday. Write a few lines after receiving of this letter and also don't forget to report what Jacob Aul is doing. Now I want to close and wish all of you a merry Christmas and a happy

---

4 The U.S. endured another financial panic in 1893, in part due to bank failures.
5 [drank it away] These words in the original are nearly illegible, this is a possible translation based on context.
6 Paul Schmidt, 80 and 82 Michigan St. sold imported wines and liquors (1879 Cleveland City Directory).
7 Writing illegible.
8 In 1892-93, the Harm & Schuster business model shifted; they discontinued the manufacture of carriages and did repair work only. (Per a notice published in *The Hub*, March 1893, Vol. 34, No 12, p. 593.) In 1896, Fred Schuster retired, and the business became the Harm Carriage & Wagon Co. An Ohio factory inspection in 1901 reported the Harm Co. employed 40 males and 3 boys ages 15-18. But the heyday of carriage manufacture was over. In the 1890s, Cleveland became the center of automobile manufacture in the U.S. In 1897 Scottish immigrant Alexander Winton began making and selling the gas-powered Winton Buggy. In 1899, Baker Motor Vehicles began manufacturing electric-powered cars. The White Sewing Machine Company of Cleveland produced steam-powered cars beginning in 1900, and also sold other vehicles such as trucks, bicycles, tractors and buses. German carriage-maker Charles Rauch of Rauch & Lang shifted with the times, beginning to manufacture the Rauch & Lang electric car in 1905. Examples of all of the above vehicles are on exhibit at the Crawford Aviation Museum, a division of the Western Reserve Historical Society in Cleveland.

New Year. Your brother, brother-in-law and uncle always M. Harm

Greetings to Richard Amarie and her husband also to J. Fuhrmann,/ Philip Reichert and Lui Harm also to all of the brothers Aul. In 1896 if everybody's healthy we will see again, A thousand greetings from my wife and children

[Vertical in margin]

N.B.   Michael Harm[9] has been visiting with my Henry, while I was in Germany, so far I have not seen him.

1893 postcard written by Michael Harm. Translation on page 306.

---

9   Michael Harm was a common name in Freinsheim. There were several Michaels who were contemporaries of my great-great grandfather, born in 1841. In Freinsheim, one Michael Harm was born in 1842, one in 1850, one in 1864, one in 1874, and so on, all of different parents. It is unclear which Michael Harm is referenced above.

Letter written in the year 1900 by Michael Harm is found in Part
One, Chapter 35.

Cleveland 15 December 1906

Much beloved sister-in-law and children.[1]

Forgive me that I have left your two letters unanswered.
You don't know how hard it has become for me now to
bring together these few lines. You all had to carry such
a heavy burden and such big sorrow has fallen on you
nobody was spared. The last letter by Katchen[2] uncle
why don't you write? Yes what shall I write there.

I have for many years been the recipient of the Pfalz in
America.[3] There I have read all of your bitter losses
about the death of Richard about the death of Kitsch also
Pirrmann and Katchen falling off the barn. That was too
much for me. I cancelled the subscription because I didn't
want to know or hear anything anymore from outside. In
this mood I was and if I should have written to you and
given you comfort, that I could not do, but be assured
that we all have mourned [with] you and sympathized with
our heart. In the last letter Katchen wrote we have good
courage. I was glad about that. Yes we have to be of good
courage because we can't change it, what is meant to
occur for humans in this life no one can escape so [look]
toward the future with good courage and trust. I have
already written above what shall I write after all? Here
with us nothing happens at all everything goes its usual
path.

No tales of sickness I am not in my business[4] anymore
so I'm also not interested anymore to mention it. God be

---

1   Philipp Harm died 10 August, 1900.
2   Katchen was the nickname for Philipp Harm's youngest daughter, Katherina
    Harm (Kitsch).
3   The German language newspaper "Der Pfälzer in Amerika," a weekly, was
    founded by German immigrant Conrad Voelcker in New York in 1884. It was
    published until the onset of WWI in 1917.
4   Sometime in the early 1900s, Michael Harm handed his business over to his
    son Henry, who for another decade or so co-owned the Harm Carriage &
    Wagon Co. with Gustav H. Willbrandt. (Per a 1912 Cleveland City Directory)

thanked we're all healthy. The grandchildren[5] grow up they all go to school now and are all without exception very talented well-behaved diligent and obedient loved and recognized by their teachers and female teachers. Emma Hoppensack[6] the oldest has been confirmed on Palm Sunday now goes to high school and wants to become a teacher. The second oldest her sister[7] will also be confirmed on Easter 1907. She will be a little housemother. Edna Harm, Henry's only daughter, 14 years old, also is facing confirmation. She also attends high school,[and] is the strongest of all in the family, tall and strongly built like an adult woman. Gretchen Becker[8] is exceptionally musically gifted and [has] such power of perception of her mind that she is called the wise one by her teachers. Then comes Leonie[9] our youngest and last (if nothing else follows) the darling of all of us. She has the biggest heart of all wants to do good for all people. She will be 8 years old on the 5th of Feb. 1907. [She] is already for one entire year head of her class against cruelty to animals and she takes that very seriously like an adult. Namely, here it has been introduced into all schools and all classes to have an effect on the feelings of a child that animals should be dealt with in a humane way and the love of the child towards all animals will be awakened.

Also, as mentioned above, in the last years little of importance has come calling as there are sicknesses and other unpleasant things. Only a small damage has occurred to us through an explosion of dynamite close to our factory which has destroyed all windows and cost 40 dollars. Unfortunately also human lives have been lost

---

5   Michael and Elizabeth Harm had five grandchildren. Edna Harm (the only daughter of Henry and Barbara Harm), Emma and Olga Hoppensack (daughters of Lucy Harm (Hoppensack) and W. F. Hoppensack), and Marguerite and Leone Becker (daughters of Emma Harm (Becker) and Paul Becker).

6   My grandmother, the daughter of W. F. and Lucy (nee Harm) Hoppensack.

7   Olga Hoppensack, my grandmother's sister.

8   Marguerite "Gretchen" Becker.

9   Leonie Becker, younger daughter of Paul and Emma (nee Harm) Becker.

and eight residential houses which stood close by have been collapsed to the ground. Besides the deaths, also many injured have been carried away from the place. Subsequently, I also want to write from Michael Harm who has been with his young wife here for a while in Cleveland but now moved to New Jersey, N.Y., now [he] has a quite nice and hardworking wife. Yet he himself is such an independent human being who never bows himself under the yoke of an employer. I had arranged for him two [work] places during his stay here but he doesn't endure long. According to his letters he has written to me, he is now on a farm and in his element and makes good progress and I believe myself that he is at the right place.

Of the old Freinsheimers who live here in Cleveland like the Höhns I hear once in a while that they are still healthy and alive, I haven't seen any though within the last two years.

Yet two Freinsheimers of the Selzer family play a big (important) role here, one son of Jacob Selzer, who was for a long time mayor of Brouklin [Brooklyn], a suburb of Cleveland, is now town council member of the city of Cleveland and very prominent. One son of the book binder Selzer who is a shareholder of three of the nicest pharmacies here, was elected last week on a large convention of all pharmacies of the Unit. States of America as secretary. His image was in all of the larger daily newspapers.

Currently, a group of old pioneers is working at planning a journey for all of them together to Germany. As I have many friends among them, so it could still be that I participate but then not alone, then I will take my married love with me or really she will have to want to. We would once again shake our hands and look each other in the eye and it will be a comfort for all of us.

I don't love to write of myself but still I have to remark how healthy and strong I am currently in spite of my age of almost 66. And the same with my wife. I haven't been as solid in all of my life like now. What I did go through in my younger years—rheumatism and once even the pocks

[pox] and other things and slowly in winter all is gone, and [for] all that I thank to Pastor Kneib (Kneipp)[10] according to whose directions I live, haven't drank coffee in three years, few alcoholic drinks simple German food. Kneib's coffee and much more. Our whole family sticks to this and we are well with it.

That our dear old friend R. Pirrmann is having hard times and even is getting sick with it is hard on my mind. Tell him my heartfelt greetings and my sincere sympathy and when I think of all of you each day so he stands with you because I can't separate him from you as always your sincere friend and adviser.

As this letter is supposed to arrive for the holy Christmas feast I wish all of you a merry Christmas and a happy new year. Many greetings to all from me and my wife.

I remain Yours, M. Harm

N.B. Further greet from me John Fuhrmann, the Harm brothers (except for the Judas Ischariot [Iscariot]) also Ana Maria Gumbinger if she is still alive. A photograph of our Ema will follow to this letter. The address for the future N8 6404 Francis Ave. SE.[11]

---

10 Presumably, Michael Harm is referring here to the naturopathic treatments of the 19th Century Bavarian priest Sebastian Kneipp.

11 Michael and Elizabeth Harm did not move. In 1906 new addresses were assigned to homes throughout Cleveland. An index of old and new addresses is available online at the Cleveland Public Library.

Cleveland, O. December 16th 1908

Worthy beloved sister-in-law and children,

In life sometimes feelings of great depth occur that can't be shaken off easily. It is the so-called homesickness for the old soil where one has spent the time of one's youth, where those call, and others still rest, to whom one belongs. And that [feeling] overcomes each and everyone who has left his homeland. So this mood also came over me, which pushed the quill into my hand to let you hear once again something about me and mine. These lines won't be large because at our home nothing really happens that would be worth letting you know about.

In particular, as far as our health is concerned, so we are all healthy and indeed very well on top of the dam.[1] I am indeed steadier than in my young years when I always had to suffer from painful rheumatism as well from piles.[2] That has all gone now just once in a while a little bit of asthma and my little woman, she won't even get tired that's how spritely and healthy she is. Of course our grandchildren grow, they are all still going to school and through their diligence and good progress as well as through their good behavior they not only bring us and their parents great joy but also to their teachers. Emma has left high school and now goes to technical school[3] which the city built very close to us for half a million dollars.

What can be said at this moment in relation to business. So, it is a little better. In the 51 years that I am living here it has never been as wretchedly bad as in the last 1-1/2 years.[4] Entire work places where between 300 to1,000 people worked were entirely closed. As most of the

---

1 German expression—"on top of the dam" has a similar meaning to "back in good shape."
2 Hemorrhoids.
3 East Technical School opened in Cleveland in the fall of 1908.
4 The "Bank Panic of 1907," involving a run on the banks, was also known as the "Rich Man's Panic." The New York Stock exchange almost collapsed, but was saved due to the intervention of J. P. Morgan.

workers live from hand to mouth, the Germans are no different here so you can imagine which poverty comes to light here. Even those workers who earned between 5 - 10 dollars a day for those it went the worst, that was business for the pawnshops. The city of Cleveland supports at this moment still 2,600 families with groceries and pays additionally to one or the other the rent. And other associations who support the poor have also had their hands full. Thousands still keep on leaving the land and return back to their old homeland.

During the writing of these few lines J. Höhn[5] has visited me. He brought me four sausages and in addition, a bottle of wine of his own vintage. He instructed me to greet all of you; the brothers and sisters are all still alive, except for Kattel, she died this summer. Johannes Höhn has had a stroke brought about by agitation and sorrow caused by the failure of a bank in which he had deposited 6,000 dollars. At the same time, his grandchild is said to have lost at the same occasion her inheritance on her father's side in the amount of 15,000 dollars. We will right away also send a photograph of Olga[6] who is now also confirmed. Further I wish you a merry Christmas and a happy New Year and that these lines will meet you as healthy as they have left us. With that I stay yours,

Michael Harm[7]

Further, greet from me our neighbor R. Pirrmann J. Fuhrman and all those who still remember me

---

5 Michael Harm was acquainted with Höhn families in Berea and in Parma, two adjacent Cleveland suburbs.
6 Olga Hoppensack (1893-1929) my grandmother Emma Hoppensack's younger sister. Olga married Edward Gressle 6/17/1916.
7 Michael Harm died 7/31/1910

Index

Acknowledgements

One beauty of writing a memoir is being able to focus on one thread of life to the exclusion of others. By tugging just a few threads of the fabric of the three years of this narrative, the pattern of the main story becomes more plain for all to see. Naturally, my experience in those years included many dear friends and colleagues who played significant roles in my life, and in the events unfolding here, but who did not make their way into this book. Named or not, I am most grateful to all of you.

My deepest gratitude goes to Angela Weber, who worked so diligently on the letter translations and manuscript review to make this project a reality. During the MFA program, Ana Maria Spagna's insightful course on memoir offered excellent resources and tools for writing in this genre. If not for my Family Ink writing group, with its structure of a five-page submission for critique every two weeks, I believe this book might never have been written. The intelligent, encouraging writing feedback of that group—Karen Brattesani, Sue Hoekstra, Dorothy Landeen, Delorse Lovelady, and Emily Phillips—kept me going at the most difficult of times. My other writing group—Inside Out Writers Lois Brandt, Connie Connally, Michele Genthon, and Ushani Nanayakkara—also provided invaluable feedback. I extend my heartfelt thanks to beta readers and friends Ann Bristow, Michele Genthon, Miriam Gershow, Jackie Haskins, Stephanie Lile, Craig Patterson, Laura Pritchett, Ana Maria Spagna, Angela Weber, and Dave Williams.

I am grateful to each of you for the care you took with this project, and for friend Jo Gustafson, who lends a listening ear when I need it the most. Thanks to editor Jennifer McCord, Aubrey Anderson, and the rest of the crew at Coffeetown Press for their excellent skills and book business acumen. And, as ever, deepest gratitude and love to those who put up with me the most: my children George and Vivian, and my constant, loving husband Dave.

photo courtesy of Jennifer Tucker, JMC Photography

Claire Gebben was born and raised on the southeast side of Cleveland, Ohio. After earning a BA in Psychology from Calvin College in Grand Rapids, Michigan, she settled in the Pacific Northwest, where she worked in various jobs as a resource center manager, newsletter editor, communications director and ghostwriter, all the while raising a family. In 2011, she earned an MFA in Creative Writing through the Northwest Institute of Literary Arts. Her debut historical novel *The Last of the Blacksmiths* (Coffeetown Press, 2014) is based on the true story of her German immigrant ancestor who pursues the American dream. Since the novel's publication, she's been invited to to speak at various venues on the untold stories of 19th-century immigration history, on creating legacies using family genealogies, and on research and writing. An adventurer at heart, she enjoys hiking, bicycling, traveling, and even on occasion blacksmithing. Ms. Gebben is married, has two adult children, and lives on Mercer Island, Washington.

You can find Claire on the Web at www.clairegebben.com.

Angela Weber, contributor of the German-to-English translations of the letters, was born in Bad Dürkheim, Germany and grew up in the nearby town of Freinsheim. After studying cultural anthropology, visual arts and Spanish at the University of Marburg, she pursued various artistic and publication projects while raising two daughters. In 2017, through the University of Bonn, she completed her PhD thesis, a cultural studies approach to Indigenous positions in Canadian art discourse. Ms. Weber has shown her artwork in group exhibitions at Marburg, Cologne, Berlin and Frankfurt. She is published in various periodicals and anthologies, and writes for the *Allgemeines Künstlerlexikon* [Artists of the World]. She and her family live in Marburg, Germany.

CPSIA information can be obtained
at www.ICGtesting.com
Printed in the USA
LVHW01s0147231018
594493LV00010B/337/P

9 781603 817011